We who served...

Stories of Addingham
and
The Great War
1914 - 1918

To Bill

Catherine Snape

Catherine

First published in 2015 by Addingham Civic Society

c/o The Old School,

Main Street, Addingham LS29 0NG

email: info@addinghamcivicsociety.co.uk

ISBN-13: 978-1508859536
ISBN-10:1508859531

Front cover: Burnside Mill, Beamsley Beacon & Southfield Terrace, from Southfield. Photo: Don Barrett

DEDICATION

For my grandchildren Freya and Ffion Williams and Oliver McKenzie in the fervent hope that they and other children of their generation will never see the horrors of another world war

CONTENTS

INTRODUCTION   vii

CHAPTER 1   **THE NEW CENTURY FROM 1900 T0 1914**
- A changing society   1
- Businesses and shops   10
- Children at work   17
- Industrial unrest   19
- The outbreak of war   20

CHAPTER 2   **TIMELINE 1914-1919**
- 1914   25
- 1915   33
- 1916   45
- 1917   56
- 1918   69
- 1919   82

CHAPTER 3   **ON THE HOME FRONT**
- Attitudes to Germans   91
- Postal services   92
- Fear of invasion   96
- Skipton – a garrison town   99
- The White Feather Movement   100
- Women in the workforce   101
- Women's magazines   104
- Volunteering   104
- Local war hospitals   107
- Defence of the Realm Act 1914 (DORA)   109
- Conscription   112
- War memorials   113

CHAPTER 4   **TAKING THE KING'S SHILLING**
- Joining the Army   117
- Army requirements and service conditions   120
- Daily life in the army   122
- Pastoral and medical services   123
- Prisoners of war   125

CHAPTER 5   **FOR KING AND COUNTRY**
- Service of Addingham families   127
- Medals   149
- Where servicemen lived   153
- News from the front   155

CHAPTER 6   **WE WHO SERVED**
- List of all Addingham men who served   171
Classified lists:
- Regulars and Reservists   300
- Territorials   300
- Places men served   301
- Naval personnel   302
- Lord Derby recruits   302
- The ultimate sacrifice   303

ACKNOWLEDGEMENTS

I would like to thank the following people and organisations for their input and assistance: Richard Thackrah for his time spent extracting information from newspaper archives; Carol Hindle and Jonathan White for proof reading and checking; Don Barrett for his meticulous formatting, cover design, and arranging publishing; Ken Birch for his cartoons; Lynda Robinson for the interviews she has carried out; George Rishworth, Lucy Shann, Margaret Norris and the Ellis family for allowing publication of their family photographs and letters, and to Kasheen Hastings and Phyllis Robinson, and other village residents, for their input with village stories. All photographs are from the Addingham Digital Archive (see *addingham.info/addingham-digital-archive*) unless otherwise indicated. My thanks also to the members of Addingham Parish Council, Addingham Civic Society, The Royal British Legion and, especially, Addingham World War One Commemoration Group for their on-going support and encouragement and for providing a forum to discuss content and the many details essential for a publication of this kind.

I am most grateful for the sterling work of my sister Ruth Binns for inputting the whole of the text, and for her amazing ability to decipher my handwritten scrawl.

My husband Harold Snape deserves a special mention for his great patience as I spent many hours on the computer and visited libraries and other places in search of information and, not least, for his knowledgeable "listening ear".

atherine Snape

ingham

2015

INTRODUCTION

This book came about in response to publicity surrounding the centenary of the outbreak of the First World War - "The Great War".

A group was formed from local organisations and individuals with the aim of marking the anniversary in a tangible way. One objective was to research the names on the Addingham war memorial in the Main Street, but it soon became clear that there were names of village servicemen who are not on the memorials. After discussion it was felt to be important that all local men who served their country in the armed forces should be recorded. The brief was to research the lives, times and service of all men who were either born or lived in Addingham at some time in their lives or are recorded on any village memorial.

After eighteen months the research is finished and 414 servicemen with village connections have been identified; of these 83 paid the ultimate sacrifice, a high number from a village population in the 1911 census of less than 2000 people.

Most of these served in the army and a few in the navy and what was to become the Royal Air Force. They enlisted from age 16 to age 45 and served in many different theatres of war.

Some lived in the village for all their lives and others only for a short time, but all are recorded so that their service is not forgotten.

The book is not a war history, nor indeed a history of the village, although it contains elements of both. Instead it aims to give an insight into the life and times of the families who lived through the Great War.

The content is of necessity, selective, as a vast amount of information has been accumulated from a wide range of sources, all of which has had to be validated and cross-referenced. Any mistakes or omissions in the text are my own and for these I apologise in advance.

The common images of the First World War are of muddy trenches, gas attacks and young men mown down by machine gun fire. The pictures of obliterated landscapes in France and Belgium still have a powerful effect on us today.

These, indeed, were amongst the many horrors of the war but there are stories of great courage, patriotism, compassion and human devotion.

The war had a devastating effect on British society which has to be understood in the context of the complex mix of social change, politics, and the demands of war.

Addingham, like most communities, was changing in the years leading up to the war and, indeed, throughout the war years.

This book will look at life in the village throughout those years and it provides snapshots of the lives of some of the families.

At the outbreak of war, adult literacy was high as everyone under the age of 40 years would have received at least a compulsory basic seven years education, and the village had two good schools.

Newspapers, both local and national, were the only form of mass communication and were widely read. The 'Timeline' chapter is a mix of the mundane and the shocking, and gives an idea of the way in which the general population would have received information.

Emergency powers were enacted by the Government within a few days of the declaration of war, and the restrictions they created greatly influenced village life and are examined in 'On the Home Front'.

To most men, life in the armed forces came as a great shock. The early volunteers in particular expected the war to be short lived. Patriotic fervour and Government campaigns encouraged many men to sign on 'for the duration' and some gave little thought to what that might mean. In Addingham there were several families where brothers enlisted on the same day, or within a few days, of each other.

Whether a volunteer or, later, a conscript, the men gave hard years of service for their country and, in spite of the hardships, letters show a sense of optimism, patriotism and a concern for the loved ones at home. Extracts from letters sent home to Addingham families can be found in the "Timeline", "Taking the King's Shilling" and "For King and Country" chapters.

The final chapter lists alphabetically all the men with Addingham connections who are known to have served, and records the men who paid the ultimate sacrifice

Please note that, in the text, where a street, house, church, or other building is mentioned, it is in Addingham unless otherwise stated.

Monetary amounts are given in pre-decimal currency – there were 12 pence (12d) to the shilling (1s) and 20 shillings to the pound (£1). A guinea is one pound and one shilling (£1/1/-).

1902 parade passing The Swan – probably a Coronation celebration
(photo: Ilkley Gazette)

We Who Served…

1 THE NEW CENTURY FROM 1900 TO 1914

A CHANGING SOCIETY

At the time of the death of Queen Victoria on 22 January 1901, the British Empire remained a powerful force and her people proud and patriotic. Although in many ways the Old Order was changing.

Britain was a major exporter of goods around the globe from heavy engineering to textiles. Millions of tons were handled by vast ports such as Liverpool and London and armies of workers toiled in a myriad of industries such as shipbuilding, mining and textiles.

In Keighley heavy engineering was a major employer with machine makers and ironfounders such as George Hattersley and Sons and Prince Smith and Son and machine tool makers such as Dean Smith and Grace providing for the needs of industry. Companies also manufactured for the domestic market and as early as 1884 Whalley Smith and Paget of Parker Street were making washing machines *(hand operated)*, wringers, mangles and sewing machines.

Britain also imported raw materials and luxury goods from around the world and people aspired to better themselves. In 1900 Britain saw the first sales of an American import, a soft drink which was an alternative to beer. This was Coca Cola.

Class differences were still very marked and the wealthy enjoyed a lavish lifestyle, encouraged by the new king Edward VII, whilst those at the other end of the social scale still lived hand to mouth.

The emerging middle class of the Victorian era now had a strong presence and were widely represented in science, literature, education and manufacturing.

In Addingham, the headteachers at both schools were university graduates and sent their sons to university, as did the local textile manufacturers and a few other more affluent local families.

The concept of childhood was now established, with children's toys and games enjoyed by all classes. Children's literature had been written from the 1880s, often in serial form in magazines. Beatrix Potter published several titles from around 1900, including "The Tale of Peter Rabbit" in 1902, and E Nesbitt wrote "Five Children and It" in 1902 and "The Railway Children" in 1905. A fortunate child might receive a book at Christmas or as a school or Sunday school prize.

The idea of an annual holiday was taking hold and many mill and industrial workers expected to have at least a day excursion to the seaside and some saved for a week away at popular resorts such as Blackpool and Morecambe. At least one Addingham mill had a holiday club into which people paid a small sum from their weekly wage.

From around 1890 there were excursion trains from Addingham to Blackpool.

Scarborough was seen as a more gentile, middle class resort and a postcard of 1900 shows the imposing Grand Hotel and the South Sands thronged with people, donkeys and horse-drawn bathing machines.

Society was also changing politically. For example, in 1903 Emmeline Pankhurst formed the Women's Social and Political Union. From the first, the small number of women who joined were highly organised and soon many women joined its ranks to fight for women's equality, particularly in relation to enfranchisement.

The change in attitudes towards women and by women would later greatly help the war effort as women took on work previously seen as men's work, and became highly skilled and efficient in their fields.

The Government later accepted that without the contribution of women, Britain could not have won the war.

As early as 1906 the Government had been mindful of the shifts in attitudes of working people and had made a number of reforms; however, these largely benefited the more affluent. In 1902 an Education Act set up grammar schools and a number of new universities opened in industrial towns such as Leeds. Later came other legislation regarding a national insurance scheme, unemployment benefits and old age pensions for the poorest elderly.

In 1908 the Scout Movement was formed by Lord Baden-Powell followed in 1910 by the Girl Guide Movement. The Scout Movement quickly gained popularity and as early as 1910 local newspapers were mentioning troops in Keighley and Ilkley. Addingham certainly had a Scout troop by 1914, but it may have formed much earlier.

The Workers' Educational Association was formed a few years earlier, around the time that the first Carnegie library opened in Keighley in 1904. Several other libraries donated by the wealthy industrialist followed.

The cinema was increasing in popularity and by 1910 many short films were being made each year and when King Edward VII died in May 1910 his funeral was seen by thousands on film in the cinema. Early film was amateurish and primitive but people were willing to pay to see the phenomenon and the few cinemas were packed to the doors. In 1910 some titles were "Tilly the Tomboy Visits the Poor" and "The White Slave Trade". Also in 1910 "Fred Karno's Circus" with Charlie Chaplin was showing in Bradford. Early in the war in 1914, the Government made much use of the cinema, which by then was available in most towns, to show its own newsreels and propaganda films.

The health of the nation overall was improving following a range of Public Health Acts of the late 19th century. Local authorities had the power to supply clean water and sewerage systems. There was greater access to better qualified medical practitioners and cleaner hospitals. Vaccination was being seen in a more positive light, especially for some of the major diseases such as smallpox. However, there were major smallpox outbreaks in 1902 when over 100 schools in the Bradford area were affected, and again in 1905. Where war service records of Addingham men are available, these show that almost all were vaccinated in childhood.

Large families were common and although people still succumbed to infectious diseases such as diphtheria, measles and scarlet fever, life expectancy had risen. By 1910 life expectancy was 52 years for men and 55 years for women, although 60% died before the age of 60 years. An analysis of the burial records for St Peter's Church, Addingham, indicates that infant mortality was on the decline. In the decade of the 1880s about 98 children aged 2 years and under were buried and in the decade 1900 to 1910 there were around 60. There would be burials elsewhere of

Addingham children and the overall population was only a little less in 1901 at 2143, than it had been in 1881 at 2163.

Transport links had greatly improved with the expansion of the rail network in the 19th century and by 1900 fares had become affordable by most people. Commuting to work was now possible and local towns all benefited as "workmen's" trains at special fares were available. People no longer had to live in a town to work there and Addingham people travelled to Ilkley, Skipton, Bradford and Leeds and all stations in between. Links were poor between Addingham and Keighley and in the 1911 census there were very few Addingham people who worked as grinders, moulders, fitters or, indeed, had any other occupation of that type, unlike in Keighley where a significant part of the male workforce was employed in the engineering industry there.

Roads were beginning to be inadequate for the increased amount of motor traffic with the popularity of the motor wagon and lorries in businesses, the charabanc for general transportation and the motor car. In 1910 Bradford registered its one thousandth motor vehicle and in Addingham in 1911 there were several men employed as chauffeurs. The village saw several motor accidents, usually to pedestrians as the road through the village and onto both Bolton Abbey and Ilkley was far narrower than now with a number of dangerous stretches and corners on which the motor vehicle, people and the pony and trap were in daily conflict.

By 1910 people generally were becoming more prosperous with more disposable income and able to take advantage of new opportunities. Girls were increasingly able to work in less traditional roles and to enter education at a higher level. Ilkley in particular provided a number of opportunities in businesses associated with a spa town, such as some office work, nursing, waitressing and shop work. A number of village girls had apprenticeships in dressmaking and millinery and may have worked in Ilkley or Addingham, whilst some worked in the village in family businesses as shop assistants. However, most adults and young people in Addingham still worked in textiles and were subject to the boom and bust associated with this industry.

Addingham developed as an industrial village although in the mid-nineteenth century it had suffered serious decline with half the houses empty and limited work.

At the dawn of the twentieth century the population was again buoyant.

There were five working textile mills and the three which had the largest workforce were owned by Listers. In 1851 the population was 1558 and by 1891 it had risen to 2225.

The railway from Leeds to Skipton, completed in 1888, greatly added to the prosperity as trains traversed the Pennines carrying coal, limestone and cotton and allowed for speedy transport of finished goods to the docks and large cities. Samuel Cunliffe Lister used the railway to transport materials from his mill in Addingham to his larger mill in Manningham, Bradford. The line also became popular for excursions as people became more prosperous.

Local quarries were active until well into the 1920s and, in the 1901 census trades associated with quarrying and stone were second only to textiles. Local stone was used to build the mills and houses for both workers and employers.

Supplied by the Addingham Gas Company, gas was the main fuel for street lighting, and in the mills and the school, but it employed few people. Only the most prosperous had gas lighting as had a few of the most recently built properties. Electricity did not arrive until the 1920s.

Many of the dwellings were mill workers' cottages and "tied" to the mill so that when a person left employment the family lost their home. There was little incentive for the mill owners to modernise these properties.

The Co-operative Society built a row of houses on Bolton Road for private rent and there were other private rented properties, some in poor condition and very small.

The textile boom in the late nineteenth century saw the building of terraces of back-to-back housing, such as Rose Terrace and Victoria Terrace; Southfield Terrace was unusual in that the properties were part rendered and not fully stone built. A few more substantial homes were built with gardens, such as those in Southfield Road.

Addingham School had opened in 1874 with 26 scholars and was situated in Chapel Street *(now the Methodist Church)* and built by the Wesleyans. Numbers rose rapidly as education became compulsory. A second school was in North Street. The two schools were known as the 'High' school and the 'Low' school because of their position in the village. Both had an infants' department and took pupils up to the age of 14 years. Although many became part-timers at the age of 12 years they had to continue with some formal schooling up to the age of 14. In 1910 it was proposed that the school leaving age be raised to 14 for "full time" schooling. This was not well received and it was not until 1918 that this happened, and so all through the war "part time" schooling continued.

The Wesleyan/High Council School

In 1903 the National *(low school)* had 174 on its roll and the Wesleyan *(high school)* had 248. Numbers fluctuated depending on the economic fortunes of the village; education was not free and epidemics such as diphtheria and demands of agricultural work for the farmers' children seasonally reduced numbers.

The Headteacher of the Wesleyan School from 1885 to 1923 was Mr Harry Hewerdine who lived at 5 Springfield Mount. In 1911 three of his children were also school teachers. Mr Hewerdine opened a school library with 45 books and began a newspaper club for half a penny a week and older pupils could borrow publications such as Cassell's (Family) Magazine and Chambers's Journal. He held regular examinations in grammar, geography, reading, writing, spelling and arithmetic. In 1911 "handwork" was added to the curriculum. Outings were regularly organised including to Hambleton Quarries and Beamsley Beacon. In June 1903 the boys played a friendly cricket match with Boyle and Petyt School at Bolton Abbey. In 1906 the Wesleyan closed for the day for the funeral of Lord Masham *(Samuel Cunliffe Lister)* formerly of Farfield Hall.

The Headteacher at the National school was William Kidd. His wife Clara was a teacher and their daughter Winnifred an assistant teacher. Clara was born in Addingham as were all their children. William Kidd died in 1923 when still a serving teacher. In 1911 the family lived at "Lynholme", Bolton Road. In 1911 Mrs Hadley of 8 Church Street was head of the infants' department.

In 1906 there was a major slump in the textile industry and it was noted that "large numbers of pupils are leaving owing to very poor trade and more children are applying for their part time certificates to help eke out; even though it would be little; the poor earnings of their parents". At times of slump some children were provided with a free breakfast at school in the winter months. This slump seems to have lasted well into 1907 by which time, with so many families dependent on textiles, short time would affect all trades and shops in the village.

During the early part of the century, Education Committees within Local Authorities were given increased powers, including powers to introduce school meals and medical examinations, but these were not compulsory. In 1907 a scholarship system for secondary schools was introduced. At that time fees had to be paid to attend all secondary schools.

Ilkley boasted a number of fee paying schools for boys and girls, both day and boarding. Ilkley Grammar School offered scholarships and education up to the age of 17 years. Full fees were around £16 per annum. Ghyll Royd, founded in 1890, prepared boys for scholarships, the Royal Navy and public schools.

Girls were catered for by the High School for Girls in Wells Road and Oaklands House, run by the Misses Lawrence, had 60 day pupils and boarders. Ilkley Ladies College, also in Wells Road, was a boarding school. Crossbeck House, another school for girls, closed in 1914.

Ilkley was a popular spa town and its population had risen from around 800 in 1840 to around 7400 in 1901. The bracing moorland air encouraged charities to send city children for holidays and one such establishment was Highfield Children's Holiday Home for sick or poor children from Bradford and Leeds, founded in 1907.

The extensive pleasures of the spa town could be enjoyed by visitors and local people alike and Ilkley was popular for day trips from the cities of

Bradford and Leeds. All the large hotels advertised a variety of leisure facilities such as bowling greens, tennis courts, croquet and pleasure gardens. Dances were held, and the Craigland's ballroom could accommodate 200 guests. Concerts were also held there. Boats could be hired on the river from Wray's Pleasure Gardens *(now the riverside gardens)*. Here there were, at various times, an aviary and a menagerie with monkeys, raccoons and armadillos. In 1912, Mr Wray, the owner of the Pleasure Gardens, laid out a cycle track on the fields. A cinema, The Picture House, opened in 1913 in Back Grove Road with a capacity of over 700. There was a bandstand in West Park built in 1914 for summer concerts and the Tarn Gardens had bands and shows in the summer, paths for walking and winter ice skating.

The town also had a military presence in the summer on east and west Holmes Field which was the site of a tented camp for officer training.

Addingham had grown as more housing was built for workers but the traditions were maintained. There were sheep and cattle fairs held on land behind the Craven Heifer and the Swan Inn. The annual feast holiday was in July when fairground rides and other attractions were provided behind the Swan. A circus came to the village on at least one occasion. This was Sangster's in May 1905 and in May 1911 a menagerie visited.

More regular entertainment was held in the Oddfellows Hall on Lodge Hill, with lantern slides and concerts and in the various chapels and churches. Every July the Oddfellows, Ancient Order of Buffaloes and Foresters, all of which had many members in the village, marched down the Main Street with brass bands. This tradition is still upheld today in July with the annual procession and gala. It is likely that there were also drama groups and it is believed that there was an annual pantomime which, in 1904, was "Bluebeard".

Sports were popular, with both cricket and football clubs having a large membership. Some local men played rugby and golf in Ilkley.

The 1900s saw a number of eccentric sports; walking backwards and speed walking became popular. In 1903 a man cycled facing backwards, from Skipton to Keighley. The feat took him just under an hour.

At this time people were beginning to have more leisure time. Wages were also increasing and skilled men could earn 40s. a week and labourers from 18s. to 22s. Contrast this with the 7s. a week earned by a soldier. In 1914 around 25% of women worked.

Prosperity was increasing and a number of Acts of Parliament helped to make old age and unemployment less of a financial problem. The Pension Act of 1908 awarded a pension to persons aged 70 and over but was means-tested. The pension was 5s. *(25p)* a week or 7s. 6d. for a couple. In the 1911 census, for the first time people were categorised under "occupation" as old age pensioners and there were a few of these in Addingham.

The National Insurance Act of 1911 introduced unemployment benefit for some men. After one week's unemployment the benefit was 7s. a week for up to 15 weeks.

There were local clubs and insurance schemes to which working people could contribute to receive payment should they become unemployed, bereaved or require a doctor. Most people would contribute to a burial fund.

The same family held the living at St Peter's Church for around 100 years and the Reverend Thompson had been rector for the latter part of the nineteenth century following his father. Various curates had served them both and lived at the property now known as Potters Hall. The curate, the Reverend Hall, became rector after Reverend Thompson as neither of his sons were clergymen. In the census returns Reverend Thompson's sons described themselves as gentlemen. The older son, William, was Master of a pack of Otterhounds in the village from around 1903. These were 30 pure bred hounds and they hunted every week in season along the River Wharfe. In 1910 William purchased the pack and later transferred them to Giggleswick where he lived in 1911 at Beck House. The younger brother also had an interest in the hounds, later taking over as Master. The hounds were eventually taken to the Lake District where they became the Kendal and District Otterhounds.

There were a number of absentee landlords, notably the various descendants of the Cunliffes and Listers, who owned several hundred acres, including most of the farms and tenanted houses such as Farfield Hall, Hallcroft Hall, Holme House and several in Church Street.

The Addingham Water Company owned the sewage works and "branches" *(sic)*, Bradford Corporation the reservoir conduits, Ilkley Urban District Council the water mains works, the Gas Company owned the gas mains and an office and the Parish Council the allotment gardens.

Lord Northfield owned sporting rights on sections of Middle Moor and High Moor which he leased out. Under the Land Valuation Tax of 1910 all were required to pay tax on these holdings. The valuation lists both the owners and the tenants of a property.

Main Street in about 1910

Most of the village properties were spread out along the Main Street; indeed the village in earlier times was called Long Addingham. The total village population in 1901 was 2143 and of these 848 were born elsewhere and around half of the population was under 21 years of age. This number would be significant during the war as large numbers of men were eligible for the armed forces.

Business and Shops, 1901 and 1911

An analysis of the properties in Main Street in 1901 shows that the majority of the shops were in the centre of the village whilst the extremities were mostly workers' cottages and a few small farms interspersed with the occasional small shop. By 1911 the number of shops and small businesses had increased from 65 to 83 as had the variety of employment and occupations of the residents. Sometimes two businesses occupied the same premises.

In 1901 there were ten grocer's shops and seven in 1911; however, the number of confectioners and bakers increased. In each census only one was specified "bread baker". Whilst the number of grocer's shops had decreased between 1900 and 1911 there was a dramatic rise in the number of confectioners from one to eight. Sugar was cheap and available granulated instead of solid cones from which it was tedious to remove, and the nation had developed a "sweet tooth".

Some of the brands we would know today were already well established. Huntley and Palmers made a range of biscuits sold loose out of large tins by the pound. The digestive biscuit was popular and had been invented in 1892. Confectioners vied with each other to produce the widest, most appetising range of pastries, biscuits and cakes, and home baking in busy households was on the decline. Chocolate was popular, with Cadbury, Rowntree and Terry all producing the confection from the 1d. bar to elaborate boxes of chocolate. Favourite beverages were Bovril, Horlicks, and Bournville cocoa. Sauces such as HP and Lea and Perrins added flavour to everyday food.

Margarine was a cheaper alternative to butter and was readily available since its invention in the 1870s. Tinned food, such as corned beef and condensed milk, was sold by grocers and although it was relatively expensive, most families aspired to having a few tins in the cupboard for special occasions. Tinned peaches and salmon were the height of luxury for an average family who spent around 60% of its income on food. The major brands advertised widely in newspapers and magazines and shop fronts were adorned with product promotions. Families became used to such products and in 1910 the United Kingdom was the largest importer of tinned food in Europe.

The Cooperative movement had shops in every town and village, including one on Bolton Road. Usually imposing buildings, some were department stores in their own right with foodstuffs on the ground floor and a drapery on the first floor. They sold every kind of household item and everything the "housewife would require" from a packet of needles to ready to wear garments. Generally local traders did not welcome the arrival of the Co-op because of its competitive nature and system of dividends which encouraged people to buy there. The Cooperative stores are not listed in the 1911 census as no-one lived on the premises.

There were four (1901) and two (1911) greengrocers, and four and five butchers, although some living in the Main Street described themselves as farmers and butchers so they may not have sold direct to the public. A surgeon, Mr Manson, who was most probably the village doctor, had moved from 118 Main Street and does not appear in 1911. Until around 1900 Dr William Bates lived at his surgery in Main Street but was in Ilkley in the 1901 census.

In 1911 there was one poultry dealer at 4 Railway View and for the first time a dealer in "dairy" at 43 Main Street. This may have been a small dairy attached to a farm as number 41 is a farm. It is likely that farmers visited various streets, selling measured amounts of milk into customers' own jugs from churns on the back of a horse and cart, as one milk dealer would be insufficient in a village of this size.

S Bilton, Drapers (adjacent to The Crown)

By 1911 the number of tailors, milliners and dressmakers had increased. Most families would make at least some of their own clothing, particularly for women and children, although men may only have had one suit of clothes and their working clothes. Increasingly men's shirts were available ready-made and most women expected to have several dresses, skirts and blouses in their wardrobe. A few of the "for best" garments would be made by a dressmaker, often using the customer's own fabric and to her own design. Cotton was available for as little as 3d. a yard and there was a wide range of dress materials in cottons, wool and artificial silk. Skipton and Keighley markets had several stalls selling fabric and drapers Harrisons, Hartleys, Simpsons and Nuttall in Main Street would sell dress fabric and sewing materials. It became a status symbol amongst women who had a little more disposable income to visit a dressmaker and the large rise in women sewing for others in Addingham is indicative of the trend.

In 1911, for the first time a monumental mason, district nurse, music teacher, barber, "peddler in small wares", yeast dealer, chemist, two newsagents and booksellers appear. However, a newsagent and bookseller in 1911 at 100 Main Street was a stationer in 1901. The second was at 3 Southfield Villas. The artist and sculptor in 1901 at 44 Main Street had gone by 1911 as had the musician and vocalist at 4 Ilkley Road.

In 1911 there were two premises described as boarding houses *(listed separately to the inn keepers)*, at 9 Bolton Road and at the Junction Temperance Hotel.

In both census records the post office was at 103 Main Street with living accommodation above and a Lister family had this for several decades. There must have been sufficient "club" business to support two insurance agents in 1911.

A fishmonger at 137 Main Street was, by 1911, a fish shop. These premises were, until recently, occupied by a fish fryer and it is possible that in 1911 it had the same purpose. Fried fish and chip shops had become popular from the late nineteenth century in areas with a large number of mill workers as they provided working families with a relatively cheap meal at the end of a long working day.

By 1911 the tripe shop at the bottom of Druggist Lane had gone and there was a bizarrely named "marine dealer" at 1 Bolton Road. The fishmonger at 76 Main Street was no longer trading there.

Overall, the village, in spite of the textile slump in 1906/7, appeared to be thriving and indeed, if the variety of trades is an indication, the population had more disposable income.

A new doctor arrived in the village around 1906, newly married; he served the village for many years. William Lancaster Crabtree qualified in London in 1905. The family lived, in 1911, in a ten roomed house at Springfield Mount and this was also the Surgery. In addition to the district nurse mentioned earlier, there was a sick nurse living in the village who may also have been a midwife as no one else is listed as such.

The shops and businesses in the village in 1911 are listed below.

Commercial premises where no one lived, such as banks, warehouses and lock-up shops, were not included in the census. The list runs from the Craven Heifer down to the Ilkley Road junction. There were around 90 self-employed or small businesses:-

Name	EVEN NUMBERS, MAIN STREET	
Name	**Occupation**	**Street Number**
Town	Boot maker	22
Prior and Schofield	Grocer	28
Steel	Boot maker	34
Steel *(female)*	Milliner	34
Smith	Carrier	36
Throup	Greengrocer	40
Whitaker	Ironmonger and plumber	72
Demaine	Confectioner	74
Smith	Painter	74
Whitham	Grocer	82
Roe	Dressmaker	Jubilee Terrace
Batty	Joiner	1 Chapel Street
England	Joiner	84
Lowcock	Carrier	86
Atkinson	Grocer	96
Harrison	Milliner and draper	98
Richardson	Newsagents	100
Whitaker	Boot maker	102
Richardson	Confectioner	104
Parsons	Innkeeper	Swan 106
Atkinson	Farmer	23 Brumfitt Hill
Wilkinson	Coal merchant	110
Horsman	Barber	112
Anderson	Pig dealer *(possibly pork butcher)*	114
Snowden *(female)*	Poultry dealer	2 Railway View
West	Butcher *(possibly his home not shop)*	Manor House
Stapleton	Insurance Agent	112
Adams	Watch and clock dealer	126

Bancroft	Cast off Clothing Dealer	130
Nuttall	Draper	132
West *(female)*	Grocer	134
Binns	Hotel Keeper	The Crown 136
Firth	Police Constable	8 Bolton Road
Dempsey	Confectioner	15 Bolton Road
Ashton	Boarding House Keeper	9 Bolton Road
Rishworth	Marine Dealer *(wet fish shop?)*	1 Bolton Road
Thompson	Dressmaker	140
Wall	Maltster *(Malt Kiln Yard behind Mount Hermon chapel)*	142
Whitaker	Music teacher	144
Atack	Grocer	146
Smith	House Painter	152
Smith	Publican	Fleece Hotel
Mason	Barrister-at-Law	High House
Brear	Chair Manufacturer	Low House
Brear	Timber Merchant	Low House
Bartholemew	Builder	4 Adelaide Terrace
Dixon	Boot maker	6 Adelaide Terrace
Dixon	Butcher	6 Adelaide Terrace
Wall	Insurance Agent	1 Church Street
England	Land Agent	Croft House
Hadley	Co-op Store Manager	8 Church Street
Emmott	Joiner	10 Church Street
Smith	Monumental Mason	12 Church Street
Lister *(female)*	Dressmaker	Church Street
Hartley	Sick nurse	Church Street
Hall	Clergyman	Ashgate House (now Potters Hall)
North	Hotel Keeper	Junction Temperance Hotel
	ODD NUMBERS	
Herd	Farmer at home	41
Whitaker	Dairy Farmer at home	43
Shuttleworth	Publican	Sailor Hotel
Steel	Shoemaker and Farmer	61
Wroe *(sic)*	Greengrocer	69
Wade	Cabinet Maker and Farmer	79

Hibbard (female)	Baker and Confectioner	93
Cockshott	Butcher	97
Lister	Postmistress	103
Hartley	Draper	107
Ridley	Stone Mason at home	109
Bell	General Dealer	113
Bell	Baker	113
Whitham	Tailor	117
Simpson	Draper	119
Whitham	Tailor	121
Hedley	Stationmaster	123
Flint	Grocer	127
Richardson	Confectioner	131
Sutcliffe	Fish Shop (possibly fried fish)	137
Ashton	Beef Butcher	139
Town	Fish Dealer	141
Wilkinson	Confectioner	147
Wilkinson	Clog Maker	147
Harrison	Chemist and Water Manufacturer (may have had lock-up premises)	Beech House 157 Main Street
Benson	Butcher	2 Hudson's Yard
Emmott	Blacksmith at home	11 Southfield Terrace
Schoon	Yeast Dealer	33 Southfield Terrace
Brayshaw	Plasterer at home	37
Barker	Newsagent and Bookseller	3 Southfield Villas
Atack *	Grocer	5 Southfield Villas
Shipley (female)	District Nurse	2 Victoria Terrace
Flesher	Farmer at home	30 Victoria Terrace
Lightbody	Pedlar on own account	16 Rose Terrace
Emmott	Blacksmith	1 Stockinger Lane

* (Mr Atack is believed to have been in business as a grocer at 146 Main Street with his brother)

Most of the houses were occupied by textile workers and there was still a significant number of stone masons and timber workers, the latter probably employed at the saw mills and, perhaps surprisingly, a significant number of domestic gardeners.

Children at Work

In 1901, as mentioned earlier, children could become part-timers in the textile mills from the age of 12, and a number are identified in the census. This was a very long day for them.

A memoir of a Worth Valley girl born in 1893 gives great detail of her ten hour day, plus the long walks in all weathers. Martha tells of starting work, aged 12, at 6 a.m. in a local mill some twenty minutes' walk from home. The walk meant that her breakfast "bit" and lunch had to be packed up the night before. This consisted of two cans of soup or tea to be warmed up at work, oatcakes and butter for breakfast, bread with a wedge of cheese, hard-boiled egg if the hens were laying or a slice of cold bacon for lunch. There was no time for breakfast nor time to light the fire for a hot drink before leaving home. The mill started at 6 a.m. and at 8 a.m. there was a 30 minute break for breakfast. Work continued until 12.30 p.m. when the girls would wash and change out of their oily over-clothing and tightly wound headscarves. Then lunch was eaten in the outhouse at the mill. Then on to school, a ten minute walk, where lessons began at 1.00 p.m. for three hours. If on "afternoon turns" the children would be in school from 8.45 a.m. until 12.30 p.m. then at the mill from 1.00 p.m. working until 5.30 p.m. Six hours were worked for five days if on the "morning turn" and four and a half hours a day if on the afternoon shift. Those on afternoon turns had to work on Saturday to make up the thirty hours. Pay was 1s. 6d. per week with increments, so by 13 years of age and "fully trained" they would have 3s. 9d. per week. Full-timers from 14 years of age had 8s. per week. The work clothes of strong cotton were made at home and became very greasy. They had to be washed in hot suds on a Saturday to be ready for Monday morning.

Children who worked part-time and lived on farms would have extra duties. Another Martha tells of being on the afternoon turn but still getting up at 5 a.m., helping to light the kitchen range, prepare breakfast, help the younger children get ready for school and pack up their lunches. She preferred the morning turn!

Boys who lived on farms and were on the afternoon turn would help before school, perhaps with the milking, feeding the pigs, mucking out and collecting eggs.

Most of the children became full-time workers at 14. Apprenticeships to "other trades" began at 14 and the two years of part-time work was seen as good training. Not all young people were sufficiently fortunate to obtain an apprenticeship as there was usually a fee to pay, unless you were apprenticed to a family member, and few apprentices received a wage. This meant that the poorer families who needed the weekly wage could not afford the apprenticeship. In 1907 scholarships to secondary schools became available but these were only for the brightest children and the cost of books and uniform still had to be met by the family.

In some areas there was a strong tradition of girls going into service. Few from Addingham appear to have gone down this employment route. The families in Addingham who had domestic servants tended to employ them from further afield, perhaps because of a privacy issue. One example is Mr Harrison, chemist, of 157 Main Street who employed an 18 year old general domestic servant from Wakefield. In 1911 only one family, that of Mr Hewerdine, employed a local girl as a live-in servant.

In the new century the spectre of the workhouse still loomed large. Addingham's destitute went into Skipton Union Workhouse and the village collected an annual Poor Law Tax from householders to cover these costs. The workhouse had 100 beds and a reputation for being clean and humane. In 1900 a hospital wing was added which had 48 beds. In 1911 there were seven inmates/patients who were born in Addingham.

In the Edwardian era there seems to have been little crime in the village, although at least one young lad was involved in criminal activities. In 1907 he was at Calder Farm School at Mirfield as an "inmate" having been sent there for a custodial sentence of five years for an offence committed in August 1905. Shortly after his release he was in Leeds Prison on remand for three cases of shopbreaking, one of which was "entering the Counting House of the Midland Railway Company in Addingham and stealing an overcoat, seven keys and 2s. on 21 January 1912". The case was heard in June 1912. Pleading guilty, he was bound over to keep the peace for 12 months on payment of £5 and placed under the supervision of Skipton Probation Service. Arrested three days after the offence, he had already spent six months in jail awaiting trial. He was 19 years old.

A number of Addingham men, usually young and single, went to both Canada or Australia to seek work. Both governments needed manpower and attractive terms and cheap passage was available to the right applicants.

The textile slump in 1906/7 had encouraged men to consider emigration and alternative employment out of the area. A few families went to coal mining areas and at least twelve young men joined the armed forces as Regulars after 1900.

Industrial Unrest

The Labour Party had been growing in strength and, backed by trade union support, found itself with seats in Parliament in the 1905 General Election. However, the well organised labour supporters who had put them there found that they could influence little of government policy and industrial unrest followed.

The General Election of 1910 saw no clear party majority. Keighley's MP died in 1911 and a by-election followed. Keighley had fielded a Labour Party candidate in 1905 who was unsuccessful. It did the same in 1911. The results are surprising as the votes cast show much support for the Labour candidate, especially as voters had to hold property in order to be eligible to vote. The results were Liberal 39%, Conservative 32.1% and Labour 28.9%. A further by-election in 1913 showed almost identical results.

The four years from 1910 to 1914 saw major industrial unrest as groups of workers came out on strike with various demands for increased pay, a shorter working week, better working conditions and enfranchisement not based on property. The Government was at times obliged to call in the military and in Liverpool when seamen went on strike, two warships were sent up the Mersey. The strikers were not always men, indeed several thousand women who assembled Singer Sewing machines in Glasgow were out on strike for many weeks.

In May 1914 in Keighley 1,000 engineers went out on strike following over a year of unrest, and demanded an extra 2s. a week. The next week an extra 500 men joined them and groups of angry men assembled in the streets. On one occasion the town's Mayor confronted a belligerent striker, and the police began escorting non-strikers home to avoid them being attacked. The situation deteriorated as the weeks wore on and the activities of the strikers made headlines most weeks in the Keighley News. One non-striking worker had his allotment wrecked by his striking worker colleagues and a trip wire set up to catch a non-striker injured a cyclist instead. The Education Committee decided to feed the children of strikers as some were too hungry to attend their lessons. Angry groups assembled outside the homes of employers and the town's magistrates who had imprisoned, bound over or fined a number of strikers. Although Keighley developed a reputation as a rough and somewhat lawless town, the same scenes had been played out elsewhere in the country as the strikes had escalated.

All this would have had an impact on the attitudes of the population in relation to Government policies and the economy, and greatly affect Britain's ability to fight a war.

The Outbreak of War

In 1914 the map of Europe was very different from the way it is today. There were three vast Empires, the Austro-Hungarian, the Ottoman *(Turkish)* and Russian. The first two were ailing and dealing with factions demanding independence in their conquered countries. These two Empires existed side-by-side and were not in conflict with each other. Beyond them to the east was Russia. Britain had an interest in several countries outside Europe, for example in Egypt, to protect her trade routes through the Suez Canal, and in Africa. Northern Egypt was officially part of the Ottoman Empire but Britain had had a presence there since 1882. The vast Ottoman Empire was shrinking due to local wars and by 1901 it had lost some Balkan States and some parts of Greece that it had formally occupied. The extensive Austro-Hungarian Empire also held some Balkan States and its influence there was slowly eroding.

In the years from 1908 all the major powers were increasing their military strength as the situation in Europe became less predictable. Britain, as an island, relied on her naval strength and increased her navy. On land, in 1908, the Territorial Army was formed and the various local volunteer units became a formal part of the British military strength. By 1912 France, Germany and Russia, as well as some other countries, had introduced military conscription.

In the first years of the 20th century there was unrest in several countries in Europe. For example, in 1911 Italy invaded Libya. Serbia and Bulgaria formed an alliance to rid Serbia of the Turks and to throw the Austro-Hungarians out of Bosnia-Hertzegovena. Serbia, Bulgaria, Montenegro and Greece then declared war on Turkey. A conference was held in London to try to broker peace. It failed. Germany offered aid to the Turks and trained and re-organised the Turkish army.

There were many factions and the situation was both volatile and constantly changing. So the event which is commonly accepted as the start of World War I – the assassination of Archduke Franz Ferdinand, heir to the Austro-Hungarian Empire, was at the time seen as another element, although a serious one, in the fight for independence by several Balkan States. This event occurred on 28 June 1914 in Sarajevo when a Serbian National, Gavrilo Princip shot the Archduke. On 28 July 1914, in retaliation, Austria declared war on Serbia and it was this act which caused the crisis. The Austrians secured a German promise of support for the retaliation against Serbia. Turkey, which was ally to both Austria and Germany, agreed to take action if Germany was forced into war by Germany's treaty with Austria.

Many in Britain thought that the Balkan conflict did not threaten Britain and so the British Government waited. Britain had close links with Germany. Kaiser Wilhelm of Germany was a grandson of Queen Victoria and, therefore, cousin to King George V of England and Czar Nicholas of Russia. By his various alliances he was positioning himself to become more influential in Europe.

Once Austria had declared war on Serbia, Germany, as Austria's ally, considered what action to take. The situation was escalating rapidly. Russia declared that she would stand by Serbia and embarked on pre-mobilisation activities along her borders with both Austro-Hungary and Germany. The German navy already had influence with Turkey, and Turkey allowed German warships into the Dardanelles Straits to prevent Russian warships leaving the Black Sea. Britain, France and Russia offered to guarantee Turkish independence if the Straits were re-opened to shipping and the German ships removed. Turkey did not comply.

Germany sent an ultimatum to Russia to cease mobilisation whilst both Germany and Austria increased their mobilisation. When there was no response, Germany declared war on Russia on 1 August 1914. As Russia and France were allies, Germany had sent an ultimatum to Paris at the same time as the one to Russia. This demanded French neutrality as Germany had borders with both France and Russia. Germany saw France as weak and ineffective but feared the power of Britain. On the basis of a spurious charge that French troops had crossed the German border and French planes violated German air space, Germany declared war on France on 3 August.

Germany swiftly overran Belgium, hoping to secure its western front. Britain, although France's ally, declared war on Germany because Germany had failed to comply with Britain's ultimatum to respect Belgian independence and integrity. War was declared by Britain on 4 August 1914 at 11.00 p.m. and the British Expeditionary Force *(BEF)* was sent to France to support French troops and to relieve Belgium.

The number of troops available to Germany vastly outnumbered the combined French, Belgian and BEF troops. Germany and her alliances were known as the Central Command. At the outbreak of war Britain had a Regular Army of around 250,000 with a similar number of Reservists who were former soldiers. The Regular Army had a presence in several parts of the world including Cyprus, Africa, Egypt and India, and these troops were not available to fight in France. The BEF was small compared to French forces and consisted of six infantry divisions with modern weapons and light field guns.

By early September 1914, Germany had over-run the Ardennes and northern France from Lille to Nancy. The French troops and the BEF were forced to retreat and dug in to prevent further German advancement towards Paris. And so trench warfare began on the Western Front. The front eventually stretched from the Belgian coast over 450 miles south to the Swiss border, although the British army occupied only a small part. Their section was from the coast and varied in length from around 20 miles at the beginning of the war, 80 miles in 1916 and over 120 miles in 1918.

Turkey remained neutral, until Britain decided to keep two warships it was building for the Turkish navy causing relations between the two countries to become hostile. In October 1914 a Turkish flotilla went into the Black Sea, attacked Russian shipping and bombarded the port of Odessa. At the end of the month Britain declared war on Turkey.

There were several other fronts such as Egypt and Persia. On 18 December 1914 Britain declared Egypt a British Protectorate in a further attempt to keep the Suez Canal from Turkish control and prepared for this Declaration by increasing its military strength. Reinforcements were sent, including Indian Divisions. Turkish troops moved across Sinai to attack the British positions. The attack was defeated but the canal still had to be protected throughout the war and there were several skirmishes. Britain also had an oil interest in the Middle East. Oil had been found in Persia by a British citizen who had drilling concessions from the Shah. By 1914 this had become a major source of oil for

Britain and it was transported through the Suez Canal. As the war progressed there were other fronts including East Africa, Palestine, Salonika and the northern Italian border.

The war, which many believed would be over by Christmas, was to drag on for four long years.

The Cornerstone Road House tea Rooms (formerly The Junction Inn) at
Church Street/Ilkley Road corner in 1930s.

2. A TIMELINE FOR 1914 TO 1919

Much of this has been painstakingly extracted by Richard Thackrah from back issues of the Craven Herald, Ilkley Gazette and the now defunct Wharfedale Pioneer.

Extracts from past issues of the Keighley News and The Times have also been included. Information from local sources such as a History of Addingham School 1874 to 1894 and the Parish Council Minute books have been inserted, together with brief notes on national events, government regulations and other relevant documents held in the National Archives. Where local newspapers record the same news, only one has been used unless they differ significantly. A few explanatory notes have been added. The day that a news item appears in the newspapers may be some time after the actual event. Newspapers from late 1914 were subject to censorship, reflected government propaganda and were not always accurate in their reporting.

1914

13 February	Robert Parkinson of Adelaide Terrace, employed at a limestone quarry near Bolton Abbey, received a fractured skull after being hit by a stone
6 March	Widening of the Bolton Abbey road proposed to make it less dangerous
20 March	The Alhambra Theatre in Bradford opened by impresario Francis Laidler
1 May	1000 engineers out on strike in Keighley demanding an extra 2s. a week

5 June	A plane passed over Addingham Moor, Silsden and Ilkley and people marvelled at the spectacle. The pilot will be making passenger flights over the summer
12 June	James Emmott of Addingham appointed to the post of Guardian to Skipton Union Workhouse
19 June	Ambulance men helped an Addingham boy who had fractured a thigh after stepping on a ball
22 June	The Winter Gardens in Ilkley was officially opened by the Chairman of the Town Hall Committee, Councillor J Dinsdale. The building was paid for by Ilkley District Council. It was built to hold promenade concerts, balls and entertainments *(during the war the Winter Gardens was used as a rest and recreation room for recuperating injured servicemen)*
26 June	Two men, who had been arrested and charged with falsely collecting for a strike fund, were fined £5 and bound over to keep the peace
28 June	Archduke Franz Ferdinand of Austria and his wife Sophia were assassinated in Sarajevo by Serbian national Gavrilo Princip
3 July	An Addingham man severed a thumb at a mill in the village
5 July	Kaiser Wilhelm II promises German support to Austrian Emperor Franz Joseph in any conflict against Serbia
	Strikers in Keighley threw stones at buildings and non-strikers and women in the Parkwood district shrieked and booed in support of the strikers. The damage to property extended across the town and police reinforcements were called in
10 July	Programme of evening classes in Addingham announced
17 July	Bolton Road causeway to be extended to Aynholme Bridge

25 July	Serbia starts to mobilise its army, and troops are stationed by Serbia's ally Russia on Russia's border with Austria
26 July	6th Duke of Wellington's Territorials annual camp at Marske, near Redcar, and Ilkley Howitzers at their camp in Wales
28 July	Austria-Hungary declares war on Serbia
29 July	German patrols cross the French border
31 July	Addingham cricket competition
1 August	Germany declares war on Russia
3 August	Germany declares war on France and invades Belgium
	Britain sends Germany an ultimatum that it must withdraw its troops from Belgium.
	Britain orders troop mobilisation
	The Bank Holiday is extended by one day to avoid a run on the banks
	The heatwave continues and families spend the extra day enjoying the countryside
4 August	Germany declares war on Belgium and the ultimatum given by Britain is rejected. War is declared at 11 p.m.
5 August	Reservist soldiers and seamen report to their unit headquarters. All Territorials required to report to their units for mobilisation
6 August	Royal Navy Ship "Amphion" is struck by mines in the North Sea with a loss of 150 men
7 August	The Addingham Agricultural Show planned for tomorrow will not now take place
8 August	Eight Keighley residents of German nationality arrested
	The Defence of the Realm Act *(DORA)* was passed by Parliament. It gives ministers emergency powers to make

any Regulations or Orders which might be required to safeguard the health and welfare of the nation in the present crisis

14 August Street lighting will begin on 15 September in Addingham

A car and a van were in collision at Town Head

The Parish Council received a letter from the village band asking for custody of the instruments to be in its care and for their safe storage in the Parish Room as the band with its now reduced numbers was no longer viable. It was noted that the band was in arrears with the rent on its practice room in Silsden Road

Lord Kitchener issued the recruitment poster "Your Country Needs You"

Consideration was given to relief measures to help families of men who have gone to war. The Parish Council thought that the Government was introducing the necessary measures

21 August A sermon at the Wesleyan Chapel on "the relationship between Christianity and war, and the duty to seize the opportunity to show the love of Christ in a time of national distress and need, so that the world might be convinced of the reality of our faith"

28 August A young lady broke a leg when hit by a car when returning from school

A collection in the village for the Prince of Wales Relief Fund raised £21 19s.

Three children were injured by a motor cycle near the Craven Heifer

1 September The Parish Council offered itself to be used as a "committee for the purposes of carrying out any and all officially adopted schemes which may be necessary through the present state of war with Germany"

4 September   Addingham Parish Council met on 1 September to appoint a committee to deal with any distress which may arise owing to the war

5 September   In Keighley a crowd of thousands was reported to have stoned and attempted to burn businesses with German names. The targets were mainly pork butchers' shops in the High Street and Church Green. There was much looting and extra police were called in to help subdue the rioters

8 September   Hundreds of men volunteered at Bradford for the new battalion of the Bradford Pals

9 September   It was suggested that socks knitted by volunteers for servicemen should not be smaller than size 10 and both 10½ and 11 will be needed

11 September   Mr Capstick, an Addingham farmer who had emigrated to Australia in 1912, wrote to the Craven Herald with his impressions of life on a sheep station

A first aid exercise was carried out by members of the Ilkley Voluntary Aid Detachment in the Backstone Beck area; 36 members took part and the "casualties" were boy scouts "suffering from all kinds of wounds and injuries"

Ilkley and Addingham recruits totalling 153 men (21 from Addingham) were sworn in. The Ilkley recruits marched to Addingham accompanied by Ilkley Brass Band and all attended a public meeting. They were seen off with much cheering

Driver O Sutcliffe with the BEF in France, in a letter to his wife dated 29 August, commented on German cruelty to old men, women and children

18 September   William Waters appointed Addingham lamplighter at 14s. a week

Addingham man John Clarke died aged 35 on 26 August in the retreat to the Marne

30 September	The first group of Belgian refugees, numbering 46, arrived in Ilkley

9 October   Corporal McRink, Regular soldier, says in a letter, "We are having it a little stiff out here; two horses killed under me and some of my chums killed and injured. The Germans are starving with hunger. Only nine hours sleep in one week. Always on the go on the fighting line"

Annual Addingham sheep fair. Prices much lower due to the war

Baby drowned after falling into a washtub in the washhouse at Sandpits Farm, Addingham

15 October   A carriage of 64 wounded Belgian soldiers arrive in Ilkley for treatment at the Grove Hospital

16 October   Overseers in the village agree to pay £100 for street lighting

It was agreed that Draughton be joined with the Addingham Distress Committee

Separate groups working to support servicemen have applied for free use of the Parish Rooms and these requests were granted

23 October   Fruit and flowers from the Harvest Festival Service to be taken to the wounded Belgian soldiers currently being cared for in Ilkley

More Addingham war deaths:-

- Private W Ogden: died on 26 September
He joined up in 1910 and his last letter to his mother was on 17 September, which said that he had not yet been in action.
- Private Ryder: died on 23 August in France
He wrote to his sister Mrs A Robinson on 17 August. He is one of four brothers in colours. Two are in India and the youngest, aged 15, was a bugler.

6 November   Laurence McRink has been made up to Farrier Sergeant. He thinks the war will not last long as the British are driving the Germans back

13 November   Road repairs are needed in Low Mill Lane

Concern was expressed by the voluntary organisation collecting and distributing socks for servicemen, that they should be paired and not secured with pins or wire as these are causing injury to the volunteers

20 November   Mr James Whitaker provided a house in Addingham for a family of Belgian refugees. It will be maintained by private subscription and occupied by a widow and her married daughter from Louvain whose husband was fighting

More football club members are in the forces; they are Fred Watts, W Pocklington and J Kettlewell

A concert for the Distress Fund was only moderately attended. Reserved seats had been nearly all booked before the event

Plans are under way to send Christmas parcels and a Christmas card to all Addingham lads in the services

21 November   A man from the north of England wrote to a newspaper saying that in his hillside village life goes on as normal and one would not think that the country was at war: "life goes on as comfortably and undisturbed as before". Food is plentiful and so is work, as the County Council has recently opened a quarry for repairing roads and with plenty of work, "at 7d. per hour, there is no inducement to sturdy young men of the village to trudge away to lead the hard life of a recruit"

A description of life in the trenches, as reported in a national newspaper, indicated that they were clean, dry and comfortable giving excellent protection from shrapnel balls and splinters of shells. The trenches "peek out amid the russet woods" close to picturesque villages. "Quarries and caves provide ample accommodation for whole battalions and ..... most comfortable are the shelters constructed within them"

The Princess Mary, daughter of King George, has launched an appeal for funds to send a Christmas box to every serviceman. She said, "I am sure that we should all be a little happier to feel that we had helped to send a little token of love and sympathy on Christmas morning." *(She hoped to raise £10,000 and £170,000 was raised, enabling parcels to be sent in future years).* The gift was an embossed brass box which would contain tobacco, a pipe, cigarettes, a bullet shaped pencil case and a Christmas card. Non-smokers would have sweets instead. *(The King gave £100, the Queen, the Prince of Wales and the Princess Mary gave £50 each and Lord and Lady Rothermere gave £1,000)*

Swan advertised fountain pens "still 10s. 6d pre-war prices" and suggested "when your thoughts fly home, send a few lines, and a Swan pen will speed your thoughts"

11 December   A meeting was held in the Council Room to consider forming a local Volunteer Corps for home defence. The Corps would be trained in basic military skills. The Army Council was prepared to recognise Training Corps which became affiliated to the Central Associating Training Corps on condition that only the names of those not eligible to serve in the Regular Army or Territorials, through age or other reasons, are registered into the Corps

Two more Addingham men have been killed:-

- George Clayton: of George Street, aged 27
- Charles Prior Clarke: who was one of the victims of the sinking of   HMS Good Hope. He was aged 30 and leaves a widow and three children

13 December   The row continued as to who should pay for repairs to Crossbank Road

16 December   Whitby, Scarborough and Hartlepool were shelled by German battlecruisers.

24 December   Gifts of flour, cheese and potatoes for Belgian refugees have arrived from the Canadian Government

Christmas activities this year will be more subdued than usual out of respect for our lads serving at the front

The Queens Theatre in Keighley was staging a thrilling drama "A Mill Girl's Secrets"

1915

January   Mrs Dunlop's working party for making bandages for wounded soldiers recommenced in the Council Room and was given the use of the room free of charge

8 January   The Distress Committee reported that many more good homes are needed as large numbers of Belgian refugees are due to arrive here soon

14 January   The Bradford Pals marched from their temporary quarters to Skipton where a new semi-permanent Raikes Camp had been erected. On the march they were accompanied by massed bands and other units including the Territorial Reserve. In total 4,000 marched via Bingley where they stopped to salute the Belgian refugees billeted in the old Post Office. In driving rain, they stopped at Eastburn House for hot tea and sandwiches, arriving at Skipton at 3 p.m.

15 January   Lectures on ambulance work were well attended by forty one ladies and seventeen men. The examination was taken by forty women and three men and all passed

The Reverent J Duncan Percy of Addingham, who is second minister on the Ilkley Wesleyan Circuit, has enlisted in the R.A.M.C. Territorials. He said that the "call of duty is imperative"

19 January   First German airborne attack: Zeppelins bombed Kings Lynn and Great Yarmouth over a two day period. Five

people were killed and a number injured

The first death in the Bradford Pals in Skipton when a young Private died from pneumonia

22 January   The Distress Committee reported that Belgian families were given a choice of three houses by the ladies of Addingham and over £5 raised for the refugees

The colonies have sent gifts of 90 lbs of potatoes and 100 bags of flour and it was decided to divide these equally between each Belgian refugee in Addingham and Draughton

Following a number of road accidents from motorised vehicles, the Local Government Board has agreed to the Parish Council request for a 10 mile an hour speed limit for cars between the Craven Heifer and Cross Ends and the Crown corner to Aynholme Bridge

23 January   The Highland Pipe Band visited the area in a recruitment drive. At an assembly in Keighley young men were told that the British soldier at 1s. per day is the highest paid in Europe

Francis Norman Bell married Edith Jackson at St Peter's Church, Addingham. *(Shortly after he joined the Royal Navy. He died in 1917 and is buried in Rio de Janeiro)*

29 January   With many men away with the colours, appeals were made to women, especially those who would not normally consider paid work, to step forward and volunteer to help the war effort

5 February   The latest Belgium refugees are from Dixmunde which was totally destroyed in the German advance

12 February   Forty Addingham people joined the Volunteer Training Corps and they now need room for drill and rifle practice

The education of the Belgian children was giving cause for concern. Discussions were reported in the Craven Herald regarding the earnings of the adult refugees, especially the setting up of a fund to be paid into from earnings so that they would have money on repatriation

26 February   POW Private Hudson was at Soltau and thanked Mr Flint for the cigarettes and the box and says he longs for cheese, butter, cakes, OXO cubes and tinned beef

5 March   A Belgian boy is attending Ilkley Grammar School and a girl is at Skipton Convent

Consideration was given to providing a public clock in Addingham but the proposal will not be considered until the war is over

A letter was read at the Parish Council meeting concerning Separation Allowances for soldiers' children over the age of 16 years, who are either apprentices or not earning more than a nominal wage or are not attending a Technical Institute or University. *(There is no note of any action taken)*

There was a proposal to widen Bolton Abbey Road to make it less dangerous

12 March   Keighley Fire Brigade suggested at a Council meeting that they visit Addingham to inspect the fire hydrants. The Fire Brigade was now costing Addingham £13 per annum. This was formerly paid by the Rural District Council

The Parish Rooms were so much in demand for use by local groups that Mrs Wilkinson was appointed caretaker at £5 per annum

4 April   More Addingham men have joined the Leeds Engineers. They are:-

- Frank Holmes
- Benjamin Brear
- Ellis Kettlewell
- Arthur Holmes
- James Hillbeck

9 April	Reported that Lance Corporal Walter Emmott was killed in action on 20 March. He had been a Reservist in the 2nd West Riding Regiment. A former captain of the Addingham football team, he leaves a widow and one child. Employed at Lister silk mill he is the fifth Addingham man to die and two others are POWs

Edward Lawson had a seizure whilst cycling from Ilkley to Addingham. He was found on the road, unconscious

14 April	Several Territorial battalions of the Duke of Wellington West Riding Regiment landed at Boulogne with the 49th West Riding Division

30 April	Still more Addingham men are joining the Army.

For the Leeds Engineers:-

- Edward Lister
- Tom Throup
- John England
- Tom Wade
- Wilfred Ettenfield

For the Howitzer Brigade:-

- Dennis Holgate
- Dale Smith
- Clifford Horsman
- Tom Lancaster

For The 6th West Yorkshires:-

-Granville Moore

£8/14s. has been received for the Belgian Refugee Fund

7 May	Addingham Education Sub-Committee read a circular regarding the employment of children in agricultural work during the current emergency

The passenger liner "Lusitania" was sunk off the coast of Ireland with a loss of 1198 lives, many of which were women and children

21 May	Ilkley Gazette added George Rishworth Snowden of Addingham to its "Roll of Honour" which is the list of men volunteering for the front

Bombardier Fred Hall wrote to Mr Shuttleworth of the Sailor Hotel complaining about the poor quality of beer the army provided

Consideration was given to the number of organisations now using the Parish Rooms free of charge and it was proposed that a number of organisations not working for the war effort should pay. This included the Gala Committee which had paid 9s. in 1914, the Yorkshire Penny Bank and the County Council Education Sub-Committee

In March Mr Bramley Lister was paid 16s. for leading *(carting)* stone to build a retaining wall at Silsden Road Allotments which Charles Towers was repairing

The Mayor of Keighley called a meeting to discuss the scope of new occupations for women, such as work in shops, on farms, in public transport, banks and offices *(some 500 women applied for the new jobs)*

28 May   Private Fawcett of the 1st East Lancashire Regiment, aged 21, was killed in the trenches near Ypres. He had played in the regimental band. Wounded in September 1914, he went back into the line. Killed instantly by a bullet when holding a critical position. He had lived in east Lancashire for 3 years and was the grandson of Mr and Mrs Thomas Myers of Main Street, Addingham

St John Ambulance equipped Spencer Street Congregational Sunday School in Keighley as an auxiliary hospital and received its first 30 wounded soldiers

5 June   Private Charles Ellis of the Yorkshire Hussars was killed on Whit Monday at 4.30 a.m. in the trenches near Ypres. Whilst under heavy bombardment he was shot in the head by a piece of shrapnel from a high percussion shell. He was killed instantly

7 June   The pump at the Sewerage Works ceased functioning and it was proposed that a windmill should be erected for pumping. Instead it was agreed that the existing engine should be repaired and made so that it would be able to work an additional chain pump which would help to lift the accumulated sediment

It was proposed that Addingham Parish Council help raise funds towards an ambulance and it was agreed that a deputation should go to Skipton on 30 July to meet representatives of other councils "under this union" to discuss providing a Craven Motor Ambulance

11 June   Skipton District Insurance Committee *(meeting in Addingham?)* are working on a complaint from a man against a member of the medical profession. It is over the injustice of losing a day's pay in order to attend the Medical Committee in Wakefield to substantiate his claim. He asserted that this should not be tolerated, "on sheer expense grounds alone"

A memorial service has been held at the Wesleyan Church for Private C Ellis, "duty was his watchword"

Prisoner Private E Hudson is now working on a farm near Hanover and writes with his thanks for the parcel

Private F R Spencer writes to his parents in Bolton Road, saying that he saw his friend Lance Corporal W Emmott killed. Private Spencer was a playing member of Addingham Football team and 12 of the team are now serving

The Ilkley Gazette entered Ernest Smith of Addingham on its Roll of Honour of volunteers

Sunlight Soap, in an advertisement, claimed that the cleanest fighter in the world was the British Tommy. "He welcomes Sunlight Soap in the trenches just as you would at home"

18 June   Bugler Strickland wrote to Mr Atack saying that the 7th West Yorkshires are having a lively time and having to take food up to the trenches at night and that he will try

and visit Walter Emmott's grave. Strickland is a playing member of Addingham Football Club

The first census of men of military age in Ilkley and District is to be taken. This is seen as the first step towards conscription

An outing to Bolton Abbey was arranged for wounded soldiers at the Ilkley Hospital and Convalescent Home. They visited the Strid and travelled in nine landaus and two charabancs. Most of the men had been wounded on Hill 60 slopes in the vicinity of Ypres and Neuve Chapelle

The licensee of the Matchless Inn in Draughton was summonsed for permitting wounded soldiers, undergoing treatment at Ilkley, to get drunk on his premises. Two soldiers were found staggering drunkenly towards Addingham and another was found intoxicated on Addingham railway station. The licensee was fined £5 and ordered to pay witness expenses

2 July   Eggs were contributed to the Eggs for the Wounded Campaign by thirty Addingham women

Gunner Keighley of the Howitzer, 4th West Riding Brigade, asked for cricket bats and balls and Mr Atack agreed to arrange to send them out to France

A motor crash near Chelker Reservoir claimed the life of 2nd Lieutenant Ernest Roscoe of the Leeds Bantams who died in hospital at Skipton from his injuries. He lived in Leeds and was travelling with eight others in a car built for five people. The accident was caused by too much weight, the tyre bursting when it got into a gutter

9 July   Feast Week in Addingham, but this year there will be no stalls or other attractions behind the Fleece. The mills will be closed only Monday and Tuesday. No cheap trains are to run and the usual Tuesday trip to Blackpool will not run

The petition to restore the Addingham Gas Light Company Limited, to the register of the Joint Stock

Company, has been successful

16 July	Repairs to Druggist Lane are long overdue and the swing bridge decking is also in a bad state

A burst water main has caused damage at Parson Lane allotments

30 July   A recruitment meeting held near School Bridge was well attended on Wednesday evening. It was preceded by a military marching band playing through the Main Street. Mr Walter Dunlop presided and said that "Addingham had not done badly *(for volunteers to the Services)* but still many more men eligible and their conscience requires stirring up". Other speeches were given by Mr J W Taylor and Sergeant Gavins

16 August   The Allies land two divisions at Suvla Bay in Gallipoli

20 August   John Spencer had news that his eldest son, Frank, was wounded. The letter came from a friend of Frank's to a young man in Ilkley and he was requested to tell Spencer's parents. A bullet struck his right arm and went through his chest

Village contributions to the Craven Motor Ambulance raised £21 16s.

A thunderbolt struck a field last Sunday afternoon as an exceptionally heavy thunderstorm, with rain in torrents and hailstones, passed over the village

A letter has arrived from Frank Spencer, written before he was wounded, saying that he was having a mundane time in the trenches and trying to catch up on sleep during the day as they were in action at night

Archie Watts wrote to thank everyone from Addingham who contributed towards his parcel

26 August   Several letters of thanks for parcels have been received – the men received cigarettes, toffees and other comforts. The letters were from Privates Dove, Driver, McCarthy, Harrison and Sergeant McRink. McCarthy was looking

forward to seeing Addingham and Ilkley again

The Addingham Volunteer Training Corps joined with the Keighley and District Corps on a training outing and route march through Bolton Woods

10 September Four Addingham lads who earlier joined the Leeds Engineers have received their first stripe. They are B Brear, F Holmes, T Heap and J Hillbeck. Private F Spencer has succumbed to his wounds

Arthur Trevor has become a Sergeant

17 September Addingham Parish Council discussed repairs to Moor Lane which were urgently needed and the Moorside road which was also in a dangerous condition

It was also proposed that if Ben Sutcliffe continues to tip fresh refuse *(possibly manure or night soil)* onto his allotment at Newtown he shall be given notice to quit

A lamplighter was appointed for the season and insurance for him arranged

Machine Gunner L R Baul wrote that a German had been taken prisoner. He asked for food and was given bread, jam and tea. He said that the Germans were half-starved having meagre rations of biscuits and bully beef. Baul expressed his pity for them, if that was the case

Corporal J W Fisher of 9th Battalion Duke of Wellington's appealed to the "slackers" to join up and fill the ranks *(his description of constant shell fire, mud filled trenches and being less than 200 yards from Boche trenches would not be encouragement to many!)*

Mr Flint who, for the past year, had organised parcels for all servicemen, formally accepted the position of organiser and fund raiser

22 September Post Offices are to take on extra staff to help deal with sorting the increasing number of letters and postcards received from servicemen

24 September   Eggs for the wounded have been provided by 17 ladies from Addingham Moorside

A flying recruitment column of the West Riding Brigade arrived in Addingham at noon on Saturday. It proved to be an inconvenient time and the rally was abandoned

1 October   The Keighley Corporation Fire Brigade Committee urged authorities and businesses to make arrangements for fire cover

Queen Mary's Needlework Guild appealed for more garments to help servicemen through the cold winter months. It hoped its last year's target of 75,000 body belts and woollen underwear would be surpassed

Fund raising and preparations are under way to provide Christmas parcels and a card for the servicemen serving overseas

The Home Defence *(Addingham Voluntary Training Corps)* at camp in Otley where a review of the whole of the Wharfedale Battalion was held by Lord Harewood

An inquest was held on an Addingham lady who committed suicide by drinking ammonia. She had been worried that her work as a weaver, for over twenty years, was not satisfactory and she suffered from depression. Verdict of suicide recorded due to an unsound mind

8 October   Letter received from Corporal H Horsman saying the Germans are jolly good shots but don't like our bayonets

Private Baul, writing from the trenches, said he was fighting fit but had lost many friends. This war makes "one feel the horrors and degradation of the whole thing". The main issue amidst all the shot and shell is that "our dear ones in the Old Country are safe"

This winter, in the darkest months, school will close early to save gas

12 October   British nurse Edith Cavell executed by a German firing squad for helping POWs escape from Belgium to neutral

Holland

29 October   A cheery letter has been received from Harold Emmott serving with the Australian Forces in the Dardanelles: "The Turks do not like our method of attacking in masses as *(we)* Australians shoot too straight for them to be comfortable"

It was agreed that Trench Committees should be formed throughout the Skipton Division comprising groups of villages to encourage recruitment under the Lord Derby Scheme. *(Lord Derby was now the Director General of Recruitment appointed by the Government)*

The West Riding County Council have written to all District and Parish Councils to suggest the setting up of an Agricultural War Committee to look at food production and continuity of supplies

Fish catches landed at north-eastern ports have been much reduced this year due to military activity in the North Sea. Fishing vessels and their crews have been lost. Crews also reduced due to men volunteering for the services

Hedley Cooper has joined the Royal Flying Corps as a wireless operator. Mr F W Atack, an Addingham grocer, joined the Army Ordnance Corps at Didcot Camp and Tom Cottam is now with the Royal Garrison Artillery at Woolwich

12 November   Questions were raised at the Parish Council meeting regarding the filter beds and the possibility of raising revenue from the site *(no decision was reached)*

Local men are being encouraged to volunteer under the Lord Derby Scheme. If they attest to be called up later they will be placed in Reserve, go back to their normal occupations and given an armband to indicate their status. However, men were encouraged to sign up for immediate service as they would be given a choice of regiment or serving in the Royal Navy. There is only one month left before the scheme closes

The Military Service Act will be presented to Parliament and is expected to become law early next year and will bring in conscription for all men aged 18 to 41 years

Private Dove wrote to say that he had met his brother and about six Addingham lads at the front

19 November   A Sale of Work raised £3 2s. 7d. for the Refugees Fund

Private W Waggitt wrote from hospital to say he had a finger amputated but he was "going on alright" and expected to be home soon

An Addingham cab driver was charged with being drunk and disorderly in charge of a cab in Station Road. He bit two policemen and assaulted them. He became very violent, kicking and striking in all directions. He had been fined on 12 June for being drunk and disorderly. Fined £2 2s. and costs with three weeks in prison if the fine was not paid

3 December   £4 11s. has been raised for parcels for the troops. The Council Rooms have been used for packing the parcels. Many more have been packed this year

Gunner Brown wrote that he was pleased that more Addingham men had enlisted

A Christmas party will be held for those children whose fathers are serving with the colours

Corporal S Selby paid tribute to the medical men and their dedication and courage. His own ward doctor, Captain Lane, had won the Victoria Cross on two occasions. *(Selby had been in France for two months – there is no indication on his service sheet that he had been wounded)*

10 December   Corporal Emmott wrote to say that he was very pleased with the pocket stove as it was ideal for the trenches

Gunner Readshaw was in the Dardanelles and wrote that he hoped the Turks would soon be beaten

15 December	In the wake of the British defeat at Loos, Sir Douglas Haigh replaced Sir John French as Commander-in-Chief of all British Forces on the Western Front
20 December	The Allies safely evacuated 83,000 troops from Gallipoli
24 December	An Addingham market day raised funds for the British Farmers Red Cross Fund
31 December	Private W Overin wrote to Addingham people on behalf of Private R Smith and Corporal G R Moore thanking them for the Christmas parcels. *(Willie Overin was made Corporal in July 1915 when serving with the 9th Battalion, Yorkshire Regiment. Granville Moore was wounded in late 1915 as was Roy Smith. It is possible that all were in hospital together as all three were in different regiments)*

1916

1 January	Reports have been received of heavy losses of Yorkshire Territorials from gas fumes under cover of darkness on 20 December. Men in the reserve trenches were amongst those overcome
7 January	One woman assaulted another in Addingham village centre
	A lantern lecture on the Boer War was given by Bombardier Ben Harrison who was on leave from Flanders
14 January	The Parish Council considered if more allotments are needed. Decision deferred for further discussion at next meeting
	It was agreed that the Addingham Platoon of the 20th West Riding Volunteers should store their bayonets and rifles in the Parish Rooms for which facility there would be no charge
	The Central Control Board on Liquor Traffic requires information as to local consumption of liquor and expenditure on it, whether it presented any public order

issues. It was agreed that consumption locally was normal, public order was good and there was very little drinking amongst women

The Red Cross Society and Queen Mary's Needlework Guild required more knitted items for the troops

21 January Letters have been received by Mr Flint expressing thanks for the Christmas parcels

Private William H Tunnicliffe writes that his section carries 18 pounders and "my lorry carries 3 tons. Roads horrible. We sleep in lorries"

The Reverend H P Walton B.A., formerly in the employ of Messrs G H Walton and Co. of Addingham has accepted a Chaplaincy with the forces. He has been curate at Jarrow-on-Tyne

Under the Lord Derby Scheme the first batch of men from groups 2-5 *(aged 19-22)* reported to Halifax for final medical inspections

24 January The British Government passed the Military Services Act and it becomes law on 25 March

28 January Several more letters of thanks to Mr Flint for Christmas parcels

February Joseph Town married Ada Laycock. Joseph had attested in December 1915 under the Lord Derby Scheme, aged 24 years. He was a grocer's assistant

Abraham Stapleton married Martha Moore. Abraham's family farmed at Gildersber

4 February Addingham Education Sub-Committee met in the Parish Rooms. Emergency school teachers are needed. There has been a drop in the numbers attending evening school *(classes?)* and a general lack of interest in what is on offer

Facilities are to be provided to release school children for farm work owing to the number of farm workers who are likely to be with the forces under conscription. Concern was expressed that release should only be allowed when it was proven that there was a real scarcity of adult labour

Private Fred Fisher is reported gassed. He was a member of Ilkley Rugby Club and pre-war worked for John Green and Son of Bolton Abbey. He joined Kitchener's New Army in September 1914.

Mr and Mrs J Spencer have been told their son Harry has been gassed and in hospital at Eden Hall, Kent. He was a postman in Addingham. His brother was killed in the trenches in August 1915

Advertisements for Lea and Perrins Sauce promised that it would make bully beef appetising and could be securely packed direct to any member of the Expeditionary Force on the Western Front for 5s.

11 February It was reported that troops at the front are concerned that they will not get the supplies and ammunition they need due to a fear of labour troubles and strikes at home. Hopefully workers will not do anything to hamper "our soldiers in their efforts to maintain the liberty of the world – the finest army in the world"

Corporal Throup, writing from Egypt, tells of a tug of war with six mules on one side and men on the other in which Tom Wade from Addingham took part. Everything is expensive and there are plenty of camels

War savings are to be organised by His Majesty's Inspector for Schools

Morton Banks Fever Hospital at Keighley will become a military hospital

School attendance is higher than this time last year

Private Hustwick is away from the trenches in a good-sized town and there are YMCA concerts every evening

Ellis, Hillbeck, Lister and Brear, all with the Royal

Engineers in Egypt, write with thanks for the Christmas parcels

Addingham Company of the 20th Wharfedale Volunteers attended an event at Farnley Park near Otley to witness exhibitions of bomb throwing, trench bombs, hand grenades, star shells and rockets

Private Emmott serving with Australian Forces had met up with Fred Lister on Lemnas Island and had "jolly times together"

Concern was expressed about farm productivity especially pig breeding and poultry keeping

Tram services in Keighley are to be cut because of manpower and shortages

There was an appeal for more munition workers for the Dalton Lane Shell Factory. The factory aimed to output 5,000 high explosive shells per week.

Arthur Trevor, serving in Salonika, wrote with his thanks for the Christmas parcel

The weather in February has seen the worst snow coverage in the UK and Europe for 20 years. In some places snow fell most days for four weeks

6 March	German airships have attacked in the east of England. Bombs were dropped in east Yorkshire, Lincolnshire, Rutland, the Thames Estuary and Kent
10 March	Private Robert W Townson was killed in action. A member of Addingham brass band, he joined up in 1914 and served in 9th Battalion, Duke of Wellington's West Riding Regiment. Gilbert Snowden was with Robert when he was killed. He wrote to Mrs Townson of the attack. Six soldiers were killed by the same shell and he *(Gilbert)* was buried "under your husband". He died "facing the right way and doing his duty to the last"
17 March	Private H Leach has been killed. He, like Townson, was in the 9th Battalion, Duke of Wellington's. Leach, aged

38, had served in the Boer War. Sergeant Fisher, in a letter to Mrs Leach and her four children, said that he died a true soldier fighting for King and Country

Oliver Sutcliffe, writing to Miss Lucy Wade, says he had been in France for twelve months and is now fighting the Turks in Mesopotamia. He saw hand fighting around the supposed Garden of Eden. He has seen many more places of Bible times.

Military Tribunals are to be centred in all towns to hear appeals against conscription on the grounds of hardship, ill-health, conscientious objection to taking up arms and reserved occupation

31 March   Corporal H Horsman of Ilkley Company, Royal Engineers, Wharfedale Howitzer Brigade, has been awarded the Distinguished Conduct Medal whilst serving with the 9th West Ridings. His award is for conspicuous gallantry during operations, in that he directed stretcher bearers under heavy shell fire and continued to tend wounded after the Dressing Station received two direct hits

The Olicana Glee Party provided entertainment for the 1st Addingham Troop Boy Scouts in the Parish Council Room

The Addingham annual rate payers meeting was well attended, especially by Moorside farmers determined to get some measure taken for improving footpaths and roads leading to the Moorside. The meeting held in the Parish Room was lively

Recruitment is under way for women to work as conductresses for Keighley Corporation Tramways. A local trade union leader expressed grave misgivings about women as tram crews and there was a threat of industrial action if that happened. *(The women, six in all, were employed and no strike followed. In November 1916 women were trained to drive trams)*

7 April   The poor winter and early spring weather had been given

as a reason for poor child attendance at school, with the comment that the weather was hardly fit for adults to turn out let alone children. The Education Sub-Committee expressed its concern regarding the situation

Campaign to urge people to eat less bread is launched

14 April   Private W Ettenfield, writing from France, remarked on the terrible wet weather conditions but optimistically felt the warm weather would soon arrive

An inquest was held on Mr Tom Demaine of Farfield Farm, who was killed on the railway. He was crossing by a level crossing to get water for his sheep when hit by a train. His son found the body. Verdict: knocked down and accidentally killed. Mr Demaine was 76 years of age and one son, Harry, worked in an estate office. The other son, Harman, was a gardener living at 74 Main Street, Addingham

Rifleman Frederick Ryder has been presumed dead whilst serving with 2nd Battalion of Kings Royal Rifles. He has been missing and unheard of for over a year.

The Brigadier General Berwick Copley inspected the Wharfedale Volunteer Corps in Ilkley. They formed up on the cricket field. The Addingham 20th Corps sported the new uniforms provided by Mr Douglas of Farfield Hall. *(Fifty uniforms were presented by Mr Douglas and a photograph of the men appeared in the Ilkley Gazette the following week)*

21 April   Driver Oliver Sutcliffe, still in Mesopotamia, is fighting hard in temperatures of up to 120°F in the shade

Further air bomb attacks over eastern England earlier this month

23 April   Addingham Parish Council has received complaints about the state of several roads, including Parsons Lane, Crossbank Road, Moorside Lane and Turner Lane. Adverse weather conditions over the winter and early spring were cited. Costings are to be obtained for repairs

| 28 April | Mr Flint received further letters of thanks for parcels. All are appreciative of the kind people at home who provide them with a few extra comforts |

Comments were made that censorship is becoming very strict and that there is little of public interest which can be recorded now in the newspapers.

Reports that Addingham was very quiet with little social activity. Good works are still being carried out, but fundraising is difficult in these straightened times.

26 May   Mr and Mrs Gill of Prospect Farm, Addingham, celebrated their Silver Wedding on Saturday

The change from old time to summertime does not seem to have resulted in any inconvenience or confusion. Evenings now have more daylight than mornings. *(This change was made under DORA – the Defence of the Realm Act of 1914)*

A list of Regulations for the recognition and take-over of Voluntary Training Corps by the Government arrived at various local Headquarters. Men must be aged 17 and upwards with no medical needs. A maximum number of 600 in each battalion. The Corps would only be called upon for actual military service for the purpose of repelling the enemy or an imminent invasion

31 May   Woollens and cotton fabric are in short supply and the price of clothing – when it can be obtained – is steadily increasing

The Education Sub-Committee expressed its concerns that Addingham National School seemed unable to deal with matters of urgent importance for the well-being of the school

16 June   The Volunteer Training Corps went to Guiseley for the memorial service for Lord Kitchener and all the men who have fallen in the war

The Friends Ambulance Service founded by the Quakers now has almost 1,000 men in France and Belgium. As pacifists they do not join in the fighting, seeking to save life and serve God. The service is funded by the Society of Friends

Wilfred Holmes wrote from France saying that they are having lovely weather. Now away from the front and band concerts are held every day

30 June   The Duke of Devonshire has been appointed by the King to the post of Governor General and Commander in Chief of Canada

Horace Hustwick just out of the trenches after eight days where "they gave us it very hot". He had met up with Jack England, Pat Holmes, Ellis Kettlewell, Wilf Ettenfield, Teddy Lister, Patsey *(Paddy?)* O'Shea and Sergeant G McRink

(Names published in the paper from letters such as this could be of real comfort to families as letters from loved ones could be lost or delayed due to the fighting. Word of mouth would also go around the village)

Addingham was quiet during Feast Week and premises were closed for 6 days. Some of the mills have a holiday fund and one had £80 to dispense

Education Sub-Committee heard that school attendance was still low due to coughs, colds and sneezes

1 July   *(This was the first day of the Battle of the Somme but no news was reported immediately and then only the barest details and censored reports. This was the worst day's fighting in British military history. Around 750,000 men attacked the German lines on a twenty five mile front and by the end of the day nearly 60,000 were dead, wounded or missing. Dozens of Addingham men took part)*

14 July   News has come through of Addingham men wounded and missing. They are:-

- Private Smith, the 19 year old son of Mr and Mrs J Smith of Adelaide Terrace, who joined under-

age in 1914. He is in Oxford General Hospital. Before the war he worked for Johnson Confectioners in Ilkley
- John Burke, aged 20, son of Mrs Burke of 13 Jubilee Terrace is wounded. First Addingham youth to enlist under the Lord Derby Scheme. He was an engine cleaner for the Midland Railway
- Private Willie Roe, aged 38, serving since 1914; in Northampton War Hospital. He had worked for G H Walton and Co.

(Over the next four weeks twenty seven Addingham men were reported wounded, missing or killed and then more in September and October giving a total of over forty in the five months duration of the battle. The details of these are not included here but are in the alphabetical list of the men who served)

21 July	There was industrial unrest reported in the national newspapers and the threat of strikes. Jack England, writing from the front, says he can't imagine why there should be strikes in England when there might be a more serious escalation in the fighting
4 August	The body of a small boy was found by a boy scout in the mill goit at Listers Low Mill. He was identified as Stephen Parkinson, aged 3, and had drowned after accidentally falling into the River Wharfe

The Military Tribunal dismissed the appeal of a 28 year old Addingham man to be classified as a Reserved Occupation. He worked for the Co-operative Stores and was a bread roundsman delivering to outlying villages

A memorial service for all those killed, missing or wounded in the current conflict was held at St Peter's Church. A large congregation attended a most impressive service

A group of men have been described by the Scottish writer as "Addingham Highlanders". They are actually men from the village who went together to join the Cameron Highlanders last year. The writer referred to their home as a village in the Craven Highlands and said "as for language, Yorkshire in most places will pass muster for Scots any day"

18 August   The Treasurer of the Central Committee in Skipton, solicitor Mr Richard Wilson, sent a receipt to the Parish Council for £21 16s. being the amount collected in Addingham for the Craven War Ambulance

A Charlie Chaplin film showing at the Cosy Corner Cinema in Keighley was advertised "it will cure you of the blues"

Addingham moors were shot over for grouse by Mr J T Hemingway's party. They bagged 162½ brace. The birds were plentiful, plump and good. Mr Hemingway also leases shooting on Ilkley Moor

25 August   Corporal S Selby wrote from France to express his concerns and the problem of unpatriotic people at home not pulling their weight while men are fighting to prevent tyrants being resident in England

2 September   The first Zeppelin shot down over Britain with the Royal Flying Corps using new explosives and incendiary bullets. *(Robert Cloughs, Keighley Gas and Oil Company powered the searchlight used to find that first Zeppelin – and others shot down later)*

8 September   It was reported to the Education Sub-Committee that owing to the harvest and shortage of labour, many children had been absent from school without permission

An old boy of Addingham Wesleyan School, Harold Hillbeck, now on furlough from the Royal Navy, and who had seen service in the "great Jutland sea fight", paid a visit to school to tell of his exploits

22 September   Private Edward Burke, writing home, said that he had a lucky escape as he had been slightly injured but his overcoat and oilskin cape saved him from further injury

25 September   A German bomb was dropped from an airship onto

Clough Fold, Rawtenstall. It failed to explode

Fears were expressed that airships might target other industrial units and factories inland

3 October   It was agreed by Addingham Parish Council that all street lights be extinguished over the winter months and that people be asked not to shine lights. All dangerous corners will be whitewashed as will street lamps. This will cost 10s.

6 October   The annual Addingham Sheep Fair produced a very light show and this was largely as a result of the restrictions in place

Corporal Benson, serving in India, spoke of his sadness at so many Addingham casualties in France. Recovering from malaria, he mentioned monsoon conditions

The Military Tribunal granted a temporary exemption to military service for an Addingham "jack of all trades". He carried out the roles of grave-digger, chimney sweep, whitewasher and general repairs of buildings and in the weaving sheds

27 October   Listers Mill manager, William Watson, received a silver tray from the employees on the occasion of his marriage to Annie Mitchell at Bolton Abbey

30 October   Because of the risk of air raids, local gas works companies asked householders and businesses to turn off all gas taps at night in case the supply had to be cut. In the event of this happening supply would be resumed at 5.30 a.m. the following morning

3 November   The milk dealer in Addingham put up the price to 4d. per quart *(two pints)*

10 November A stillborn child was found in the sewerage tank at the sewerage works. A local girl has been charged with concealment of a birth

24 November Christmas parcels to Addingham servicemen will this year contain plum loaf, tinned salmon, toffee, soap,

French paste, socks and a Christmas card

1 December   Private F Lister, with the transport section in Egypt, says he is still in the Sinai desert, long past the Turkish base at Katia. Drinking water is being carried from Port Said, over 50 miles away

It is reported that all allotments owned by the Parish Council are now occupied and it was proposed that the Stamp Hill fields be examined with a view to providing extra allotments. Over 5½ acres are currently under cultivation

22 December   The Ilkley Company of Volunteers marched to Addingham on Sunday for joint field manoeuvres

26 December   Private J E Townend of Bradford married Miss Bessie England at Addingham. The wedding was a quiet one as Townend's brother had been killed in November

1917

5 January   The Addingham Platoon of the West Riding Volunteer Corps were present at a church service. The sermon expressed hope that this year would bring peace. Huge loss of life made people think that there was no future to life and there was a need for courage born of a confidence in God and the righteousness of the cause of this national crisis. In the re-adjustment of social problems which will inevitably follow, bold and courageous measures will be required and it was the duty of the church to see that Christian ideals had their proper place. *(It is highly likely that this sermon was by the Reverend Joseph Hall, Rector of Addingham. Two of his sons, Clifford W Hall and the Reverend George R Hall, served in the forces)*

12 January   Archie Watts, writing to Mr Flint, said that country people think of their lads differently from "townies" and it makes one long for a time when we are all back

Frank Atkinson, serving on HMS Astrea from East Africa, writes "that the weather is hot with snow on the mountains – *(I am)* often wet with perspiration"

31 January Germany announces it will continue its intense submarine warfare in the hope of starving Britain into submission

2 February The United States cuts diplomatic ties with Germany as U-boats threaten American shipping

A request from West Riding County Council to all local councils for them to provide school gardens for school children

The Wesleyan school has secured the use of 270 square yards of land for the children to cultivate vegetables. It is at the junction of Back Lane and Long Ridding Lane; "potatoes are the first aim"

There was a fracas at the Fleece Inn and a man was arrested on a charge of assault. The incident occurred on 21 January and there was evidence that the defendant was greatly provoked. Defendant fined 1 shilling

9 February Two of the morning train services to Skipton and Ilkley have recently been withdrawn to meet war needs generally on the railway

12 February The Parish Council agreed that £95 of the Recreation Ground account be invested in £100 of 5% stock in the War Loan. *(There are notes in the payment book for 1920 and 1921 in regard to this loan)*

16 February The reduced rail service and the apparent apathy at securing land for new allotments were both raised at the Parish Council meeting

Sergeant H Hustwick wrote that it was tough luck on the lads in the trenches *(the weather was bitterly cold)*. Hustwick was behind the lines and keeping fit with all kinds of sport including running, boxing, football and tug-of-war

23 February Sapper England wrote to Mr Flint, "I don't think another village in England can beat our record for parcels". The

weather here is very severe, everything frozen up for five weeks

9 March

A talk was given by Mr Oddy of Farfield on how to grow potatoes. There was a fair attendance at the Mechanics Institute

The Education Sub-Committee again reported less children in school than at the same time last year

16 March

The Parish Council discussed land for allotments. It was asserted that it was a duty to produce as much foodstuff as possible and provide as much land for allotments as possible

12 March

The Parish Council agreed to pay Alfred Simpson £13 for the current half year and from September he will be paid £36 per annum for the work. *(This may have been to act as Clerk to the Council)*

23 March

Sergeant J H Brown of Main Street was killed at 12 noon on 13 March. He was standing next to the Captain when he fell and never spoke again. *(The Captain survived.)* Brown was a Territorial with the Howitzers and until 7 January this year had been engaged in training men for the front. Aged 27, he played football for Addingham, played in the brass band and had two brothers serving in France

Edward Town of the Army Service Corps died of pneumonia at Netley Hospital. Aged 23, he joined the Army in February 1916 and had been on the front for eight months. His brother Harry was serving in France with the Cameron Highlanders

Mr Ellis Cunliffe Lister-Kay died in Tunbridge Wells. A cousin of the present Lord Masham, he will be interred in the family vault at Addingham. He lived at Godmersham Park, Canterbury

Private Kettlewell writes with grateful thanks for the socks; he needs many pairs owing to the bad weather. Plenty of shell and shot flying around

1 April   A number of food restrictions become law this month. These are: Wheat, Rye and Rice Restriction Order:

- None of these foodstuffs must be used for anything other than food consumption
- Up to 25% of flour from other cereals can be added to wheaten flour
- The Government will take control of flour mills to ensure the nutritional value
- Bread must be one day old before it can be sold

Cake and Pastry Order:

- Cakes should be made of simple ingredients without an excess of sugar for decoration
- Scones must not have fruit added

The Food Hoarding Order:

- Food on premises must not exceed the amount "required for normal household use and consumption"
- No person can sell amounts to any household than that which would reasonably be used by that household

All the above Orders gave powers, to persons authorised by the Food Controller, to enter premises where it was believed that an Order had been contravened

The Government expressed concerns about the nutritional value of some foods and laid down what amount was needed for healthy activity. It recommended 3,400 calories for a man doing average manual work

13 April   Private G Foster writes that no sooner have they got the trenches tidied up when they are again in an awful state due to Fritz – but "we pay him back with interest"

Mrs Whitaker of Lodge Hill had a letter from her son saying that he is wounded but half the letter is missing and she has no more information

15 April   The Parish Council agreed to occupy one of the fields at

Stamp Hill covering 1½ acres for £4 per annum in rent. John Cockshott, who rented all three fields there should continue to occupy the other two at a rent of £10 per annum. The plots are to be prepared and services provided. A local contractor will clear the site of trees and Mr Brear from the saw mill will be asked to buy them. Walls will be built. The annual charge for a 200 square yard plot will be 4s. 6d.

Mutinies in the French army due to the appalling losses in the Battle of Aisne

3 May   The King issued a Proclamation to encourage citizens to be patriotic and avoid food waste. The Orders now in place were to ensure that everyone has sufficient to eat

4 May   Laurence Whitaker was reported wounded in both legs and arms. Five were killed by the same shell

Private James Lister of Mill Lane has been killed. He was a Reservist at outbreak of war. Wounded three times

Private Alfred Cook wounded in the body and arm

Sergeant H Hustwick received a Certificate of Merit for devotion to duty during the attack at Gummercourt Salient on 25 February

Artificer H Dickinson of HMS Swift is on leave after action in the Channel. His ship was hit by a shell and 5 men wounded. They tried to tow HMS Broke into harbour but to no avail. Took 60 to 70 enemy prisoners

Local man John Smith died of a heart attack when returning home from his allotment

11 May   Philip Brown, wounded on 30 April, died from his wounds. Mr T Brown has now lost both sons

25 May   Private H Spencer wrote that Wilf Holmes had died from gunshot wounds to his side

Private J Rishworth, aged 21, is in hospital in Cardiff with wounds to his foot. It is unlikely that he will walk again

1 June   Gunner D Holgate died of wounds on 17 May at the 49th Casualty Clearing Station. Aged 19, he was in France since December and had served since April 1915. He was the eldest son of Mr J Holgate of Main Street

Letters of thanks to Mr Flint were sent by Privates A Dewhurst, L Wall and Gunner Hartley

8 June   Private Hadley of the Canadian Forces had also received a parcel and thanked everyone for remembering him

Letters from C W Burke to say that he was out in the desert with no canteen for miles

Private A Whitaker had received a postal order instead of a parcel. He had a broken jaw because of a bullet wound to his neck

11 June   The Parish Council agreed to purchase a potato sprayer at the cost of £3 for the use of allotment holders

13 June   First major bombing raid on London killed 163 people

15 June   Mr Oddy, head gardener for Mr Douglas at Farfield Hall, has been appointed as local advisor on allotments by the Committee of the Yorkshire Council for Agricultural Education

A request for a stile at Marchup was made to the Parish Council. The farmer maintained the path himself

Concerns were expressed about the high price of bread substitutes *(this was probably potatoes and oats as these were the more readily accepted substitutes. Porridge and oat cakes were popular)*. Individuals have been asked to limit themselves to a maximum of 4lb of bread each week *(bread was sold by weight not per loaf)*

Children have been asked not to waste bread and to eat slowly. Recipes were produced to show how to use up "waste bread"

ITs A SPECIAL ADDINGHAM
CORNED BEEF, CUSTARD & RHUBARB
STEW !!!

WAR REGULATIONS
1 POT COOKING
SAVE FUEL

Ben Church

22 June	An Addingham man pleaded guilty to being absent from the West Yorkshire Regiment and remanded to await a military escort. He had been a farm substitute but when told by the farmer in Ben Rhydding that he was no longer needed he went home instead of returning to his regimental base
	Private Hodgson wrote saying thanks for the books and that he was now stationed in a good French village. Weather very hot
	Mrs A Dewhurst has heard that her husband has been seriously wounded
25 June	Troops from the United States arrived in France
29 June	Private R Smith died of shrapnel wounds in No 2 Casualty Clearing Station. The Roman Catholic chaplain gave him last rites
	Gunner E Hartley is in hospital in Nottingham with trench fever
	In April, May and June, two million tonnes of Allied shipping was lost, mostly to submarine activity by the enemy

1 July	Lord Rhondda has been appointed National Food Controller
	More Restriction Orders in force. Under the Tea Order, tea must be sold in packets of true weight and under the Intoxicating Liquor Order, further restrictions were made concerning the amount of alcoholic beverage which could be brewed. No wine or spirits could be delivered for home consumption without paying duty
6 July	Private Richardson hoped that the war would be over "for the sake of the lads who are facing the Inferno of Hell"
20 July	There had been no excursion trains laid on for Addingham Feast this year and the Parish Council again requested that the 8.17 a.m. passenger train to Skipton be reinstated
	Signaller F Stapleton, serving with the Camerons, said he could do with a week in Blackpool.
	Private J Pass sent his thanks for the trench cooker, cake, coffee and cocoa. In the trenches, he said that "Fritz was giving them a lively time with machine guns".
	Private Hudson was a POW in hospital in Hamm with a bullet wound to his arm. He asked for soap, writing paper and would like some eggs as he had none for weeks
27 July	Craven men have between them received seventy four awards for gallantry
	Sergeant Hustwick wrote about a visit to his unit from the Queen and said she was met with great ovation.
	Private Horsman said the good weather was beneficial because they could sleep in fields in tents
3 August	The West Riding Agricultural Committee wrote to Military Tribunals to ask if owners and operatives of threshing machines could be given military exemption as they were sorely needed for the harvest, especially in the

East Riding. Coupled with this was a request for skilled agricultural workers to be exempted in the national interest. *(There were no threshing machines identified in Addingham)*

Several Craven women have joined the Food Production Board and will give demonstrations on fruit and vegetable bottling and jam making

Driver Waggitt, serving with the Canadian Field Artillery and who hails from Addingham, was found dead in Hebers Gill, Ilkley. People who had spoken to him said that he was quite sober but very tired and on occasions was seen asleep in Grove Road. During a conversation of around 20 minutes he kept falling asleep. He was home on furlough and planned to walk to Addingham to his family farm on the Moorside. Found dead and believed to have drowned and may have fallen from the bridge into the stream below. The inquest verdict was accidental death. *(Waggitt is buried in St Peter's Church Churchyard, Addingham and his grave is marked with a Commonwealth War Grave headstone)*

An Addingham man "evaded" military service according to the Ilkley Gazette. The man, from Moorside, "a wealthy Yorkshire farmer", was arrested at a farm in Surrey. The article says:-

'He ignored call up papers January and March – and was eventually traced to a farm at Limpsfield. He thought he was over military age and did not report. Had he thought otherwise he would have reported. He was of independent means, yet his sisters bought the farm in Yorkshire to provide occupation for him and his brothers when conscription came in. He was employed at Broomlands Farm, Limpsfield, as a cowman and in harvest and general farm work. It was presumed he was exempt through age. Fined £10 and handed over to military authorities: the alternative being one month imprisonment. Removed to cells but subsequently paid cash.' *(There are a number of inaccuracies in this report – the Addingham farm was, as of 1911, a property tenanted by his father and there were no wealthy sisters, although his mother was from a wealthy background. There were three brothers living at home, all in their mid to late 30s).*

A letter from Durban, South Africa, has been received by Mr and Mrs Harry Gill of Main Street, parents of Lister Gill. It expressed the writer's best wishes for the family saying, "Gill and his friends visited each day for a cup of tea", and noted now pleasant all the soldiers were. Gunner Gill was serving in India when his parents received the letter

Corporal Attwood, who is related to Mr Carline of the Craven Heifer, is in hospital with shrapnel wounds. He was buried by a shell which struck the top of the foxhole he was in

Private Tom Foster has been wounded for a second time and Private John Parkinson of High Mill wounded and in hospital in Scotland

The West Yorkshire Pioneer carried an article about Addingham saying that it had been growing in favour as a health resort with walks on the moors and either side of the River Wharfe "although its architecture and general arrangement is poor and leaves much to be desired"

24 August   Letters received by Mr Flint from the front and from men recovering in hospital

Private W Richardson had been in bed for nine weeks and will now be two months in an Auxiliary Hospital to recuperate

Private G H Strickland had just finished a two day trek under miserable conditions

Gunner Brown was greatly shocked to hear that two of his brothers had died in such a short time

Through the efforts of its Food Committee, Keighley received commendation from the Daily Mail for its programme of educational lectures and demonstrations with titles such as "How to provide dinners for 4d" and for producing recipes using pearl barley, maize, rice and oatmeal. Children were taught songs about saving food and were urged not to be greedy or eat between meals

"Ideal" daily ration leaflets were given out and the Keighley workhouse inmates had their bread rations cut and substituted by porridge and pease pudding

10 September   The post of Addingham lamplighter has become vacant and Henry Spencer will be employed at 20s.a week. A new ladder and torchlight were purchased for his use

14 September   Newtown allotments have shown a good yield of produce. One holder lifted a root with 86 tubers and earlier 2 roots were taken up with 76 and 52 fair sized potatoes.

(Potatoes, cabbage and carrots appear to have been the main crop with turnips for the winter)

21 September   This year there will be more Christmas parcels to pack and fundraising events are to be held over the next few months.

Sergeant Burke sent everyone his warmest wishes from Egypt where it was very hot. He was in the "best of health"

Geoffrey Rishworth was very grateful for the cigarettes as his gun crew were nearly "smoked up"

Corporal S Selby enjoyed the tobacco and said that the way to victory is to carry on and prepare now for a few more years of war

28 September   Grocer Mr J E Atack, who was also a member of the Parish Council, is endeavouring to get support for the Sailors and Soldiers Comfort Fund. Mr Atack also asked for parents of serving personnel to notify him of changes of address for the servicemen so that parcels would arrive quicker. *(He had taken over the organisation of the local scheme from Christopher Flint who had received his call-up papers)*

5 October   More news from the boys.

J Spencer had "just played B Company at football and won 4 to 3"

Private Charles England, of the Dukes, wounded and in hospital. He was out in a wiring party under hot shell fire and has several bad wounds. Aged 25, he had worked as a warp dresser for Messrs G H Walton and Co at Wolsey Shed, Addingham. His older brother earlier wounded and was on light duties at Clipstone Camp

Private Sydney Hadley of the Canadians, son of the Addingham Stationmaster, has been badly wounded in the face by shrapnel. He joined up in Ontario and before going to Canada worked on the Duke of Devonshire's estate. *(A few weeks later came the news that Private Hadley had died)*

The annual Sheep Fair had a very poor attendance of farmers and few sheep on offer. All fetched lower prices

Grays Cigarettes, advertising in British newspapers – "capture the excitement of a cavalry charge with Grays Cigarettes"

12 October   Private W Horsman has been killed – the thirty seventh death from the village. Killed instantly by a shell. He was the son of Mr and Mrs Arthur Horsman of Southfield Terrace

2 November   Private Bert Wall now in hospital had "laid three days in a shell hole as he could not walk and had wounds to his legs"

A burst water main on Mr Hardisty's land at Crossbank caused deep ruts in the road which had only recently been repaired

Sugar rationing cards have been issued

Bradford has opened communal kitchens to cook food which individuals can purchase for a nominal sum. This will save fuel and reduce food waste. The increased purchasing power will also help to keep down the cost of a hearty meal for the family. The kitchens are popular with working women who are working full shifts in mills and factories for the war effort

16 November   The amount of compensation for flood damage to allotments near Parsons Lane amounted to £9 6s. 4d. *(This may have been the result of the earlier burst water main)*

Rifleman F G Carline of the Lewis Gun Section has wounds to his face and eye

30 November   A Merry Evening held in the village raised £14 for the Sailors and Soldiers Comfort Fund. The evening of song, verse and games was enjoyed by all

Keighley Food Control Committee discussed the serious shortages of butter, margarine, lard, tea and bacon and agreed that further rationing would be required in 1918 if supplies did not improve

Shops are being asked to hand over information on their stock in order to reduce queues which the Christmas demand will create

Private J Pass is dangerously ill with head wounds. It is his fourth time in hospital since he joined the army in March 1916. He is too ill for a visit

Sergeant B Atkinson of the R.G.A. is seriously wounded in the neck and his wife has been sent a pass to go see him. *(Only five weeks earlier he had been home on leave after recovering from burns)*

December   Addingham schoolchildren were given a special day holiday by Headmaster Mr Hewerdine "for the splendid achievement of the 62nd West Riding Division at Cambrai in November". *(The Battle of Cambrai began on 20 November and was the first battle with a mass attack by Allied tanks)*

7 December   A lecture was held at Mount Herman by the Reverend Gale, a missionary in South Africa. He spoke on the

work of the YMCA

11 December   The Allies liberated Jerusalem

21 December   Lance Corporal Maloney was wounded for a second time, this time at Cambrai

A memorial service was held for Seaman Norman Bell of HMS Glasgow

The Ladies Troupe held a concert and raised £9 for the Sailors and Soldiers Christmas Fund

Ladies were thanked for their efforts in packing 347 Christmas parcels for Addingham boys in the forces

By the end of 1917 it was estimated that 1 million women were in munitions, 200,000 in general engineering, 16,000 in the Land Army and 76,000 as volunteer nurses

1918

11 January   Mrs Foster of Cockshott Fold has received news that her husband, Private Arthur Foster, died from wounds in a Casualty Clearing Station in France. His legs had been broken and in spite of expert treatment, he succumbed to his wounds. Aged 37 and serving with the Duke of Wellington's Regiment, Foster had only recently returned to the front after being in hospital with trench foot and was expected home on leave on 21 January. He joined up on 26 August 1916 and had been employed as a carter by the Co-op

Mr W H Smith has received a long service medal from the St John Ambulance Brigade. He passed annual exams over a fifteen year period and assisted doctors in running over 40 First Aid and Home Nursing Classes

A day of prayer was held at St Peter's Church. The "Dead March" was played in memory of local lads who had fallen. There was a crowded congregation and a collection for the Ex-Servicemens' Fund

18 January   £9 8s. 4d. has been paid in settlement of claims by allotment holders following damage done to crops last year by a water main burst in Parsons Lane

At the Parish Council meeting the Clerk said the authorities wanted to know what steps were being taken to warn people of air raids and also how the public should be warned if gas had to be turned off at night. The Council believed a buzzer was the simplest way and thought it could be arranged. It was proposed that the buzzer be fixed to the shed of Messrs Walton. *(This does not appear to have been done and would, in any case, have been inadequate!)*

The will of Mr Ellis Cunliffe Lister Lister-Kay formerly of Farfield Hall and of Godmersham Park, Canterbury, has been proved at £111,393.

25 January   Private G H Thompson, now of HQ Staff in Italy, received the Military Medal for carrying despatches whilst serving in France. He had seen a good deal of active service in France and recently transferred to Italy. Before the war he had been employed at Farfield Hall

Harry Rishworth, a miner, was fined 20s. at Skipton for being drunk and disorderly which led him to mistaking the house of a neighbour for his own and falling asleep in it

1 February   Ration cards for butter are to be introduced this month and recipients are to register with a retailer to ensure supplies. Next month meat will also become rationed and Wednesday will become a meatless day. Extra amounts will be available under the rationing scheme for working men and adolescent boys

Addingham Allotments Society discussed allotment management. It was essential for the soil to be well drained and to work the sub-soil to allow roots to strike deeper, thus helping the land to conserve moisture in the drier months. The use of phosphates, nitrogen and potash were considered and soot and lime were good for top-dressing

22 February The Allotments Association held a lecture on manure

The Parish Council agreed to order and distribute 500 leaflets about air raids if the Police Authority will not provide them

1 March   The Christmas Parcel Fund Committee had sent out "one hundred, 10s. notes to men in hospital abroad and to eighty men in hospitals or in training at home. Some men have been overlooked but this was because relatives had neglected to hand in changes of address"

21 March   A second Battle of the Somme marked the German Spring Offensive

Mr Jonathan Fawcett, a farmer at Holme House, Addingham, was buried at St Peter's Church. Aged 94, he had been a tenant there for fifty years and until recently had enjoyed excellent health

5 April   Mr Green has been appointed Commissioner for Yorkshire for the Food Control Committee based in Leeds

Huge gains have been made by the German forces and they have taken many Allied trenches and strategic areas

The Craven Territorials, having spent January constructing a Reserve Line near Hazebrouck, did not have its Christmas dinner until February. Each company had beef and Yorkshire pudding, pork, cold ham, Christmas pudding and other seasonal fayre.

Gunner Gale is in hospital in Leeds. Aged 21, he joined in February 1916 and was formerly a wagoner for Messrs Booth of Silsden

Private Tom Rishworth is in the New Zealand Forces Stationary Hospital in France

Private Wilkinson of the Welsh guards is in a French hospital with severe gunshot wounds to his right shoulder. His wife lives in Cockshott Fold

12 April   The son of Mr Kidd, Headmaster at the National School, Second-Lieutenant E J C Kidd, was killed in an air accident when serving with the RAF. He had only just returned to duty after a few days' home leave

Private Ambrose Emmott was killed on 21 March. Aged 35, he had been in the Marines for 17 years. After serving in the Dardanelles, he transferred to France and was wounded there in February 1916. His brother was killed in February 1915

Private Harry Hudson, gassed in France on 21 March, was in hospital in Southport, suffering from a temporary voice loss

The Reverend Harry Percival Walton, Chaplain to a Shropshire Regiment, wounded in the shoulder and in hospital in Sunderland. Pre-war he was employed by G H Walton of Wolsey Shed, Addingham

A fine of £2 was imposed on Joseph Brear at Skipton Police Court for working a donkey in unfit conditions

Gunner Town of the R. G. A. gassed and in hospital in France

Private Harry Spencer in hospital in Nottingham

Printer Mr Wilkinson was paid 18s. 10d. for printing 500 Air Raid leaflets

22 April	Allied forces carried out raids on the harbour of Zeebrugge and Ostend
26 April	Private G Rishworth in hospital in Britain after receiving gunshot wounds to his foot on 21 April
3 May	Joe Robinson of Low Mill is in hospital with a shrapnel wound in the thigh after only two weeks at the front
	Gunner Norman Ryder in hospital with shell shock from a bombardment on 11 April. He is one of five brothers who have joined up. Two have been killed and the others are on the casualty lists. *(The Ryders were brothers to Mrs Robinson of Low Mill)*
10 May	A postcard has been received by Mr and Mrs J Berry of Bolton Road to say that their son Percy is a POW in Germany
17 May	The Parish Council received a letter from the Food Control Committee asking it to appoint representatives to deal with

Supplementary Rations for manual labourers and to scrutinise applications for sugar allowances by fruit growers

19 May   The last raid on London by the German Air Force. Of the 34 aircraft, six were shot down. The casualties number 49 civilians killed and 177 wounded

24 May   The Addingham Gardeners Association met to discuss arrangements for the show. There would be a prize for the best wartime allotment and prizes for a range of vegetables and potatoes

A lecture was held regarding the techniques of pig breeding and pig keeping

31 May   Trumpeter J Whitaker has died of wounds received on 12 May. The letter to his family said that death came suddenly and he had been "quite cheery and happy up to the last ten minutes". Aged 24, he had been with the Howitzers (Territorial) in France since April 1915. Pre-war he was employed by Lister and Co at Burnside Mill

Lance Corporal Walter Burke won the 100 yards race at the Northern Command Championship at Leicester on Whit Monday. There were over 100 competitors and the prize was a silver cup

Conscription, currently set at an upper age limit of 41 years for both single and married men, is to rise to 51 years of age. *(Conscription was not abolished until 1920)*

14 June   A meeting was held in the Wesleyan School with the objective of securing volunteers for the Women's War Work Corps. Every woman who joins the Corps sends a man out to fight. There are currently around 40,000 in the Corps and more are wanted. Volunteers are paid £26 per annum and all expenses paid. Women and girls are wanted for all categories of work including clerks, cooks and waitresses. The Women's Land Army urgently need recruits in three departments – timber, agriculture and forestry – and girls will work as close as possible to their own locality. Initial pay is 20s. a week rising to 22s. and uniform is provided. Women will, after training, be allocated duties according to strength

and abilities

The Parish Council had received 95 applications for an allocation of preserving sugar

(Jam making was common in most households and the fruit season began with bilberry picking followed by any fruits in the garden such as raspberries and strawberries, then plums, blackberries and apples in the autumn. In the winter months jam was often the only "fruit" families had)

A soldier, Alfred Smith, came off his cycle near Town Head mill in trying to avoid some children. He had a nasty wound to his head and shoulder and is in Keighley Military Hospital

Lance Corporal G Strickland has been awarded the Military Medal for outstanding bravery in France. He joined up in August 1914 and is a well-known football player. His father, J D Strickland, farmed at Highfield Hall Farm before moving to Guiseley

21 June   Arrangements for the Allotment Holders Association September show are complete. Proceeds will be given to the

Soldiers and Sailors Parcel Fund

28 June   Private Norman Beck, serving with the South Staffordshire Regiment, has been killed in action in France. His sister, Mrs Clarke, lives in Main Street. She had received a letter from him dated 14 June saying the enemy was giving them a rough time in the trenches

E Holmes and C Lancaster, both of Addingham, have been awarded County Minor Scholarships

An Addingham farmer travelling to Ilkley on his horse and cart was seriously hurt in the head when hit by a large branch falling from a tree. He is making a slow recovery

5 July   Private J Hadley has been wounded in the left buttock. Aged 19, he had only been at the front since April

Corporal Baul has been missing since 27 May. He is the holder of a Military Medal. The son of the late John Baul of Turner Lane Farm, he was before the war a clerk at Messrs G A Walton and Co

Private Ernest Stocks of the Trench Mortar Battalion is in hospital in France with gas poisoning and influenza. Aged 40, he had been in France since December 1916

An Addingham grave digger, who also worked on the Bolton Abbey Estate, has been granted three months exemption by the Military Services Tribunal. This was his seventh appeal

An Addingham old age pensioner was bound over for stealing a piece of beef valued at 2s. 10d.

12 July   The current balance of the Soldiers and Sailors Comfort Fund is £11 1s. 10d. and plans are being made for the Christmas parcels

Mr and Mrs G A Keighley heard that their son Frank of the Royal Field Artillery had been wounded again. He lost his sight for six days but is now recovering. Aged 27, he joined up in 1914, was wounded in July 1916 and gassed in November 1917

Private Emmanuel Benson reported missing on 27 May. He joined the Yorkshire Regiment in September 1917 and has been in France since March. Employed as a butcher by Mr Oakshott, he is 37 years of age and has a young family.

Sergeant E Burke also reported missing on 27 May. He joined up in April 1916 and had been wounded twice.

19 July   Ten parcels containing cakes etc. have been "sent out to men serving in India and the Mediterranean. A hundred and two notes to the value of 10s. have been sent to men in France and Italy, seventy two to men training at home and eleven to men on leave. The total expenditure was £96 14s. 5d." Some dissatisfaction had been expressed at the way the scheme is administered, but the blame lies with relatives for not complying with "reasonable request". *(This is likely to refer to an earlier note when families were asked to keep the scheme notified of any new address)*

Sapper E Kettlewell is in Morton Banks Hospital with influenza and pneumonia. Aged 38, he joined up in March 1915

26 July   Corporal Laurence Baul was captured on 27 May and is a POW at Largensalza. He will receive Red Cross parcels

Also a POW in Germany, Private Joseph Bell of the Lancashire Fusiliers who before the war was a painter and decorator in Ilkley

There had been poor weather for the annual holiday and rationing has been a restraining influence in keeping many people at home whilst it added materially to the impediments of those who went away

(Generally, in 1918 rationing per person was 4 ounces (115 grams) butter or margarine, 8 ounces (230 grams) lard, 1 ounce (26 grams) tea, 12 ounces (345 grams) syrup, 4 ounces (115 grams) jam (if purchased from a shop), 8 ounces (230 grams) soap or soap powder, 2 ounces (60 grams) cheese, 4 ounces (115 grams) bacon or ham and 6 boxes of matches per household per week)

John Wall, a pupil at the National School, has obtained a

Governors Scholarship for 3 years at Ilkley Grammar School

2 August   The Ministry of Food has appealed to owners of land to give access to their land under the blackberry scheme. School-children will be accompanied by their teachers

(The Blackberry Order prohibited the use of blackberries for anything other than human consumption. The berries would be sent to jam makers who would have an allocation of sugar. No person would be allowed to profiteer and any berries offered for sale would be at set prices)

9 August   Private J Bickle, assistant to grocer Mr Atack before being called up, has been wounded in several places and is in hospital at Great Worley, Essex

30 August   Sergeant F K Holmes of the Royal Engineers has been Mentioned in Despatches for good work and devotion to duty. He had also served in the Boer War

The Keighley News reported that some mills and factories were experiencing a shortage of materials and in particular yarn to keep the looms going in spite of a rationing system. Layoffs are likely if the situation deteriorates

Private Tom Foster, missing since 12 April, has been confirmed as a POW. Aged 21, he had three brothers serving and had been wounded twice

Mrs Burke of Chapel Lane has died aged 49 years. She was the mother of six soldier sons

6 September   Lance Corporal Tiffany of K.O.Y.L.I has been reported missing since 20 July. Aged 28, he joined up in March 1915 and had been wounded in May 1917

Three Addingham men are reported to be in hospital. They are Private D Whitaker, Bombardier Swales and Private J Dixon

13 September Private W Smith, whose parents live in Church Street, has died of wounds. He would have been 19 on 14 December 1918. A drummer in the Volunteer Training Corps for three years, he worked as a gardener for Mrs Cooke of

Summerfield, Ilkley

Sergeant L McRink, previously reported as seriously ill in the 29th Australian Casualty Clearing Station, has died in hospital

Bombardier E Hargreaves in hospital in France with a neck wound

Private E Stocks, wounded in the left leg, says he is "going on nicely"

Air Mechanic E Sutcliffe has been missing since 30 August when overtaken by a violent storm over enemy lines. He is aged 31 and has been in the services for twelve years

School was closed this afternoon for blackberry picking *(and again on 1 October and 8 October. It is believed that 290 pounds of berries were collected, although one record says 90 pounds)*

27 September Mrs Robinson of Main Street has received word that her son Driver George Robinson is in a Casualty Clearing Station after being kicked by a mule

11 October Staff Sergeant Willie Gale has been killed

Lance Corporal W J Atwood has been missing since 8 September. He joined up in April 1916 and was wounded in July 1917

Private L Whitaker of the Durham Light Infantry is in hospital in Kent with a wound to his right arm and elbow

The Parish Council said that there would be no street lighting this winter

18 October The Parish Room will be charged out at 30s. per annum for each user, namely the Tenant Farmers Association, the Yorkshire Penny Bank and the County Council Education Sub-Committee. These charges will commence on 1 January. There are a number of cases of influenza in both Addingham and Ilkley and a number of deaths. Ilkley schools will be closed for two weeks as a precaution and extra men will be

called in as grave diggers

Private L Whitaker of Stockinger Lane is in hospital. He was "ambushed in a wood by Germans and eighteen of them were killed"

Sergeant Willie Bell killed in action. He married Miss Cousins, whose parents have the Swan Hotel, and leaves a widow and a daughter. Aged 31, he joined the army in July 1915 after being rejected three times and underwent an operation before he was finally accepted. He was the captain of Addingham Football Club. His wife received his last letter in the same post which brought her news of his death

25 October   At a meeting of the Addingham Soldiers and Sailors Fund Committee it was reported that during the year 349 parcels of food and cigarettes had been sent to servicemen and postal orders to men in hospital

8 November   Signaller Flint is in France among the boys he helped so much

Fred Binns, the landlord of the Craven Heifer, has died of influenza

9 November   Kaiser Wilhelm of Germany abdicated and fled to neutral Holland

11 November The Armistice

The Parish Council, at their meeting on "the day peace declared", recorded their "thanks and appreciation of the glorious service rendered by the men of Addingham on land, sea and air in the defence of the liberty of our beloved country and for the rights of small nations. Our deepest sympathies rest with all the families who have suffered loss of loved ones in the terrible conflict just concluded"

14 November The Secretary of State for Foreign Affairs said in the House of Lords that arrangements will be made to repatriate prisoners from all countries with which this country had been at war.

Extra medical supplies were being sent to help alleviate the suffering of Allied prisoners and transport was being arranged to bring them home. A large stock of emergency parcels will be sent out by the Central Prisoners of War Committee, and 30,000 kits and 30,000 rations for a month would be sent as a first instalment

Ships with a capacity for 9,000 prisoners will go to Holland to collect the men. Two large camps, one at Dover and one at Hull, had been prepared

Those prisoners being held in areas of formerly occupied France and Belgium would be first to be repatriated

15 November In Craven District 1,500 gallant lives have been lost

At a Parish Council meeting Mr Atack proposed a formal thanks to all those who fought for freedom and asked for a dialogue on how best to remember their great sacrifice

Signaller F Stapleton has been burnt by a star bomb in an attack on a house where he was billeted

A General Election has been announced for 14 December, but votes will not be counted until 28 December to allow votes from men serving overseas to be included

(The Representation of the People Act 1918 enfranchised all men aged 21 and over with no property qualifications)

22 November Private Ellis, aged 22, died from wounds when gangrene set in

Gunner T Wood died in Whalley Hospital on 11 November, from wounds. Aged 22, he had been in France three years and had three brothers serving

30 November The Admiralty, War Office and Air Ministry issued announcements that general de-mobilization had not begun and there had been no release of men from the forces. When it did begin priority would be given to those who had employment waiting

They also asserted to both UK and overseas commanders that garrisons still needed to be provided and to this end men may extend their service for periods of 2 years and over. Men must be fit for general service and aged 19 to 35 years. If extended service was signed for before 1 January 1919 men would receive a bounty and a generous UK furlough.

6 December   Lance Corporal Attwood, captured by Germans on 18 September, has arrived in Dover

The village Ladies Troupe held two concerts which raised £50 for the Soldiers and Sailors Fund

13 December   Notice of the death of Corporal W Dixon has been received. He died on 27 October following the attack across the Piave River in Northern Italy

20 December   The house collection for the Soldiers and Sailors Christmas Fund raised £27 16s.

Turn out for the General Election last week was well below average and, but for the addition of the newly franchised women, it would have been very light indeed. *(This was the first general election since 1910 and after votes were counted on 28 December a Liberal/Conservative coalition was formed)*

27 December   Private Arthur Jacobs, formerly of Addingham and now Northampton, has been awarded the Military Medal

Lance Corporal Attwood has recounted his experiences as a POW. He had worked in Belgium at an aerodrome. If they complained of food shortages their captors blamed the British blockade. Sleeping and sanitary arrangements were abominable and there was no medicine. The guards carried sticks as well as rifles. On 14 November he and 1,400 other POWs captive in Belgium were released but could not cross neutral Holland. The Belgian people kindly looked after them for 10 days until they were put on a train for Brussels, then to Calais and finally by ship to Dover. He thought that the authorities had wonderful organisation and looked after the men very well.

Private Tom Smith, taken prisoner earlier in the year, also got back home

1919

January	The Parish Council discussed the question of a war memorial.

10 January   £19 16. 2d. received in subscriptions for the Soldiers and Sailors Comfort Fund

24 January   Corporal Arthur Holmes has been awarded the Belgian Cross for services rendered

Another former POW, Private Percy Anderson, has returned home to Church Street. A POW in Germany since 3 May 1917. He was captured after being wounded. He fought against having his injured arm amputated, which would have been done with no proper medical facilities or medicine. Sent then to Germany he was cared for by the Sisters of Mercy, then removed to Dilmerlager in Westphalia where the guards were brutes and he suffered from beatings, starvation and dysentery. He worked on the railways at Gastrow and boils and problems with his arm meant a spell in hospital, then removal from the railway to a farm

31 January   A meeting was held at Mount Hermon Chapel by the West Riding County Council to discuss how its present straightened circumstances would affect Addingham. It had a serious financial burden and efforts had been made to carry on with depleted staff and to effect the greatest possible economy

The Discharged Soldiers and Sailors Association were offered free use of the council room and the Parish Council received a letter of thanks from the Addingham Voluntary Platoon for free use of the room during the war. This was signed by W Dunlop, Captain of "C" Company of the 4th Voluntary Brigade of the Duke of Wellington's West Riding Regiment and A V Mason, Lieutenant of No 10 Platoon of the same unit

7 February   Members of the 10th Platoon of the Duke of Wellington's Regiment held a tea and smoking concert and were entertained by songs and recitations

The Education Sub-Committee reported that school attendances were unsatisfactory due to bad weather and sickness

At Town Head Mills, three Belgian refugees in the employ of Messrs G H Walton were given presents by their employer in high esteem of what they had achieved

14 February   It was agreed that the council should honour all men who served by compiling a Roll of Honour

Private J Bell has arrived home. He was captured on the Champagne Front on 29 May 1918 and received mixed treatment. With regular Red Cross parcels he was probably better off than the Germans. On leaving the camp his former captors pleaded with the former prisoners to make allowances for the hardships which they had suffered and urged that they *(the captors)* had done what they could under the circumstances.

The Craven Herald announced that it would return to its pre-war size of eight pages

28 February   Alfred Stapleton, only son of Mr Francis Stapleton and late of Addingham, has been appointed Chief Sub-Editor of the London Star. He had previously been Sub-Editor for the Birmingham Evening Post

The Draft of the League of Nations has been completed

Complaints have been made by Skipton Rural Council that the summer occupation by visitors to Burnsall and Grassington caused a shortage for residents *(presumably in 1918)*

The Rural District Council also reported that a number of houses in Addingham were in need of demolition

Blind veterans housed in Ilkley for their rehabilitation are to be sent to specialist centres

14 March   There will be an election for the Parish Council. Eleven members will be elected

Proposed that a Roll of Honour for Addingham service personnel should hang in the Council Room

4 April
Certain provisions made under the Education Act of 1918 are to be enacted. The first will be the raising of the school leaving age to 14 years for full time attendance

The Education Sub-Committee reported much better attendance, probably due to the better weather. Attendance of junior schools better than for seniors

11 April
A second honour for Company Sergeant-Major Kettlewell has been announced. He holds the record for Addingham men who served in the forces for both promotion from the ranks and in winning double honours. Aged 26, he was wounded twice and is a good footballer and boxer

25 April
Glorious weather prevailed for the Easter holiday

9 May
The freehold of Reynard Ings Farm has been sold for £2,200 and its 30 acres will be let for £90 per annum

Parish Councillors celebrated their recent election by giving a banquet at the Crown Hotel

The Education Committee was given permission to allow a one week holiday for the peace celebrations when the Peace Treaty is signed

16 May
There are problems over the proposed enclosure of roadside land at Scar Ghyll Farm, Moorside. The Parish Council opposes such a measure and will write to tell the Rural Council of its opposition

Addingham has requested an extra postal delivery as it only has one per day and Ilkley has three

Despite objections, the Midland Railway says it is impossible to grant any further concessions in train services

Plans announced for the Peace Celebrations. There will be bonfires, a procession of schoolchildren, a field day and teas. The Clerk to the Parish Council was asked to write for quotations for 300 illuminated certificates and to price a

Scroll of Honour to carry 300 names. *(The certificates would be for surviving servicemen and the names of the fallen would be on the War Memorial and not on the Scroll of Honour)*

3 May   An Ilkley girl was hit by a car and badly cut and bruised. The accident was at the point in Addingham where Ilkley and Addingham roads meet

6 June   Private Charles Hood, the son of Isaac Hood of 1 Bolton Road, who has been missing since 3 September 1917, is almost certainly dead

The Parish Council reported that the illuminated certificates are too costly especially when framed

There was poor attendance at the meeting to discuss the Peace Celebrations. Some people said that as there was no peace treaty yet, the celebrations should be when Addingham Park was opened

A 14 year old was accused of maliciously setting fire to a haystack at Low Mill. Remanded at Shipley Detention Home overnight. He came from "a rough background"

13 June   Concerns expressed about the hazardous nature of the Ilkley road through Addingham, especially for motorists. Police have recently prosecuted many motorists for dangerous driving. The need for the council to restrict speed on sections of the road was discussed and perhaps a warning sign at the entrance to the village should be erected

20 June   Twenty car loads of injured and maimed soldiers were given tea and entertainment in the grounds of Hallcroft Hall

28 June   The Treaty of Versailles was signed in the Hall of Mirrors in the palace of Versailles. It ended six months of peace negotiations. A victory parade will be held in London. All children in Addingham schools were treated to a tea in celebration.

It was announced that conscription will end

28 July   Lord Masham officially presented Addingham with five acres of land fronting the Main Street opposite the Fleece Hotel for a memorial park

1 August   The Discharged and Demobilised Soldiers and Sailors Association will hold a fete, sports and sheep dog trials day in September. Mr Flint will be secretary

                 The coal strike has not had a major effect in Addingham and the shortages of fuel have not seriously affected the mills or gasworks although householders are being put to some inconvenience

6 August   The first sod for Addingham War Memorial has been cut by Mr J England JP. The members of the Finance Committee provided the spade

15 August   The Addingham Second Eleven beat the Royal Engineers at a cricket match

                 The Council agreed to commence street lighting on 6 September

29 August   Addingham Football Club is in good fettle for the new season in spite of wartime losses and is in the Second Division of the Wharfedale League

                 Most Addingham servicemen have now been demobilized

                 The War Memorial fund was boosted by a donation of £184 5s. from the Parish Council and there has been a public appeal for subscriptions

                 The levelling of ground for the bowling green has been completed and stone has been "gifted" from a local quarry for the clubroom building. Walks will then be made and the whole complemented with ornamental flower beds and trees

                 There has been the discovery of an ancient hand-mill built into a field wall. It is the base of a stone quern used for corn grinding and is very rare. It may be 2,000 years old

5 September Public concern has been gathering regarding the graves of fallen servicemen buried overseas. The controversial decision

by the government not to "repatriate" because of the prohibitive cost has caused outrage. Instead special cemeteries will be created under the auspices of the Commonwealth War Graves Commission and, in areas of the heaviest casualties special war memorials will be raised, including at Thiepval on which the names of those with no known grave will be engraved

Coal shortages are now beginning to have an effect on Addingham but production in the mills has not been significantly affected

12 September Addingham Show was very successful and proceeds of both the show and sheep dog trials will be donated to the Discharged and Demobilised Soldiers and Sailors Association

Frustration at the shortage of post-war housing and the slow progress was expressed at a Council meeting

10 October   The Addingham Sheep Fair had little stock and a poor attendance

The proposed housing scheme seems unjust as only the better off will be able to afford them.

There was a meeting to discuss the revival of Addingham Brass Band

21 October   The Treaty of Versailles was registered with the League of Nations. The "final chapter of the conflict has ended"

Varley's general store (127 Main Street) which was run by Mr Chris Flint during the war. For three years, Mr Flint organised comfort parcels for the soldiers (see p.106).

3. ON THE HOME FRONT

This chapter examines some of the effects of the war on the civilian population and the ways in which government controls affected everyday life.

News from the war fronts of major setbacks, conscription, the huge loss of life which devastated communities, rises in food prices, shortages and the constant requirement to make further sacrifices, led to a hardening of attitudes in even the most patriotic citizens.

Children were particularly hard hit as they sometimes suffered from hunger and cold, had less access to a good education when schools were requisitioned and were expected to gladly bear the privations of life. Many found that their fathers were away for months, if not years, at a time when war had made them almost strangers. Their mothers were either required by economic necessity or peer pressure to work long hours and some children, on reaching the age of 12, also had to work to help the family economy.

War was costly, not only in terms of its social and emotional impact, but in government spending, much of which was achieved by raising income tax to 10s. *(50 pence)* in the pound. Everything cost more and there were major shortages of all commodities. All but the very wealthy suffered.

The Government had sweeping powers and exercised great control over every aspect of life. Punishment for minor infringements was common and free will was frequently sacrificed for the good of the country. Changes began as soon as war broke out when the Territorials and Reservists marched away and families overnight lost their bread winner.

Propaganda was all pervasive and people were put under great pressure to conform to government appeals and requests. Newspapers, magazines and even the pulpit became instruments for government messages.

The war came as a shock to most people as the general feeling from newspaper reports was that Germany would back down. The crisis weekend was the August bank holiday, the first weekend of the month. A few days earlier the holiday had been extended by a day to avoid a rush on the banks. Many people were away on holiday or on one of the day excursions run by the railways to seaside towns or beauty spots. England was in the middle of a heat wave.

Newspapers had articles about the situation in Europe but these were not seen as headline issues by most of them. War was declared on Germany at 11.00 p.m. on 4 August 1914 and next day made headline news. Whilst there were peace rallies and letters to the press condemning the war, these had no effect. Britain was at war and had to deal with it.

August 1914 saw a balmy few weeks of hot and sunny weather; however, winter of that year was the wettest on record with fierce storms at home and in northern Europe. There were fears that the big guns in France had triggered the rains and the Meteorological Office tried to calm those fears by reminding people that severe rainy periods also occurred in peace time. Gales in the English Channel disrupted supplies to the Western Front and caused delays to movement of troops and the wounded. To add to the misery it turned bitterly cold in mid-December with sleet and snow. Severe frosts began in late December and records of the Christmas Truce all tell of snow and frozen ground. Heavy snow fell in France on Boxing Day. In England a ferocious storm on 28 December, backed by high winds, caused several enemy mines in the North Sea to break free causing extra hazard to shipping. Newspapers reported the collapse of buildings and winter crops, such as turnips and potatoes, were still in the ground for many weeks. The following winters were also very cold with severe frosts and snowstorms.

In the first few days of the war the British Government passed the Defence of the Realm Act *(DORA)* which allowed it to make Orders and Regulations to safeguard its citizens and aid the war effort. These powers were wide ranging.

One of the first restrictions in place was that of censorship. Newspapers felt its effects immediately and any articles concerning the war had to pass the censor. Reporters were forbidden to go to France but many were highly resourceful and were able to report back to their newspaper. If caught, the reporters could be arrested and detained by the army. The

Government had not reckoned on the tenacity of the war correspondents and within a few weeks was allowing reports of defeats, and the German advance, providing they were coupled with anti-German messages. This was done to aid recruitment because of the heavy losses of men of the British Expeditionary Force.

Attitudes to Germans

German atrocities to Belgian civilians were widely reported and such reports resulted in over 300,000 men volunteering for the services in a little over three weeks.

Another, and not unexpected result of the stories in the newspapers was a backlash against Germans living in Britain. Bradford had a large community of people of German origin, although most of these had been established in the city for two or more generations. Some were wealthy manufacturers and some had even served in the British army. What identified them was their German surnames. Shops and homes were targeted and a number arrested. Keighley with its very small German population saw the greatest violence. There were reports of angry mobs of several thousand, running amok, stoning, looting and attempting to set fire to businesses in the High Street and Church Street which had German names over the door. Most of these businesses were pork butchers and one, Andrassy's, was owned by a man who had lived in Keighley since the 1870s. All his children had been born there, some had married locally and two of his sons were to serve in the British army during the war.

There was concern that some of these Germans could be spies and ordinary people became increasingly suspicious of anyone "loitering" or taking photographs – both activities were a criminal offence under DORA. A couple were questioned in Skipton, suspected of spying, as they were noticed near the new army barracks being constructed at Raikes Road. It turned out that they were there in an official capacity and checking on progress.

German resentment continued but the sinking of the Lusitania in May 1915 hardened attitudes further. In some industries people refused to work with Germans and some lost their jobs as employers feared strikes and reduced productivity. In Bradford German bands were forbidden from playing in public places.

At the start of the war there was a heightened awareness of the German origins of our royal family. Kaiser Wilhelm of Germany was cousin to King George V and a grandson of Queen Victoria who had died only fourteen years earlier. Wilhelm had been a regular visitor to Britain and held honorary rank in both the British navy and army.

An early casualty of the anti-German feeling in Britain was the resignation of the First Sea Lord, Admiral Prince Louis of Battenberg. In a letter to Winston Churchill he wrote "I have been driven to the painful conclusion .... that my birth and parentage have the effect of impairing my usefulness on the Admiralty Board". Winston Churchill accepted the resignation but complemented Prince Louis on the fine work he had done for the navy, including overseeing the "enormous influx of capital ship, cruisers, destroyers and submarines" which had been commissioned and built in the preceding few years. Prince Louis' son was then serving in the British navy and did so throughout the war.

In 1917 the family name was changed from Battenberg to Mountbatten. Also in 1917 and following the same concerns, King George V officially adopted the family name of Windsor, replacing Saxe-Coburg-Gotha.

Both King George V and Queen Mary played a prominent role in supporting the armed forces and civilian population. They visited military camps, reviewed the troops, visited hospitals, launched ships. The King alone made over 400 official visits during the 4 years of war. The Queen carried out many visits, especially to hospitals and organisations helping the troops and, in addition, she chaired a number of committees and became patron of many more.

Postal Services

At the start of the war the Army Postal Service found itself unable to cope with the increased amount of mail, especially that sent to and from servicemen. Britain had not been at war for sixteen years and there was a huge increase in personnel within a very short period. One of the early examples of the problems faced by the postal service was after the Battle of Mons, just a few weeks into the war.

Ernest Norris, an Addingham man, was a Reservist recalled to his regiment on the day war was declared. When news filtered through about the British defeat at Mons and the subsequent retreat to the Marne, Mrs Norris became anxious because she had not heard from her husband. The family were connected with St Peter's Church and Mary Ashby, who then lived with her mother and sister at the old Rectory, knew the family well.

She wrote to a friend, Edwina Lewis, who had army connections. Edwina contacted Major Wylde who commanded the battery in which Ernest served. The reply came back two months later on 3 November 1914 that as of the end of October Ernest was safe and well. Mrs Lewis wrote to Mrs Ashby, "I hope that they will get a letter soon but they have been very busy getting letters through" and "we have all got to fear the silence and so long as she *(Mrs Norris)* hears no bad news from the post office she will know her husband is well".

Ernest Norris and Mrs Norris with the children

Around a month later Mrs Ashby wrote to Ernest and her letter indicated that his wife had by then heard from him. The letter (overleaf), and the photographs, are reproduced by kind permission of the Norris family.

30 November 1914   Addingham Rectory
                                                        Ilkley
                                                        Yorks

Dear Norris

When I went up to see your wife a few days ago she told me you would like a body-belt, so I am sending you a parcel containing one I have knitted and I hope it will fit you and protect you somewhat from the cold. I have also enclosed a few of the little things which you may find useful, and there is a tinder-box from your wife as well. Little John and Mary both held it in their hands, talking of their dear Daddie, and poor Mary cried when her mother gave it into my care, fearing that I might defraud the rightful owner! The tears rolled down her shell-pink cheeks and she buried all her pretty curls in her Mother's neck until she was re-assured, poor mite! John stared in blank amazement when I told him that "once upon a time" I used to teach his Daddie in Sunday school, when he wasn't much bigger than John himself. I believe all little ones fail to realise that such superior beings as the "grown-ups" have ever been children – much less babies! I have three myself – boys aged five and three, and a girl just a few months younger than yours – and your wife and I agree that we are indeed blessed to have them to care for and train in the right way, whilst we are separated from those we love the best. We must make them worthy of the brave men who are setting us all such noble examples, defending their country and their homes with the most splendid valour, self-sacrificing heroism, and cheery endurance the world has ever seen. I am sending you a copy of Sir John French's first despatches, for I feel sure that you and your comrades will be glad to read, and to follow in the maps the clear and correct account of what really took place in the earlier stages of the War. Even if you have seen the newspapers regularly, as I have – and I don't see how you could get them out there – you would still get tremendous help from the despatches in understanding the difficult positions, the great odds, the almost insurmountable obstacles that have been so gallantly and brilliantly overcome. If only for that, I do hope my parcel will safely reach you 'ere long.

I expect you will have received the photo of your wife and the little ones, which I thought very good. They all look very much better than when Mrs Thompson and I first went to see them –

they were then suffering from the effects of the measles. Curiously enough I had only just recovered from a severe attack myself – I'd never had the complaint before – and I have not yet fully recovered my usual health and strength. I was laid up at the time of mobilisation. My husband is Medical Officer of the 3rd West Yorkshire Regiment, one of his brothers is in the garrison at Gibraltar, and another has given up his parish in Canada to join the R.A.M.C. He expects to go to Paris next month. I wonder if you will meet any of them – I have not time to write more, so with all good wishes – in which Mrs Thompson joins – for your good health, good fortune, and a safe return.

Believe Me

Yours sincerely

Mary Ashby

(The child was called Annie and not Mary)

By the end of 1914 a major concern of the Army Postal Service was the huge number of Christmas letters and parcels to be sent to the front. Mail for the Western Front, then the major theatre of war, was sorted at the London Home Depot at Regents Park. Mail was sent by sea to sorting depots at Calais, Le Havre and Boulogne and was carried by trains to the front along with other supplies. The postal service overseas could be disrupted by enemy hostilities, especially from 1916 when the German U-boats and mines were sinking shipping. Many letters and parcels were lost.

Appeals had been made for parcels to be packed in boxes of a prescribed standard size for ease of handling and to save space.

An article in the Times in late December 1914 said that up to 12 December 250,000 parcels were despatched for men at the front and 200,000 the following week, together with 2,500,000 letters and postcards. This number had increased tenfold by 1918. In order to meet this demand the General Post Office *(GPO)* had to requisition 900 vehicles and had secured 23 halls of various kinds for regional sorting. All of this was in addition to its usual day to day requirements. In the London district alone over 6,000 regular staff had enlisted and volunteers were temporarily taking over these duties. Throughout the war the GPO delivered around 12 million letters and postcards each week. The GPO was, before the war, already an extensive and efficient organisation employing around 200,000 people and raising around £30 million each year.

The Government decreed that all letters and postcards to and from servicemen should be post free; the usual fee was 1d. These would be sorted, transported and delivered overseas by the Army Postal Service, but letters to the UK would be delivered by the General Post Office via its post offices in towns and villages. The increased costs of servicing the post meant that the cost per letter went up to 1½d. in early 1918.

With the large number of Addingham men in the forces, the village post office at 103 Main Street must have been under great strain. Mrs Lister was postmistress and in the 1911 census there seem to have been only two other people involved with the postal service which also covered Bolton Abbey. It is likely that extra staff would be needed from 1914 for deliveries, especially to the outlying areas. Mail came in on the train, was sorted in the post office and delivered once a day to homes, the exception being telegrams which were delivered as soon as they were received.

The extreme weather in December 1914 added to the difficulties of the postal services as it struggled to deal with the huge volume of mail. As now, weather conditions affected the daily lives of people; however, severe weather during the war years had a direct, adverse effect on everything from hospital admissions, food supplies, crops and the lives of servicemen and women.

Fear of Invasion

In late 1914 there was a fear of invasion when German battle cruisers attacked the Yorkshire coast. The raids were widely reported as an example of German barbarity because of the number of women and children who were killed and injured. The raids were at Whitby, Scarborough and further north at Hartlepool and took place on 16 December. Several battle cruisers were involved and struck almost simultaneously around 8.00 a.m. although the Whitby attack was a little later at 9.00 a.m. Eye witness accounts put the total number of cruisers at between four and six, but two were involved in the Scarborough attack.

In Scarborough the east end of the town suffered the worst damage with around 100 homes set on fire. The castle received a hit, as did the Balmoral Hotel, the Royal Hotel, a church and the hospital. A number of Belgian soldiers being treated at the hospital escaped injury. In one house four people were killed outright as a shell burst in the centre of their house and in another house three people lost their lives. A postman had his head blown off whilst on his delivery round and people were also killed in the street. In Scarborough 18 died. At Whitby two people died and the abbey was damaged. The greatest loss of life was at Hartlepool where 102 died. In the three attacks over 600 people were wounded and 1,500 shells were fired.

The propaganda element of the raids was quickly realised and soon recruitment posters were released, asking men to sign up and avenge Scarborough. Scarborough was used because, although loss of life and damage was greater in Hartlepool, Scarborough had a national reputation as an attractive holiday resort. The posters had such comments as "the innocent victims of German brutality call upon you to avenge them" and "show German barbarians that Britain's shores cannot be bombarded with impunity".

Winston Churchill, in a letter to the Mayor of Scarborough, wrote that the bombardment was an act of military and political folly and "whatever feats of arms the German navy may hereafter perform the stigma of the baby-killers of Scarborough will brand its officers and men while sailors sail on the sea".

These attacks came only a few weeks after the "Rohilla" had run aground on the Scaur near Whitby on 30 October 1914. The ship had been fitted out as a hospital ship and had sailed from Leith the previous day bound for Dunkirk, where it was to take on board men wounded on the Western Front in the Battle of Ypres. The weather was bad but the ship was needed urgently, so it set out with a full complement of medical staff. Because of the war, the shore lights had been extinguished. These could have provided additional navigation aids in the storm that was then raging. At around four o'clock in the morning the Whitby coastguard saw the "Rohilla" too close to shore and signalled to her. The ship's officer believed that they were several miles out to sea. Then she struck an undersea rock and was driven on to the shore where her hull was split apart. The Whitby lifeboat launched but not from the harbour because of the storm. The men manhandled the boat over onto the Scaur and laid aside the "Rohilla". They brought off 35 people but soon the lifeboat was wrecked by the pounding. Captain Neilson was the last man to leave the ship but only after 52 hours of struggle by the lifeboat men. In all 92 people lost their lives and Barnoldswick lost 12 of its 15 members of the St John Ambulance who had been aboard.

These events, coupled with the loss of many trawlers in the North Sea due to German mines, caused the Government to consider that the threat of invasion was a possibility and that its coasts were vulnerable. Coastal defences were hastily built, the first of these being on the Yorkshire and Lincolnshire coasts, not only for defensive purposes but to allay the fears of the local populations. Airship and airplane stations were built from Kent to Scotland. In Yorkshire these were at Redcar, Scarborough and Spurn Point, and an airship base was built at Catterick. Soldiers were stationed on the coast at "watch points" and were kept for a time on high alert.

Whatever reassurance these defences gave was short-lived when the Zeppelin raids began. These defences did not prevent over 100 airship bombing raids which intensified during 1916. Raids were carried out from Kent to the Tyne and well inland. Blackout became essential and local people were fearful because targets were manufacturing units and munitions factories. The airship had an extensive range and on 25 September 1916 shells were dropped as far inland as Lancashire. The details of that raid indicate that over 40 incendiary bombs were dropped over Bolton, Bury and Bacup by Zepplin Airship LZ61. Most damage and loss of life was in Bolton but on its return to cross the coast near Whitby a final bomb was jettisoned "at Bolton Abbey". I have been unable to verify this.

Skipton – A Garrison Town

In late 1914 Skipton was designated by the War Office as a garrison town and, although it never equalled the size of troops and troop movements as Ripon, Catterick or York, it still played an important role in the training and garrisoning of servicemen.

Skipton was the home base of the $1^{st}/6^{th}$ Duke of Wellington's West Riding Regiment, a Territorial unit which recruited throughout the Yorkshire Dales. They were based at the Drill Hall and went to camp at Immingham Dock for further training on 5 August 1914. By early 1915 there were around 1,500 servicemen in Skipton, most notably the Bradford Pals, who were the first to occupy the new wooden huts at Raikes Camp and later the 5th Border Regiment. Troops were also garrisoned at various large buildings in the town and they would have been a familiar sight in the town. Day to day life for civilians in Skipton was greatly disrupted and parents feared for their daughters.

The troops brought constant noise, including that of gunfire as they practised on the rifle range. The men in uniform were allowed out of camp and were entertained at concerts, cinemas and other leisure facilities such as the roller skating rink. The Craven Herald was concerned with "unsuitable behaviour", fighting, brawls, gambling and although not by name, with prostitution. Garrison towns had extra restrictions placed on them to avoid such degeneration including reduced opening hours for public houses and curfews, all of which affected trade.

In early 1915 the Skipton traders decided to cancel their annual dinner because trade had been poor in 1914, although it was anticipated that 1915 would show an improvement.

Generally Skipton seemed able to absorb the effects of the extra men, but when the War Office asked for billeting for a further 3,500 men, the Town Council objected strongly as it would have meant turning children out of all the schools to provide beds for the troops. The War Office backed down.

By 1918 all troops, except the small remaining Territorial unit, had left the town and German prisoners of war occupied Raikes Camp. In all, around 500 arrived of which over half were officers. The Germans had their own "university" offering a wide range of subjects taught by some of the well-educated officers. A few later wrote of their experiences and, whilst they complained of draughty cold huts with little fuel to heat them and the unpleasant climate, it seems that generally they were well treated by their guards and the townspeople. However, a certain arrogance shows through as the guards and citizens were described as the poorer sort of individual and given derogatory nicknames.

As the war progressed, Skipton became the administrative headquarters for some Government local Boards such as that issuing ration cards and for a Tribunal hearing cases for exemption under the Military Services Act.

The White Feather Movement

By October 1914 army recruitment was high, the Kitchener posters were everywhere and all towns and villages were visited by "flying" recruitment teams accompanied by military bands. Their arrival was announced beforehand to ensure that local men were aware of their coming. Patriotic songs and music, together with rousing speeches, were all aimed at encouraging recruitment. Men were put under extreme pressure to join "the lads" and "play the game". Newspaper articles added to the pressure and women were told that it was patriotic to encourage their men to enlist.

The White Feather Movement started on 30 August 1914 when an Admiral who felt strongly that all able men should be in uniform instigated "The Order of the White Feather" and gave feathers to women and asked them to hand the feathers out to all men not in uniform. The white feather was a traditional symbol of cowardice.

Soon there was a very active campaign taken up by women in all towns and cities. Posters were issued asking women to urge their men to enlist. One said "Women of London. Is your best boy wearing khaki? Don't you think he should? If he neglects his duty to King and Country, might there not be a time when he will neglect you. Get him to join today!"

Letters from women addressed to women appeared in newspapers as part of an orchestrated campaign. Women wrote of men being cowards and a disgrace and "shaming" usually took place in public places. The white feather being the ultimate weapon in shaming men as the war entered 1915. The women handing out the white feathers were initially mainly middle or upper class but later working class women also joined the movement.

The women could be over-zealous and often gave feathers to men at home recuperating from wounds or illness, or honourably discharged. Men who wanted to serve but were physically unable to do so had the added shame of receiving white feathers. In smaller communities feathers were sent by post perhaps to avoid identifying the sender.

The Craven Herald had strong opinions and expressed outrage at the actions of some women. The movement was said to have contributed to a change in attitude towards women; the "sweet girls at home" whom the men were fighting to protect were described as "ignorant, vulgar and impertinent with a lack of understanding of the true sacrifices of men and the demands of war".

Women in the Workforce

When women's recruitment into auxiliary services began many men welcomed the idea that women would also "do their bit" for the war effort. The very first newspaper article regarding the contribution of women to the war effort was in the Times on 5 August 1914. It advocated being calm, keeping your head and going about one's business in a quiet and sober manner. Consideration must be given to helping others such as neighbours "think of the common wheal, and contribute your share". Be economical, avoid waste. Remember that to hurt others is "an act of mean and selfish cowardice". Pay creditors and "servants" promptly and "give them wages for as long as you can". Women were encouraged to "gladly help an organisation for the comfort and cheer of soldiers". This was the first of many such articles aimed at changing women's attitudes towards employment and voluntary work.

Although the suffragette leader, Emmeline Pankhurst, had earlier declared that war was not a woman's way as, to women, human life was sacred, shortly after the start of the war, she encouraged women to become useful citizens, whilst not taking up arms or working in war zones. In July 1915 she organised a rally for the "Right to Serve", demonstrating that women should be allowed to work in what was seen as traditionally men's work, to help the war effort. This approach may have been calculated but it, and the work of the millions of women in the war, led to the Representation of the People Act of 1918 giving the vote to some women and the Sex Disqualification Act which made it illegal to exclude women from jobs based only on their gender.

The idea of paid work was not new to working class women; almost all, usually until they married but sometimes after, had worked. Some worked away from home as servants but most, in textile areas such as Addingham, found work locally. The war was to bring changes as many women worked away from home, living in hostels and working in traditionally masculine jobs. Much of the work into which women went was to prove hazardous to health in ways which had not been fully understood before. New chemicals were developed, especially for weapons, which caused skin and bone problems. The work was also often repetitive, heavy and for long shifts.

Towns such as Bradford and Keighley required huge numbers of workers, mostly in engineering. In Bradford alone around eighty companies produced parts of aircraft, warships and tanks. Before the war Keighley was geared up for this type of manufacturing and produced a range of goods. New government contracts greatly increased production and there was a demand for new products and military equipment such as searchlights and field kitchens. Munitions was the single largest employer of women and there were large munitions works at Thornbury in Bradford and Dalton Lane in Keighley.

In 1915 a National Women's War Register was opened and recruitment posters issued for a wide range of work. Women could obtain enrolment forms at local post offices. The Ministry of Agriculture set up the Women's Land Army in 1917 to cover the loss of farm workers who had enlisted. "God Speed the Plough" was one of their recruitment posters. In a few months it had 110,000 recruits.

The work which women did depended, to some extent, on local industrial needs. For example, women worked at the coal mines on surface work and they prepared rolling stock for the railways in places like Derby and Doncaster, and made glass. They repaired locomotives in rail depots such as Bradford, made asbestos mattresses to line the boilers of battleships and made glucose, soap, tyres for vehicles, gas masks and army boots. Most of these women worked for private organisations but as the Government increasingly nationalised industry their work conditions became more standardised with health care and sometimes child care becoming available, particularly in munitions work.

There was a great variety of non-manufacturing work including, by 1916, women tram drivers, locomotive cleaners and, a particularly unpleasant job, cleaning the carriages of the hospital trains which carried the wounded from port to hospital. These trains, after cleaning, would carry troops to the same ports for transport to the front. In York alone, by 1918, there were 2,500 women workers on the railways. Pre-1914 the number had been 43. By the end of the war 50,000 worked on the railways.

It is estimated that over one million women were added to the workforce between 1914 and 1918. This figure does not include women who worked as volunteers such as for the Red Cross, St John Ambulance, the Refugee Committee, on food committees, the Sailors and Soldiers Relief Fund and a myriad of local groups and committees. For example, in Bradford the Lady Mayoress's War Guild was organised on a ward basis and reached every Bradford Street. It helped families of servicemen, the bereaved and the returning wounded. There were similar organisations in every town and city.

Women's Magazines

Women's magazines were popular before the war, all aimed at women as homemakers, with articles on child care, recipes, sewing skills and treating the sick. During the years of war they were increasingly used as part of the Government's war propaganda; using traditional skills such as knitting and the sewing of "economy" garments for the family at home. One such was how to make a smart jacket for women and girls from old, worn blankets. More obvious propaganda were articles about "keeping the home fires burning" and about how wives and sweethearts should keep up morale by writing uplifting letters to servicemen.

"Waste not want not" was a mantra from late 1914 and there were ingenious recipes to deal with the shortages of certain foods and what would make suitable substitutes. Dripping had always been popular in northern areas spread on bread, but when meat became scarce and expensive, women were advised to pour off fat from the pan when frying bacon and use this to flavour vegetables. The magazines carried advertisements for such products as Fry's cocoa showing men in uniform with steaming cups and for beef stock like Bovril, again as a warming, nourishing drink.

As more women volunteered for war work their traditional clothing of elaborate corsets, many buttons and long skirts became impractical to wear and time consuming to make. They were also expensive as much fabric was needed for them. Ready-made garments became popular as working women had less time to sew. One advertisement was for women's "fashion" overalls in a range of fabrics in checks, stripes and prints. As early as 1915 dress patterns were following a new shape of looser fitting dresses with skirts above the ankles, and for large wrap-around aprons to protect dresses, thus reducing the amount of laundering required. Undergarments became more practical and trimmings were discouraged.

Magazines were a useful tool in keeping families involved in support for the war and so, in spite of production costs, printing continued throughout the war.

Volunteering

By 1917 the trickle of women serving overseas had become a flood as many thousands were trained to carry out roles behind the lines. For example, the Women's Army Auxiliary Corps *(WAAC)* arrived on the

Western Front in March 1917 with the aim of freeing up able bodied men for the front line. At home most hospitals had volunteer nurses and Red Cross volunteers would be found at every railway station providing hot drinks and food, for the wounded and for servicemen, at free buffets. It is not known how many local women worked or were volunteers for the war effort.

Mrs Dunlop of Hallcroft Hall is known to have had a working party to make bandages and from various snippets of information it is believed that many women were sewing, knitting and baking for soldiers' comfort packs, including the hundreds which left the village each year to be distributed by the Sailors and Soldiers Fund.

There were a number of sewing and knitting groups including a Senior Girls' Sewing Class which also met in the village, and farmers' families supplied eggs to local hospitals. Money was raised by volunteers from musical productions, sales of work and street collections. Mr Flint, who organised the parcels for servicemen, seems also to have arranged for local girls to write to them and for people to make regular subscriptions to the fund.

Local Defence Army volunteers at Hallcroft Hall

Not all volunteers for war work were women. At first men aged over 40 years of age could not join the forces and remained at home in their usual employment. Some men, in particular farmers, were in essential occupations and these Reserved Occupations kept many able-bodied men at home initially. As the war progressed such men were increasingly called for military service if older, less able men or women could be reasonably expected to do their jobs.

Men who remained at home volunteered for a range of activities, in particular the local home defence unit, the police service as special constables, and they transported the wounded. They helped in hospitals as orderlies, as grave diggers, or indeed with any part-time work which was required locally.

Mr Flint, as mentioned earlier, was one such volunteer. A grocer in the Main Street, his voluntary work was clearly extensive and when he was called for military service a collection was made and a presentation as indicated by this newspaper report on 28 September 1917:-

> "A presentation was made to Mr Flint at a social in Mount Herman schoolroom. For three years he had carried out useful work sending out parcels. The public had showed their great appreciation by raising £23 16s. 9½d. which included 12s.from Nessfield. This was a splendid testimonial. A gold lever Waltham watch inscribed "Presented to Chris Flint, 24 September 1917 by J England Esquire on behalf of Addingham parishioners for services rendered to the Sailors and Soldiers Parcel Fund and their despatch during three years of war" was presented. There was a gold bracelet for Mrs Flint and the balance of cash in a purse. Mr Flint's kind and sympathetic heart was a bit of true Christianity"

A number of boys were in the Scouts and during the war they were called upon to assist in many ways. In Keighley they were sent to "guard" the tarn and the town's water supply as there was a fear that it might be deliberately contaminated. In Ilkley they became "war wounded" for nurses in training. They helped in the convalescent hospitals, writing letters, playing games and providing occupational therapy for patients. Scouts were actively involved in fund raising and the 1st Ilkley Troop funded and equipped a Ford ambulance which was used in Egypt from 1917.

Many people helped out as and when needed and when the Belgian refugees came to Addingham, villagers provided clothing, bedding and household items. It is believed that at least four families were housed in the village and one in Draughton. All arrived with pitifully few possessions. Addingham, at that time, had several empty properties and so, unlike in many places, the refugees could have a proper home and not be billeted in public buildings as they were in Bingley.

The Addingham Home Defence Force was formed in early 1915 and had, by early 1916, around 50 members who trained in defence skills such as shooting and various forms of combat. They were required to keep fit and met every Saturday for drill and training, sometimes attending training exercises with other units. It seems that some of the expenses of the Addingham unit were met by Mr George Douglas of Farfield Hall. Mr Douglas provided the Home Defence Force with uniforms. Before he did so the men had to train in civilian clothes with only an armband to indicate that they were in the unit. A newspaper report of 21 April 1916 describes a presentation:-

> "A Gathering was held in the clubroom at the Crown Hotel to present Mr Douglas with a framed photograph of the 20th Volunteers in recognition and appreciation of his kindness. Unfortunately Mr Douglas was unable to attend and Mr W Dunlop, Commandant of the Company, was deputed to hand over the photograph to Mr Douglas. Mr Dunlop reported that Mr Douglas took a keen interest in the welfare of the Company although he could not often be with them. Adjutant Voight called upon Quartermaster Sergeant Nuttall to make presentation of a similarly framed photograph to Mr Dunlop. Sergeant Nuttall said that Addingham had got the best officer in the Wharfedale Battalion and they were proud to obey his orders, they held him in such respect that it was a pleasure to serve under him. Commandant Dunlop, in accepting the gift, said he would treasure the gift and it would always hold an honourable position in his home. Several toasts were proposed and responded to. The volunteers will continue to meet every week to further their training in readiness for when called upon to do their duty"

Mr Walter Dunlop was also an active volunteer as Commandant of the company. Aged 43 in 1914 he was too old for active military service.

Local War Hospitals

Many people willingly volunteered to help the wounded and worked in hospitals. Funds were raised for comforts, local groups went into hospitals to entertain the men and outings were arranged for those who were more physically able. As the number of war hospitals in the UK grew so did the number of volunteers.

Whilst the large army run General Hospitals such as those in Leeds and Bradford were generally staffed by military personnel such as the Royal Army Medical Corps, smaller auxiliary hospitals and convalescent facilities were often staffed by the Voluntary Aid Detachment *(VAD)* (photo left) and the local, often highly trained, St John Ambulance and Red Cross units. The atmosphere in auxiliary hospitals was generally more homely and relaxed than in the main hospitals. Some had local doctors as "consultants" on their staff, rather than a resident doctor or surgeon, who dealt with minor surgical matters. All had a fully qualified nursing staff and a matron. In Ilkley a matron, Miss S E Mather, was listed in 1917 in the British Medical Journal.

Ilkley War Hospital was an auxiliary hospital for the less seriously wounded and received its first patients in late 1914 when wounded Belgian soldiers arrived at Ilkley railway station. Later numbers increased and extra beds were added. This building, Grove House, had been built in 1862 as a hospital and convalescent home for the benefit of those who came to partake of the town's spa facilities. The servicemen could enjoy those same facilities of light airy bedrooms, a library, fresh vegetables from the garden, a bowling green and a putting green. Middleton Sanatorium was built during the war with a hundred beds, mostly for patients with tuberculosis.

Skipton had a war hospital which treated the wounded but also soldiers garrisoned in the town. Keighley had four auxiliary hospitals. The first opened in May 1916 at Spencer Street Congregational Sunday School. It was equipped and staffed by the local St John Ambulance Brigade. Later a section of the Victoria Hospital was used by the military, followed by the Highfield schools and in 1916 Morton Banks Fever Hospital. The Fell Lane Workhouse Infirmary was requisitioned in 1917. Each hospital train arriving in Keighley had around 200 wounded and 73 such trains arrived during the course of the war. The trains were met by volunteers, often with only a few hours' notice. Casualties were categorised by

York Military Hospital

urgency and around 50 stretcher bearers loaded them into makeshift ambulances; vehicles which at other times were used by the mills or as public transport. The non-stretcher cases would be offered hot drinks whilst they waited for transport, also cigarettes and a steady arm if they needed it.

Defence of the Realm Act

As the war progressed the Defence of the Realm Act increasingly affected everyone as the number of Orders and Regulations increased. Censorship, mentioned earlier, affected private correspondence including letters to and from servicemen, the navy, people working in military installations or doing any type of war work. Newspapers seemed able to publish a surprising amount of information, some of it by implication, and especially where they could tell of the valiant work the brave lads were doing. Blackouts became compulsory as lights might guide enemy aircraft and shops were required to close at 8.00 p.m., restricting the amount of time people could be on the streets.

What would seem to us to be silly restrictions were deadly serious at the time. For example it became an offence to whistle, lest it scare people into thinking a shell was landing; flying a kite might be a signal to airships; similarly bonfires; showing a light at night might attract enemy attention; and people were not allowed to keep homing pigeons. There were restrictions on the movement of foreign nationals.

The strength of beer was reduced and pub opening hours restricted. In garrison towns such as Skipton restrictions were particularly harsh and several establishments went out of business. It became on offence to buy another person a drink. These measures were to crack down on drunkenness which was seen as detrimental to the effectiveness of the population and servicemen in particular. In June 1915 there were further controls to the sale of alcohol and consumption of liquor was forbidden before 12 noon and after 2.30 p.m. for daytime opening. The amount issued to public houses was restricted and some simply ran out. The gravity of beer was further decreased and sale of spirits greatly restricted. The price of beer increased from 2d. to 10d. per pint.

At first there were few very other noticeable changes but gradually there were shortages of many raw materials which helped increase the price of food including staples. By June 1915 food prices were generally 30% higher than a year earlier and by September 1916 they had risen by around 60%. Whilst wages had also increased, the unwaged were particularly hard hit.

Of all the Orders and Regulations made under DORA the ones which most affected the daily lives of everyone were those connected with food. In 1916 and into 1917 a concerted German attack on shipping including supply ships from America and Canada was beginning to have a devastating effect. At times Britain had only a few weeks' supply of flour for bread.

The 1916 Acquisition of Land Order allowed for land to be acquired by government and local authorities for several purposes, including growing food, but growing took time and so there was a campaign to ask people to be mindful of not only the amount they ate, but the importance of avoiding waste. Addingham Parish Council acquired land at Stamp Hill for allotments. Children at school in the village acquired a piece of land and grew potatoes and vegetables under the guidance of Headteacher Mr Hewerdine. The produce helped support local families and provide a school meal.

With the increased production of fruit and vegetables in 1917 and 1918 preservation became essential for these perishable foods. Classes had been held locally in 1917 to advise people not accustomed to raising vegetables, on the best methods to use, including lectures by Mr Oddy, head gardener at Farfield Hall. Local women were trained to demonstrate jam and chutney making and the bottling of fruit and vegetables. Pickled onions, cauliflower and beetroot became winter foods and spiced up what would otherwise have been a somewhat monotonous diet.

The King issued a proclamation in May 1917 telling households to reduce bread consumption and asked people to limit themselves to four 1lb. loaves a week. A Ministry of Food leaflet said "we must eat less food, especially bread, as the enemy is sinking our wheat ships" and "if the enemy succeeds in starving us our soldiers will have died in vain". A number of Regulations and Orders in early 1917 imposed restrictions. A "national loaf" was produced and the Government took over flour mills. It became a requirement to use a minimum of 81% of the wheat which meant that white refined flour was no longer available. The wheat flour must then be mixed with flour from other grains to a minimum of 10%. Other grains included corn, rye and oats. Flour was also made from these cereals. Later the content of wheat in flour was further reduced.

The Cakes and Pastry Order restricted, from 23 April 1917, sales of certain products. It became an offence to have in one's possession to sell, or to sell, any non-bread product which did not conform. The requirements were for example:-

- Cake; not more than 15% sugar or 30% wheaten flour

- Buns; not more than 10% sugar and 50% wheaten floor

- Scones; no sugar, no dried fruit and not more than 50% wheaten flour

- Biscuits; not more than 15% sugar

Crumpets, muffins, tea cakes and light and fancy pastries had similar requirements and the restrictions covered grocers, confectioners and tea shops. The supply of both flour and sugar available to bakers and confectioners was restricted.

People began to be concerned about the nutritional value of food and the Ministry of Food issued guidelines recommending 3,400 calories per day per man whilst doing average work and extra calories for those doing heavy manual labour. It was hoped that measures such as these would keep the population healthy and reduce the likelihood of compulsory rationing; and to some extent they did. Home production of food such as potatoes, vegetables and wheat greatly increased and rationing did not, apart from sugar, become necessary until January 1918.

When rationing did finally arrive not every foodstuff was restricted; for example, whilst only 4 oz. *(113g)* of butter or margarine was allowed, milk was not restricted. Vegetables, potatoes and bread were not rationed but bread was regulated by the earlier restrictions. The meat ration was fairly generous at 15 oz. *(425g)* per person each week plus 5 oz. *(142g)* of bacon. For poorer families this may well have been more than they could have afforded to purchase pre-war. Cheese was also rationed.

In villages such as Addingham people would have fared better than those in the towns as there would be supplies of milk, butter, eggs and meat produced in the local farms. However, the Government began requisitioning these foods in order to feed the hundreds and thousands of men in uniform. A regional collection system was set up with milk being collected in churns at the farm gate. Farmers were paid a fixed price and given an allocation but as fodder for animals became scarce the cost of production, especially milk and butter, exceeded the price paid to farmers. Butchers were still allowed to slaughter animals locally and families set up "pig clubs" where they would raise a piglet and it would provide a supply of meat and bacon for the winter months. It could be difficult to feed the pig because any food item fit for human consumption could not be fed to animals, so children often foraged for food for pigs.

The Government decreed that a day a week cafes and restaurants should be meatless and some days potato-less and encouraged families to make the same restrictions. A cookbook was issued to help families deal with new foods and the restrictions on traditional food staples; it was called the "Win the War Cookbook".

In 1917 servicemen had become aware of the near-starvation state of the nation and implored families not to send them food. Troops were generally well nourished although those on the front line did have delays in food reaching them. At home people became opportunists, buying what they could whenever it was available – the Government then cracked down on "hoarding" as it pushed up prices and there were several high profile prosecutions. The shortages caused long queues.

Conscription

The one piece of legislation which caused the greatest outrage was the Military Services Act of 1916 which brought in conscription. In essence, every man between the ages of 18 and 41 was required to join the armed forces and report for service as and when required. Men were drafted according to age and marital status. Men did not know when they would be called up and this affected families and the community. Once drafted they were required to serve for "the duration" and in any capacity which the military deemed to be appropriate. There were severe penalties for those who did not comply.

Enshrined in the Military Service Act of 1916 was an appeal against service because of being in a "reserved occupation", chronic ill health and the right to object to bearing arms in conflict on grounds of faith or moral beliefs. Judges on local tribunals had to decide if men were motivated by conscience or cowardice. Few of the conscientious objectors who went before tribunals were given total exemptions. Most were ordered into the armed services, or told to join the Non-Combatant Corps, or the Royal Army Medical Corps. However, some men were "absolutists" who refused to make any contribution and were usually ordered to join the forces. There is an article in the Craven Herald about one such man who is not named:-

> "An Addingham man, aged 21 and a clerk, was before the Tribunal asserting that he objected to taking any active part in war. He objected to making munitions or war materials of any kind. The Commanding Officer stated that a man is assisting in the war if he lives in the country at all and that simply undertaking remunerative labour of any kind he is assisting likewise. The man replied that he would leave the country, but the military would not let him. He said that he had held these views pre-war but had been unable to put them into practice. He was not prepared to join the RAMC and, if a wounded soldier came to his door for assistance, he would not give it in war but would in peace time. This appeal was dismissed."

Once conscripted it became on offence to disobey orders and those who did were sometimes court martialled. Many were imprisoned, often in shocking conditions.

War Memorials

When peace finally came attention turned to discussion as to how the great sacrifices men had made should be remembered. There were almost a million Allied war dead and many men were maimed and mentally scarred. As early as January 1915 a letter to the Times questioned the future role in society of these men. He felt that they should be provided for because they, like those who died, had done their duty and fought heroically and suffered for their country. Whilst offering no solution he entreated the Government to consider the matter and, once decided, save the men "from mental torture which adds so much to their suffering". The Government did provide work schemes but these were very limited and most disabled men simply returned to their families who cared for them as best they could.

In 1916 a Commission was set up to consider how best to deal with the dead who had been buried abroad. Artists designed the plain white headstone we associate with war graves after rejecting a cross as the shape because of the numerous religions and beliefs held by men from all over the British Empire who had fallen. Families could choose what symbols to carve on the headstone but for the unknown a few simple words, "A soldier of the Great War, Known under God", were chosen. The phrase was chosen by writer Rudyard Kipling whose son John was killed and had no known grave.

The Commission made the controversial decision not to repatriate the bodies. This was seen by many as an outrage but the Commission knew that repatriation was impractical. In Parliament there was also outrage that the headstone would not be a cross; outrage that all soldiers and all ranks would be treated the same and outrage that families would not be allowed to design and erect their own headstones.

These sorts of discussions were also taking place in local communities but the hard facts were that no government money was available to fund war memorials. Most were built by local donations from the public and local government bodies. Some churches and chapels wished to commemorate their own fallen and so villages such as Addingham have a number of memorials ranging from Books of Honour to elaborately carved Cenotaphs. In some cases it took a number of years to raise the funds and complete the memorials and there were those who felt that the war was over and should be forgotten rather than dragging out the process.

Addingham Parish Council minutes are not very expansive but entries for late 1918 and 1919 indicate a desire for the village to commemorate, to the best of its ability, and several avenues were explored including the presentation of a framed, illuminated certificate for every man who served and a Scroll of Honour to hang in the parish room. The scroll was commissioned and may be the one now hanging in St Peter's Church. The main focus for the Parish Council was a stone war memorial to be erected on a five acre piece of land which Lord Masham gave for the purpose. An architect was commissioned to draw up plans and Mr Douglas agreed to defray the initial expenses. The plans included a memorial building with meeting or "club" rooms with the names of the fallen to be inscribed on the wall facing the Main Street. There was to be a bowling green, tennis courts, children's play area and a small park laid out with shrubberies and paths. The cost was estimated at £2,000 and it is clear that the scheme had to be greatly reduced, probably because of a lack of funds. The building has one club room with a large stone fireplace. There are WCs which originally were accessed from outside. Two tennis courts were built between the bowling green and the present Memorial Hall but the park with trees and paths was not. The tennis courts were in use until the 1940s.

In St Peter's Church in addition to the Scroll of Honour is an engraved marble tablet which, apart from one difference, records the same names of the fallen as the war memorial in Main Street. On both the name of Abraham Dewhirst has been added at the bottom instead of being listed chronologically. Abraham died on 20 July 1921 as a result of wounds.

It seems a little strange that there should be two war memorials and the reason for this is not known. However, there may be a clue in the name which is recorded only on the tablet in the church. That name is John P Cunliffe. John never lived in the village but was a member of the Cunliffe family who owned much land here and have a family vault in the church. There are many memorial plaques to them in the church. During the latter part of the war, two Cunliffe sisters came to live at Holme House from their home in Kent. They were John's aunts and extremely wealthy. Both are on the electoral roll at Holme House from 1918 to 1920. It is possible that they wished to have John's name recorded in the "family" church especially as they installed a memorial plaque to John's father Henry who died in 1919 and was their brother. However, John's cousin, who had the same name, was not included on the plaque and it is possible that the stonemason did not realise that two men of the same name had been killed, especially as neither of them were known in the village.

The Addingham War Memorial

4. TAKING THE KING'S SHILLING

Joining the Army

Until spring 1916 all recruits to the armed services were volunteers. Soldiers entered the Great War in a number of ways.

Regular Soldiers:
Signed on for twelve years with either three years' active service and nine years in reserve or, less commonly, six years' active service and six years in reserve. Men had to be aged 18, unless enlisting as a boy soldier, and 19 to serve overseas. There were height, health and fitness requirements.

Territorial or part-time soldiers:
The Territorial units were formed in 1908 from various ad-hoc militia and volunteer groups. Men signed for one year at a time and were expected to train regularly in military skills and attend an annual training camp. Men could join aged 17 and boys as drummers or buglers at 14. It was not initially envisaged that Territorials would be required to do other than home defence service. Territorials were attached to Regular Army regiments. Because the age range for Territorials was wider than for Regulars, many under 18s and over 40s served overseas from the beginning of the war. Territorials could opt out of overseas service but in practice very few did.

Volunteers to the Regular regiments or in Lord Kitchener's New Army:
Until mid-1916 men could join any service or regiment they chose. From August 1914 most chose to join the New Army.

Each phase of recruitment was given a number: K1, K2, K3 etc. The aim was to sustain military activity through a long war. The Kitchener volunteers were required initially to meet the same height and fitness standards as Regular soldiers. Later, when manpower was desperately needed, the minimum height requirement was reduced and special "bantam" battalions were recruited. The Leeds Bantams was one such.

A regiment would have battalions of Regulars, Territorials and, after 1914, New Army. For example the West Yorkshire Regiment had two Regular, two Reserve, nine Territorial and later twelve New Army. Territorials were identified by a prefix such as $1/6^{th}$ or $3/8^{th}$ and New Army identified by a prefix such as 9th (Service) or 16th (Reserve).

The Government had many recruitment drives and Lord Kitchener, appointed Secretary of State for War in August 1914, spearheaded these.

The recruitment of the Bradford Pals is a good example of the patriotic enthusiasm that people felt following the famous "Your Country Needs You" poster. The Lord Mayor of Bradford made an application to the War Office to raise a battalion of 1,000 men to be equipped at the expense of Bradford citizens. A Citizens League of wealthy gentlemen set the terms and it was agreed that recruitment should include Shipley, Bingley, Keighley, Ilkley and surrounding areas. Notices went up and on 8 September 1914 hundreds of men queued to enlist, the process taking many hours. The first number was 1 and so on until around 1,200 were signed up. A full battalion of 1,000 fit men was reasonably expected from this number. Terms of enlistment were very attractive with half wages to be paid to married men whilst in the army to compensate families for loss of earnings and single men were to receive a flat rate allowance.

We might assume that whole streets of men working in local mills would form the bulk of recruits, but this was not the case as many were from local towns and villages. Around 20% were office workers, 25% in semi-skilled occupations and shop work and 14% were skilled employees. Recruits were generally better educated, taller, fitter and younger than might have been expected. The largest single year group was nineteen.

There was capacity for a second battalion as recruits were still coming forward and this was formed a few weeks later. The two became the 16th and 18th Battalions of the West Riding Regiment and later a 20th Battalion was formed. It was Lord Derby who coined the phrase "Pals Battalions" where friends would "fight shoulder to shoulder for the honour of Britain". At least six Addingham men joined the Pals in 1914.

The New Army was essential to the war effort as in 1914 the standing army numbered around 250,000 available for immediate active service, but scattered throughout the Empire. A similar number were in Reserve and another 250,000 were Territorials, and these would require some further training to equip them for combat. By early 1915 recruitment was slowing and patriotic rallies were held in towns and villages. Recruitment teams visited football matches and railway stations but very few signed up on these occasions.

For some men, especially those with particular skills such as engineers, motor vehicle drivers or those used to working with horses, volunteering could have advantages as men could generally choose the regiment and type of work they preferred. This decision could greatly enhance their chances of survival.

Lord Derby Scheme Volunteers:
There were rumours that if insufficient numbers volunteered there would inevitably be conscription. By early 1915 volunteers numbered nationally around 100,000 a month but this did not meet military demands. The upper age was raised from 38 to 40 years in an attempt to attract more men. A National Registration Act of 1915 aimed to discover the number of men aged 15 to 65 years and their occupations and trades. Registration was compulsory. There were almost 5 million men of military age who were not in the forces and 1.6 million who were deemed to be in protected high skilled or scarce skilled work. The registration was unpopular but the prospect of forced conscription even less popular. In an attempt to delay conscription a scheme was announced in autumn 1915 where men aged 18 to 40 years, single or married, were informed that under the Lord Derby Scheme they could voluntarily enlist to serve now or attest with an obligation to come if later called up. The men who attested and chose to defer were in Class A, paid a retainer, given a grey armband with a red crown on it and officially transferred into the Army Reserve. They were sent back to their normal occupations until called up. It was planned that those who enlisted for immediate service would have a choice of regiment and go into training. Those who attested would have no choice of regiment or type of service. Around 215,000 enlisted by the closing date of 15 December 1915 and a further 2,185,000 attested for deferment. The scheme was re-opened in early 1916 but overall it was seen as a failure and hastened conscription.

Conscription:
The Military Services Act of 1916 was introduced by Prime Minister Asquith in January 1916 and came into force in March 1916. Under this Act all men aged 18 to 41 years were eligible for conscription with the qualifying date being 15 August 1915 and who, on 2 November 1915, were unmarried or widowed and without dependent children. There were a number of exceptions, such as being in an essential or "reserved" occupation, with serious business or financial obligations, poor health or infirmity and conscientious objection to combatant service. Local tribunals would determine if a man could be exempted from military service. Call up papers, as determined by the information from the 1915 Registration, were sent out from March 1916. Whilst the navy as the "senior service" had first call on recruits, by far the greatest number served in the army. Basic army training was six months, later reduced to four months. Training camps were often under canvas and vast camps were set up, particularly in the southern counties, described by some as "army cities". The Act was later amended to include married men and those with children.

Army Requirements and Service Condition

Even if categorised as A1 fit, men under 5 ft. 3 ins. should not have been allocated to a front line infantry service as the packs and equipment they were required to carry were deemed to be too heavy. Clearly though some were front line combatants.

A number of local men were under height but accepted for service. They include:-

Robert Akers: The shortest at 4ft. 11ins. and saw home service

Maurice Clegg: Enlisted aged 22 in 1916 and served in a Training Division. At 5 ft. tall he was discharged early as unfit.

Alfred Midwood: A married gardener, height 5ft. 2ins. Service in a Reserve Regiment and later joined the Machine Gun Corps.

James Parkinson: Enlisted aged 18 years in 1916. He was a 5ft. 1in. overlooker of Adelaide Terrace. Served in the trenches with the Durham Light Infantry. In 1917 transferred to a Reserve Regiment.

Ernest Stocks: With the West Riding Regiment. At 5 ft. 1 in. tall he served in the trenches where he was wounded and also served in the Trench Mortar Battalion.

For front line duties men had to be medically assessed as A1 fit. Those who were not were still accepted as there were many less strenuous but essential duties behind the lines. Those with specialist skills, such as blacksmiths or motor mechanics, would often carry out the same work for the army. During initial training men could volunteer for specialist training such as in the Machine Gun Corps. This was an elite unit of over 70,000 who were trained at Belton Camp. The Machine Gun Corps became known as the "Suicide Corps" because it suffered 62,000 casualties in the war. Some Addingham men transferred to the Machine Gun Corps.

From 1916 those in training could be sent to any regiment attached to any division. It was very much the luck of the draw where a division would be sent on service. Some men had a relatively quiet war whilst others saw service in all the major battles in France and elsewhere. Whilst the majority of local men served in France, others served in at least eight other theatres of war.

It was rare, once overseas, for a battalion to be at full strength of 1,000 men because of illness, casualties and furloughs. A battalion was attached to a brigade and a brigade to a division. In France, at any one time, usually only one of the division's three brigades was actually in the front trench system. A second brigade could, depending on the spacing between trench lines, be about 2,000 metres behind in support and the third about 3,000 behind that "in reserve". All three brigades could, in theory, be within enemy gunfire range from their batteries. Only the training area occupied by Headquarters and Administration could be said to be reasonably safe. In stalemate situations, the brigades alternated with each other under a rotation of between three to seven days in the front trenches but this, as letters from the front show, could be much longer. On the Somme front line, for example, there were attacks on average every few weeks.

Support units were also in danger as they carried out the duty of "sappers" and dug or repaired trenches – a particularly hazardous task in shelled areas or heavy rain because of the risk of collapse. Support units installed and cut barbed wire, collected bodies and carried supplies from base, usually at night to reduce the likelihood of sniper fire. As most trenches were exposed to the elements they became waterlogged, filled with snow, baked in the sun or freezing cold at night and the men suffered accordingly.

Daily Life in the Army

"Resting" or "training" usually meant the battalion withdrawing from the trench system and marching to the rest area. A few days were spent bathing, acquiring clean clothing, de-lousing, sleeping and medical examinations. If declared fit, men would participate in drill, football, sprint races, boxing and other activities designed to keep up their fitness levels. Special activities such as night attacks and wire cutting were practised. If unfit, treatment was given, with the aim of getting the man fit for front line combat. Some men stayed in the hospital area when their battalion went forward again. They could, at this stage, be transferred to a new battalion or even a new regiment. Depending on the location of the rest area, soldiers could go into town. They had access to welfare units such as those of the Salvation Army and Red Cross who helped men contact family and deal with personal issues. There were also religious gatherings and social activities. After a few days the men went back to the trench system carrying their kit. When troops returned to and from the trench system they travelled at night and this could be several miles over muddy, potholed ground, carrying their own weapons, ammunition, rations, spare clothing, shovels etc., and often exposed to fire. Whilst travel to the front line was fraught with danger, travelling from it was even more so as the men were very tired, usually cold and often wet. An officer in the 2nd West Riding Regiment in which some local men served, recorded in his diary:-

> "the march back to billet was a nightmare. Not 'til then did I realise how tired I was, nor how done the men. We had slept less than six hours in three days. The men were overloaded with sodden kit and the mud so deep. They requested a stop but I could not let them for we were still in a shelled area. Some of the younger men could hardly walk"

The brigades in which most Addingham men served in France were in the most arduous and active sectors of the Western Front. In spite of this many of the letters home show a determination to do their duty whatever the cost. The Service Records for these men show that they obeyed the rules and army discipline. Only a handful have any notes on their record of misdemeanours or punishments and where these occurred they were for minor offences.

Army discipline was, of necessity, strict and punishment was harsh. Tired men returning from the front line could still be worked hard. Many became exhausted and debilitated. The quality and methods of officers also varied with some coming down hard on minor infringements of rules which others chose to deal with less harshly. In his diary J B Priestley records that in a bitterly cold winter spell, early 1916, in the trenches his company officers "badger and hamper the men with silly little rules and regulations". By now a Lance Corporal, he disliked being "compelled to bully the men". Officers could also be out of touch with the actual mental and physical hardships men faced.

One example is a "pep talk" given by Major O'Gowan on the night before the first day of the Somme. In a letter to his wife he says that he gave the men an inspiring address. The men he spoke to viewed it differently. Private Morgan of the Bradford Pals recalled that the address warned that anyone who funked the attack would be shot on the spot by the Military Police. He felt sickened by such an attitude to men already facing death.

A number of local men were on charges, one of the most common being late for reporting after a furlough. Although this may have been only for a few hours, pay was deducted. The rail system was haphazard and men recorded their frustration at long delays at railway stations and slow journeys. Several men were charged with hesitating, not failing, to obey an order and punishment varied from one day confined to barracks to permanent demotion to the rank of Private. A few men were on several charges over a number of years and the punishments for them seem to have escalated. Punishment was particularly hard for men who deliberately injured themselves to get a "Blighty" and this act was dealt with severely.

Theft was another major offence and one Addingham man found in possession of an item belonging to a Belgian civilian was imprisoned with hard labour. It is not recorded what the item was.

Desertion was the most serious offence. Two Bradford Pals, who had become separated from their unit during battle, were arrested, court martialled and shot at dawn when found guilty desertion.

Pastoral and Medical Services

The army also had an Army Chaplain's Department which recruited around 4,400 clergymen as military chaplains. They were to be found on every war front and many risked their lives to help others. All held the rank of officers and were affectionately known as padres. They were expected to minister to any soldier whatever his faith, or lack of it. They played a vital pastoral role, reading letters, encouraging men to write home, helping the wounded cope with the devastation of their wounds and assisting medical staff. Padres served in the trenches, in Casualty Clearing Stations and in Headquarters.

Three men with Addingham connections joined this service. They were:-

The Reverend George R Hall: A Church of England clergyman. His father was Rector of St Peter's Church Addingham and he was brought up in the village.

The Reverend J Duncan Percy: On the Addingham Methodist Circuit and living in the village from 1912. Served with the R.A.M.C. In 1915 served abroad as a "4th class chaplain".

The Reverend Harry P Walton: Accepted for the Forces Chaplaincy in January 1916 when Curate at Jarrow-on-Tyne. Served with the Royal Artillery. From an Addingham family.

The Royal Army Medical Corp provided a wide range of medical services: In a war zone the first stage was a First Aid Post with between two and six beds for very short term use and situated just behind the front line. It was often in a dug-out or communication trench and staffed by the battalion Medical Officer, orderlies and a team of stretcher bearers who could also be the battalion's bandsmen. Facilities were basic and its aim was initial first aid and dealing with minor ailments.

The Advanced Dressing Stations were usually well behind the First Aid Posts. There was one to every brigade and they were staffed by Medical Officers, auxiliaries and field ambulance, R.A.M.C. orderlies and Army Service Corp staff. The station was divided into areas of activity such as laundry, stores, bathing and cemetery. Injuries were assessed and men were treated here with the aim of returning them to the front line as soon as possible. For those with more serious injuries, those suffering from the effects of gas, trench foot and other conditions, transfer to a Main Dressing Station was the next stage in their treatment.

At the Main Dressing Station there was a wide range of medical and surgical equipment available. Those who needed surgery for serious wounds would be transferred to a Casualty Clearing Station. Later in the war the facilities at the Main Dressing Station became more sophisticated with a view to saving life by earlier intervention.

The Casualty Clearing Stations were located about 15 to 20 miles behind the lines and there was generally one for each division. These large units could treat over 200 sick or wounded at any one time. Often situated near a railway line they had motorised ambulances attached to them. As with all the medical posts, the Casualty Clearing Stations were fully portable and could be moved as required as the front line moved. All had demountable wards, huts, living quarters, kitchens, mortuary and incineration plant. Those needing further treatment would be transferred to Stationary Hospitals.

Stationary Hospitals were situated near railheads and ports and could hold up to 400 casualties. Specialist hospitals were attached to them to treat shell shock, chest infections, tuberculosis, venereal disease and gas gangrene. All had full hospital services and an excellent reputation for the work they did. Many had St John Ambulance and Red Cross volunteers working there. Although called Stationary Hospitals, they could be moved as required.

In other theatres of war where no suitable land base was available, hospital ships were used initially to treat the wounded as floating hospitals and as transport to safe land bases such as from Gallipoli to Malta and Mesopotamia to India.

Men serving in France were, if seriously injured or requiring long term convalescence, transferred to the United Kingdom. Most towns had war hospitals and auxiliary hospitals for those recuperating.

Prisoners of War

The first POWs taken by the Germans were held initially in Belgium following the Anglo-French defeat at the Battle of Mons in late September 1914. The International Red Cross soon became aware that there were no records of these prisoners and where men were reported missing, no-one searched for them. The organisation opened an International Prisoner of War Agency in Geneva. Its job was to work with all countries in the conflict to obtain lists of captured servicemen and then notify their families. By the end of 1914 the initial team of ten had grown to 1,200, including volunteers who were mostly women. All had to be linguists. By the end of the war in 1919 they had amassed personal details on almost five million POWs and sent out millions of letters. Many of those initially reported missing were later found to be casualties or killed and regimental war diaries would have noted this, but painstaking work had to be carried out to correctly identify all those missing.

The International Red Cross also arranged for prisoners to receive regular parcels from their home country and returning prisoners felt that the parcels had helped to keep them alive as the conditions in many of the camps, particularly those in Germany, were very harsh. The prisoners often fared badly with hard punishments for minor misdemeanours, poor quality food, meagre rations and heavy arduous physical labour.

Addingham men who became prisoners of war include:-

Emanuel Benson: Served with the Territorials and reported missing in early 1918. Came home in very poor physical condition and suffering from severe malnutrition

Edward Hudson: Captured at Mons in 1914 and moved to several camps

Percy Hudson: Wounded when captured and in hospital in Haan in 1917

Benjamin Pass: A regular soldier in France from 1914

Joseph Tiffany: West Yorkshire Regiment. Captured October 1916

Percy Anderson: Returned in January 1919 after 18 months a prisoner

Most POWs were released in late 1918 and early 1919, around 185,000 in all. Some received medical treatment in France and Belgium before returning to Britain.

The men, whether in hospital, as prisoners of war or on active service, had hoped that after Armistice there would be a swift peace. However, it was not until seven months later that the Treaty of Versailles was signed. The Regulars who were now "time served" were demobbed quickly but the others had signed on for the duration. Indeed, it was announced on 30 November 1918 that generalised demobilisation had not begun and the military situation did not admit of any general release and when it did priority would be given to men who had employment to return to. Some men have letters on their military file sent by former employers offering them jobs if released from service. Men were also encouraged to be part of a Peace Army to staff overseas garrisons and were invited to extend their service for two or more years for which they would receive a bounty. Some men were in uniform until early 1920.

5. FOR KING AND COUNTRY

Service of Addingham Families

Addingham men served in all three services and in many different regiments. Here are a few of their stories which help to illustrate a wide range of experiences and service.

There were at least 20 village families in which three or more sons saw military service. The most notable are the Burke and the Smith brothers.

Widow Annie **Burke** of Jubilee Terrace had six serving sons and although not all served at the same time, all survived the war. Annie was left a widow when some of her children were very young. She and husband Charles had sixteen children and it is believed that thirteen survived to adulthood. Some of the girls married local men who also served in the war. Annie herself died during the war aged only 49 years in August 1918.

Fred and Emily **Smith** also had six sons in uniform; two were killed, three others injured and one became a prisoner of war. Fred was originally a blacksmith from Horsforth and Emily, and all their thirteen children were born in Addingham. They raised eleven to adulthood. In 1891 and 1901 the family lived at Low Mill Street, just below Holme House, and these properties were then called New Houses. Fred was an engine tenter in a mill. By 1911 they lived at 2 Church Street, and later 6 Ilkley Road. The sons who served were:-

- **Allan** born 1899 was an Able Seaman

- **Craven** born 7 February 1884 was a Private in the West Yorkshire Regiment 16th Service Battalion known as the 1st Bradford Pals. With a service number 16/525 he was an early recruit. When the 16th disbanded in February 1918 he joined the

Royal Engineers. By occupation he was a stationary engine driver. His first overseas service was to Egypt on 6 December 1915 and, due to sickness, he was discharged on 9 November 1918 aged 34 years. Awarded the 1915 Star and the Silver War badge

- **John** born 1897 joined the Duke of Wellington's West Riding Regiment shortly after the outbreak of war when aged 17 years. He served in France and was wounded in July 1916 aged 19 years. Treated in hospital in Oxford, he returned to the front. John was a confectioner by trade

- **Rueben** born in 1894 enlisted in one of the Kitchener New Army battalions in September 1914 at Halifax. This was the 10th Duke of Wellington's West Riding Regiment and the battalion in which J B Priestley served. In France with his unit from August 1915, which had previously spent time in Kent building the South London Defence System. First wounded in October 1916 and then in June 1917 when hit by shrapnel in the left arm, shoulder and femur. Treated at No. 2 Casualty Clearing Station, Rueben died of those wounds on 11 June 1917 aged 23 years

- **Thomas** born 1887 is believed to have served in the Yorkshire Regiment from 1914 and was in France when taken prisoner in early 1918. A newspaper reported that Tom was wounded when captured

- **William** born 1900 was the youngest brother to serve. Willie was a drummer in the Addingham Volunteer Training Corps before he enlisted. It is likely that he enlisted under age in the Hallamshire Territorial Force Battalion of the Yorkshire and Lancashire Regiment as he was killed on 2 September 1918 in France when aged only 18 years. A report in the Craven Herald of 15 September said that Willie "died a noble death for his King and country". Before the war he had been a gardener at a private house in Ilkley

One of their brothers-in-law, Harry Wilkinson, was in the army, as was their cousin Dale Smith.

Four **McCarthy** brothers served. Their parents were local girl Catherine and Michael who was born in St Giles, London. Michael arrived in

Addingham before 1880 as their eldest child was born here in 1879. By 1911 Catherine was widowed and lived in Clifton Terrace, Ilkley, but before that the family lived at 9 North Street, Addingham. Their sons who served were:-

- **John;** it is not known where he served

- **Timothy;** it is not known where he served

- **Cornelius** born 1886 was a butcher who married Sarah Rennison in 1912 at Ilkley and shortly afterwards went to live in Leeds. At 29 years of age, when living in Leeds, he travelled to Dublin and enlisted on 5 December 1915 in the 10th Royal Dublin Fusiliers as Private 10/26858. Serving in France, he suffered shell shock on 14 October 1916 and Cornelius was also wounded in 1916 and had influenza in 1917. There are other hospital admissions but now too faded to read. Cornelius served until 6 April 1919 and sailed from France just before he was demobbed

- **Michael** born in 1885 enlisted on 11 December 1915 in Dublin, a few days after Cornelius, and in the same regiment. His service number was 10/20765. Initially Michael was in Reserve and not mobilised until 22 May 1916 when he joined the Wellington Barracks at Dublin as an Orderly Room clerk. At the time he was a 30 year old journalist, unmarried and living in Batley. There are other postings but he was a shorthand writer during 1917. In early October 1918 he left Dublin for Aldershot where he was to be a Liaison Officer providing that "he is medically BI or BII" *(i.e. of non-combatant grade).* He was examined and assessed as BII. This post appears to have been an attachment to a United States Army group at Mychett, USA Camp, presumably at Aldershot. This posting was short-lived as on 16 November 1918 Michael was instructed to join the Royal Dublin Fusiliers at Grimsby. His health seems to have been quite a problem as even these last two postings were "unsuitable". Michael was discharged as unfit on 11 December 1918 with a pension of 9s. 9d. for 26 weeks. He served for three years to the day and was "of very good character". Michael married, possibly in 1918, as a marriage certificate was returned to a Mrs McCarthy of Vulcan Road, Dewsbury, on 27 July 1918. He returned to journalism.

Cornelius and Michael took the unusual step of signing on in Dublin although, apart from the family surname, they had no obvious connections with Ireland.

Other families with four sons serving included the Whiteoaks of Gildersber, the Wades of 18 Rose Terrace and the Sutcliffes who lived at 137 Main Street. The **Sutcliffe** brothers were:-

- **Edward** born 1887. Edward (Ted) was an air mechanic and was killed on the Salonika Front in Greece on 3 August 1918. From 1916 he is recorded as serving as F11951 in the Royal Navy Air Service, service number 211951. Aged 31 years, he was listed as the son of Benjamin Sutcliffe and of 12 Bolton Road. He is recorded on the Doiran Memorial along with 2168 others who were killed on that front and whose graves are unknown.

  In January 1919 Mr and Mrs Sutcliffe received news of how Ted died. The only survivor of the air crash, the pilot, contacted them. He said that the plane, in bad weather, had dropped two pills (230lb shells) after leaving Italy at 7 a.m. The objective had been "frightfully shelled". His plane was hit twice and fell to pieces, crashing on to rocks. Sutcliffe had been his observer and the pilot regarded him as a "most obliging and deserving man". Four of the machines went out on the raid and the other three crashed into the mountains.

- **Gamwell** born 1890, was a farm servant and at only 5ft. 2ins. he was not eligible to serve as a front line infantryman and yet he did see service on the Western Front in France where he was wounded. He enlisted in July 1916, aged 25 years and a labourer, and served with 1/6th Battalion of the West Riding Regiment as Private 5169. This was a Territorial unit and it is likely that he served with them before July and then signed for overseas service. Allocated service number 267238, Gamwell disembarked at Le Havre in February 1917 and received a gunshot wound to his face in May 1917. Shortly after Gamwell arrived in France Ellis Kettlewell reported seeing him. Initially treated at Etaples and then three other hospitals, he re-joined his unit on 23 July 1917. A few months later he was re-classified medically with defective vision, possibly as a result of the facial injury. Shortly afterwards transferred to the Labour Corps and had several postings when serving with them. Gamwell served until October 1919. His only UK leave from France had been two weeks in early January of that year. Discharged to 137 Main Street, which was also his address in the 1918 Electoral Roll.

- **Oliver** born 1879 was a regular soldier who enlisted in the Royal Regiment of Artillery serving with them in the Boer War and in India from 1905 to 1906. He may have become a Reservist in or before 1908 as he joined the 2nd West Yorkshire Royal Engineers Volunteers. Listed as "home service" from 1906 to 1914. Oliver was in service in 1914 when he should have been "time served" as a Reservist and yet served abroad from 20 August 1914 until 22 November 1918. Initially he served in France, then in Mesopotamia from March 1916 and in India from May 1918. His service number may have been 30549. When discharged in March 1920 he had 26 years' service and was granted a pension for 12 years and 312 days.

- **Thomas** born 1889 was a Territorial with the 4th Howitzer Brigade, Royal Horse and Royal Field Artillery and was mobilized with his unit on 4 August 1914 when aged 24 years 5 months, and a labourer. He served abroad from 15 April 1915 until 30 March 1919, for some of this time as a driver. Service numbers 762, 776229 and 2910. In 1911 Thomas lived with his father Benjamin and stepmother Sarah who had married in 1907. Benjamin had a fish shop and Thomas was a gardener. Thomas should have had the 1914-15 Star but there is a note on file to say that he had not submitted an application for it.

At the outbreak of war in August 1914 thirteen Addingham men were serving in the Regular Army.

Stephen and Mary Ann **McRink** had three sons who served, and two of them were soldiers before 1914:-

- **Bernard Benjamin** was born in Addingham in 1887. In 1911 Bernard, aged 25, was already serving with the colours in the 3rd Reserve Battalion of the Yorkshire Regiment, based in Richmond, North Yorkshire. Service number 7652. At outbreak of war his unit was stationed at York and in August 1914 moved to Whitley Bay where it joined the Tyne Garrison. By the end of his service Bernard had the rank of WO2 *(Sergeant Major)*. In 1915 he married Florentina Smith in Hartlepool, but then in 1922 married Clara Brayshaw in Wharfedale, so presumably he was widowed. Bernard lived in Addingham until enlisting in the Army and after army service he returned to live in Wharfedale until he died in 1953.

- **John** was born in Addingham in 1890 and enlisted in April 1909 aged 19 years. In his army application John asked to serve as a Hussar of the Line and served in the 18th Battalion of that regiment. Before enlisting he had been a Territorial with the 4th Howitzers based in Ilkley and by occupation was a gardener. A few days before the outbreak of war John married Kathleen Britton. He was then a Lance Corporal and on 24 August 1914 he was made Corporal. The 18th Hussars were in France within a few days of the outbreak of war and on 9 October the Ilkley Gazette published extracts from a letter which John had sent to his father in Addingham.

"We are having it a little stiff out here. I had two horses killed under me and several of my chums that came with me are killed or wounded, so I must be one of the lucky ones. I don't think it will last much longer as the Germans are starving with hunger. It is rather a hard time with us. I have only had nine hours' sleep in a week and eleven in another, so it will give you an idea. We are always in the fighting line and on the go".

On 3 November 1914 John was made Sergeant. In early January 1915 he wrote that he was cold and wet, "my battery suffered the loss of five drivers when shells came over. We caught the Germans napping, mowed them down and captured many guns and men, some old and some quite young. Sir John French *(Commander in Chief)* says it is an honour to belong to such a unit".

Shortly after John had home leave then returned to France. In March 1915 he wrote to his wife and extracts from the letter were in the Ilkley Gazette:-

"You will be thinking something has happened to me as by now you will have read our recent work in the trenches. We were relieved on Friday 5 March and I can assure you it was the hardest ten days I have ever experienced since the war began. On the night of the 4th and early morning of the 5th we were ordered to take a trench which the 16th Lancers had lost and my word it was a stiff bit of work to take on. We took the trench with great loss to the Germans. We lost a good few though the Germans must have suffered much more severely as we took a good many prisoners. We have had a very hard time and were fighting continuously. The weather has been wretched, snowing and raining and we were up to our knees in thick mud and water and got no sleep only now and then. From this you can understand what it has been like. You would not have known me. I had ten days' beard on and never had a wash all the time, while my clothes were covered with clay. We could not help but laugh at ourselves when we got back here. I am feeling first class now. I got praise for taking my troop into action and bringing them out again with only three wounded, and they were only slight flesh wounds. I was in the thick of it but was lucky to pull through alright. I think we have finished trench work now and are leaving the firing line shortly to prepare for spring"

For a time John was attached to the 1st Cavalry Division before re-joining his old regiment. He was appointed Acting Sergeant-Quartermaster in June 1917 and Sergeant-Quartermaster in November 1917. Mentioned in Despatches on 20 December 1918, John served until 17 May 1919, and so had ten years' service. His address was then Woodlands Terrace, Ilkley. Awarded the 1914 Star.

Another Regular was:-
- **William Ogden** born 1893 who enlisted in the Regular Army at Leeds in the 1st Battalion of the West Yorkshire Regiment as  Private 9529. This cannot have been before April 1911 as in that census he is recorded as aged 18 years, living with his mother Lucy and step-father Thomas Barnes at 38 Main Street. William died in France on 26 September 1914 aged 21. This was within two weeks of his arrival with his unit at St Nazaire as part of the British Expeditionary Force. The battalion had left Litchfield, where William was based at the outbreak of war. His death is recorded at the La Ferté-sous-Jouarre Memorial at Ile-de-France. This is a

memorial to those who fell at the early battles of Mons, Marne and Aisne and who have no known grave. The Battle of Aisne began on 13 September 1914. The Germans had settled on high ground above the river and bombarded the British troops with heavy artillery, using searchlights at night. The next day the Commander Sir John French ordered trench digging as there was no shelter for the troops. There were few tools and the troops lacked training in trench building, and the work was done in full view of the Germans. These British troops were seasoned regulars which the army could ill afford to lose. There was great loss of life and in those few days in September there were 13,500 British casualties, many simply blown to bits. This was the start of trench warfare on the Western Front.

A former Regular who re-enlisted was:-

- **Brumfitt Atkinson** born 30 January 1878 in Addingham. He  joined the Royal Garrison Artillery as a young man in 1898 and served in the Boer War in South Africa. As a former regular soldier who was time-served, he re-enlisted aged 37 years, and re-joined the same regiment in Keighley on 12 January 1915, as Bombardier, and was promoted to Corporal on 12 May 1915 then to Sergeant on 4 March 1917 when serving in France. At the time of his re-enlistment Brumfitt was a limestone quarry breaker married to Mary Alice née Whitaker and living at 8 Victoria Terrace, Addingham. The couple married in 1907 and had several children.

Brumfitt was gassed and wounded on 2 July 1917 and on 23 August 1917. His various injuries were gunshot wounds to his shoulder and throat and he was later treated at 2nd Australian Field Hospital with gunshot wounds to his thigh. A message from the General Hospital at Wimereux on 10 December 1917 said that he was dangerously ill then a week later was "out of danger" and his next of kin informed. At some stage Brumfitt was injured again and he lost an arm. This effectively ended his army life and, after leaving hospital, he was discharged from service on 2

October 1918 and awarded a Silver War Badge. Brumfitt was said to be of very good character and he was granted a pension for a total of 12 years of his service effective from 5 October 1918 and received 1s. a week for life in addition to his disability pension. At the time of discharge he was in 106th Siege Battery and on 4 November 1918 received the King's Certificate for Service. Returning in 1918 to 8 Victoria Terrace, he later lived at 30 Victoria Terrace until his death in 1940 aged 61 years.

Brumfitt kept a diary for around 18 months of his service in France. It was a punishable offence to keep a diary whilst on active service but many men did. The concern was that if the diary fell into German hands it might give the enemy an advantage, an insight into Allied activities and risk lives. The last entry was on 15 July 1916. The diary has been transcribed by a Mr Leslie Syree and is reproduced in full on the Addingham Village website *(addingham.info)*; however, the extracts here will help to give a flavour of life in a siege battery in France. Leslie Syree described the diary as a pocket-tattered notebook written in fading pencil and said it recorded experiences mostly in the Béthune/Loos areas. The bracketed information in the extracts was added by Mr Syree. It is not known where the diary is now. The extract below covers the Battle of the Somme which began on 1 July 1916.

1916

1 June   Have not kept up diary for a good time but am starting again. We moved into position behind Bully nearly a fortnight since and have just got settled down a bit. We had a warm time of it the first day we were in action, the Germans using gas, and taking 1,500 yards of trenches on the Vimy Ridge. The enemy fired a barrage on all the roads and batteries about here.

             Our position is a funny one, lying between two roads and as *(Germans)* fire on these we come in for the spare shells that fire a bit wide, and they were in good number. The position is a very open one behind stacks of unburned bricks but we have made a tunnel that we can get into when they commence shelling us heavily.

Today our people tried a new system; all the heavy guns in the district opened fire at a certain time, firing on *(German)* batteries and in all it was said that there were seventy odd guns firing all at once. It was a novel way but it must have been a good one as there was no reply from the Germans. They have been very quick in returning our fire before, but there was no answer at all until late at night when one heavy *(German)* gun opened up and fired a few rounds on our right, and a few shrapnel *(shells)* came over on the road to try to catch anything that was about.

Had talk with some infantry and they said that our people were going to try to take the double crossing and straighten out the line and that it would be a hard job too. There are great rumours that the Germans have been greatly reinforced on our front and were going to try and break through, in fact, to make another "Verdun" of the place, but we have seen no signs of it yet.

During our stay at Fosse 3 we have had some lively times, especially the last month, and if it had not been for the position, which was a good one, we would have had many casualties. But we were very lucky and only had one in the left-half battery. In the right-half they have had five or six *(casualties)*. The wall behind the guns saved us a great deal, shells bursting fully 200 yards behind us, the splinters knocking pieces out of the wall, and if it had not been for that we should have suffered heavily. A battery on our right had two guns put out of action and two men killed.

We came into action in the evening and continued at a slow rate of fire until midnight, firing in all fifty rounds per gun. The infantry attacked about 8.30 p.m. and got over all right, and we were firing on *(the German)* communication trenches to prevent reinforcements coming up. All *(our)* heavy guns were on the same job and the flashes could be seen all around us. The Germans put a lot of shells around our position in the afternoon and early evening, some of them falling within 50 yards of the guns, but no damage was done, only knocking the Frenchman's potatoes and cabbages up!

12 June to 1 July
Came off leave and arrived at Bully in the evening and found that my section had moved to Albert *(a town in the Somme district)*, and *(I)* followed a few days later. When we got there we found that great preparations had been made for a big bombardment.

Siege batteries had come from all over the British front and taken up position in the district. A few days were spent in finishing the position and then we commenced registering on our different targets. Enormous supplies of ammunition were ready – 2,000 rounds being in our position alone, and we kept getting more and more in as the bombardment went on. The noise was terrific, one great battle of guns, and the same up at the trenches showed what effect it had on the enemy. The ground was a great mass of shell holes and some were an enormous size, probably the 15th and the 12th, of which there were several in the district. It was like a huge pepperbox.

Several villages were taken and all the lines of trenches and woods were battered down, and only a few stumps left to show where the wood had been. The villages were levelled to the ground and at Fricourt the one prominent thing left standing was the church, which showed up amongst the other ruins.

Wet weather hindered the operation but one good job was when it got fine it soon dried up. The infantry suffered through it all. But one thing that struck you was the good spirits that the men were in after coming out of the trenches. The success had cheered them up although they had suffered heavily.

The dead were lying about, belonging to both sides, and awaiting burial. One German machine gun was lying in the trench and had been hit with a shell and the gun men *(the gun crew)* were lying in the bottom of the trench. A number of prisoners were taken, and some of them testified the accuracy of our gunfire, and were glad to surrender. They were a lot of fine fellows but they looked as if they could have done with a good square meal.

9 July   We have not moved yet and the fight has been going on for eight or nine days; perhaps we will be making a move before long. Some batteries have moved nearer to the line to take up firing as the Germans are driven back.

Our guns must have fired about 1,000 rounds each since we have been here and the other batteries have done the same. The plans have been well thought out throughout this affair and every little detail attended to. Nothing has been left to chance. Ammunition and material and supplies of food have been brought in, horse and motor vehicles, and it has been one continuous line of traffic day and night, some men saying that the busiest street in London could not compare with the traffic that had passed one corner in Albert.

One feature about this is that we are not troubled by enemy aircraft. Very few have been over us since we came here and their artillery has been quiet or they have been in the trenches all the time, only one shell falling anywhere near our battery until today. The field guns and the heavies are knocking away now in front and it sounds as if we should be getting action again.

12 July   Things have been a bit thick these last few days, but are beginning to quieten down. This afternoon we fired a good few rounds but all is quiet tonight and it looks as if we shall have a night in bed. A few shells dropped in Albert whilst we were in action, but it has been a very quiet time for us, only one shell dropping anywhere near the battery since we have been here.

    Heard last night that the 9th West Riding *(Duke of Wellington's Regiment)* had had a rough time of it since the advance started and had gone back to be reinforced and for a rest. They had lost over 200 men in the attack.

15 July   Our troops are still making progress and we shall soon have to move forward as we are nearly out of range, and are expecting *(to move)* anytime now. A lot of batteries have already gone forward a few moves last night.

    Prisoners are still coming in and there must have been a very good haul up to now. A telegram posted up in the battery yesterday said that we had done well and if we only kept on in the same spirit as we did on the first *(day)* of July our objective would be accomplished. The cavalry had broken through and we were in pursuit of the demoralised enemy.

This is where the diary ended.

Two Addingham men were killed on 1 July 1916, the first day of the Battle of the Somme. They were:-

    -Percy Hustwick, a Territorial who went to France on 16 April 1915.

    -Wilfred Holmes, one of two men of this name to die and an early recruit to the 1st Bradford Pals, when he was 26 years old. In 1911 he was a single man living with parents at 21 Southfield Terrace, and a domestic groom. Perhaps because of his occupation he became Orderly to Captain Alan Clough and was with him in Egypt and Suvla Bay in Gallipoli. In March 1916 they were in France.

David Raw, in his publication about the Bradford Pals, wrote what happened to Captain Clough. Clough and Wilfred Holmes were killed on 1 July 1916 and both are recorded on the Thiepval Memorial.

When Alan Clough applied to be an officer in September 1914 his former headmaster at Tonbridge School supplied a reference which said "in all respects most desirable as an officer. Small in stature *(but)* afraid he is not".

Clough and Holmes were with 'D' Company and at 8.00 a.m. on 1 July were in the front of Bradford trench. Eye witnesses said they went forward and Clough was hit twice, and on each occasion got up and moved forward. On the third hit he lay where he fell – about 15 yards from the German trenches. The bodies of neither Clough nor Holmes were ever found. Clough was 21 years old and showed astonishing courage. His father was Sir John Clough, an MP and mohair spinner in Keighley. It is likely that Holmes went over the top with him.

Men dreaded being captured as the enemy, be he German or Turk, had a reputation for treating prisoners harshly. At least six local men were captured and all tell horrendous stores. Here are two of them:-

- **Edward Charles Hudson** born 1887, who came to Addingham as chauffeur to Mr Dunlop at Hallcroft Hall. This was around 1913 as daughter Marjorie was born here in July 1913. A former Regular soldier, Edward had been transferred to Reserve in April 1911 on his payment of £10. He and wife Ellen married in Chester in April 1909. Edward had enlisted in 1905, aged 18, and served in the Cheshire Regiment as Private 8039.

When war was declared Edward was re-called to his regiment and went with the initial British Expeditionary Force to France a few weeks later on 14 August 1914. Reported missing on 15 September 1914, he had in fact been taken prisoner on 23 August during the British defeat at the Battle of Mons, remaining a prisoner for 4 years and 107 days. Edward wrote home occasionally sending details of his internment and letters to acknowledge parcels he had been sent by local people.

In 1914 he was interned at Soltau, a large POW camp which became known as a particularly harsh camp. Then in June 1915 he was working on a German farm and in October of that year was at Munsterlager, Hanover. Repatriated on 9 December 1918, Edward was not discharged from the Army until 31 March 1920 and this may be due in part to his physical condition after so long in the prison camps.

In early 1919 the local newspaper recounted Edward's harrowing tales of his imprisonment. For the first year he was on starvation rations and often had to stand outside in the cold. After nearly a year he was sent to work on a farm but was already severely undernourished. Without regular parcels he would have died. He felt that the British prisoners were treated worse than their other Allied comrades and that the men captured in 1916 and 1917 received better treatment than those *(like him)* captured in 1914 and 1915. He had a brief spell in a prison hospital. Overall he felt that the Germans were afraid of the British.

Edward was born in Thetford, Norfolk, and his family seem to have been "in service" at gentlemen's residences. When he enlisted in 1905 his next of kin was mother Hannah who lived in Nantwich and Edward may have been working with horses on an estate in Cheshire. There is a note on his service record that after a year of military service he had gained in height and 15 pounds in weight. He appears to have been based at the regiment's riding school in Shrewsbury.

Daughter Ella was born in autumn 1914 which was shortly after Edward had been taken prisoner. In 1918 Edward was recorded as a serviceman voter at 4 Church Street and it was to this address that a letter regarding his medals was sent in 1921. In 1920 on termination of his service, Edward returned to 7 New Houses, Low Mill.

Whilst a prisoner his 12 years contracted service expired. This was in 1915 and under army terms he would have been released from service; however, as a prisoner of war he could not do so and it seems likely that a £20 bounty sent to "The Office, No. 2

Riding School, Shrewsbury" was to automatically continue his service and ensure that his family continued to receive his army pay.

- **Emanuel Benson** born in Draughton in 1880 also became a prisoner of war. Emanuel served in the 1/6th Duke of Wellington's West Riding Regiment Territorials as Private 54854. The son of William and Margaret, who farmed at Lobwood House, Emanuel married Sarah Cockshott in 1905. They had five children and the youngest, Lucy *(as of 2014)*, still lives in Addingham. The couple lived at Hudsons Yard later moving to 4 Moor Lane, and Emanuel was a butcher.

Emanuel became a prisoner on 27 May 1918 whilst serving near Ypres when the German Spring Offensive took much ground previously held by the Allies. His family were informed on 12 July that he was missing. Emanuel had gone to France with his unit in April 1915 and served through many of the major battles.

Emanuel Benson and postcards notifying his family that he was a P.O.W.

His daughter Lucy has the postcards shown above (with her kind permission), addressed to her mother Sarah at 4 Moor Lane. One is from the Red Cross Enquiry Department and is probably in response to her request for information as Emanuel may have been reported missing or stopped writing home. The date is 26

July and notified her that he was a POW in Germany. Another, which is dated 4 June 1918, but may have taken some time to arrive, says POW but "sound". It is from Limburg an der Lahn.

Emanuel appears to have remained in this camp and he was required to do hard manual work on very limited rations. He recounted that the diet was invariably cabbage soup and a Russian prisoner, who seemed able to get extra rations, shared with Emanuel, in his opinion saving his life. When Emanuel was repatriated, probably in December 1918, he was very weak and had the distended stomach associated with severe malnutrition.

It is believed that at least seven Addingham men served in one of the branches of the navy.

- **Charles Prior Clarke** was killed in an early naval battle on 1 November 1914 when serving as an Able Seaman on HMS Good Hope. The "Good Hope" was sunk off the coast of Chile with the loss of all hands in the Battle of Coronel which was a major defeat for the British Navy. The ship was flagship of the fleet.

  Recorded on Portsmouth Naval Memorial as husband of Martha Clarke of 9 Rose Terrace, Addingham, Charles had joined the navy as a rating when in his teens. He was aged 32 when he died and his body was not recovered for burial. In the November 1914 Naval Lists, Charles is listed as "R.F.R. B1190, Number 205888 (Dev)".

  Charles had lived at Union Yard, off Main Street, and at Farfield Cottages. He married Martha Gibson at Harrogate in 1906 and in 1911 the couple lived at York Street, Worth Village, Keighley.

  Older brother John was a Regular soldier serving as Lance Sergeant in the King's Own Yorkshire Light Infantry. He was killed at the Marne in France on 26 August 1914.

- **John Clarke** who served in the navy was killed as a result of enemy conflict on 18 September 1917 when aged 26 years. He was serving on HMS Stonecrop. The "Stonecrop" was sunk off south west Ireland. She was a converted merchant ship used as a decoy and known as a "Q" ship. Designed to draw out German U-boats, she had hidden guns. Her crew consisted of former merchant seamen, Royal Navy and Royal Navy Voluntary Service. A married man, John lived at 114a Main Street, Addingham.

- **Harold Hillbeck** may have joined the navy at the outbreak of war when he was 17 years of age. Harold was born on 28 June 1897 in Cumbria and was one of the sons of James and Rachael who then lived at Kirklands, Kendal. Harold, whilst living in Addingham with his older sister Mary and her husband Philip Pass, joined the navy. Harold became a career navy man remaining in the service until at least 1935. He was serving as early as August 1915 in HMS Woolwich and in a letter said he would like to have a crack at the "Terpitz".

Harold gave his home address as 49 Southfield Terrace as late as 1932 when he returned from Brisbane, Australia.

In his Story of Addingham Schools from 1874, William Lemmon indicates that when on furlough Harold, an "old boy", had gone into school to talk about his naval experiences and in particular the Battle of Jutland. This battle took place on 31 May 1916 and involved 250 warships. The British Grand Fleet under Admiral Beatty sailed out of Rosyth and the battle was strategically a triumph for the British; the German fleet returned home and did not fight any further major battles.

Harold was awarded his medals in 1919 when he was serving on HMS Barham. The "Barham", newly launched in 1915, did take part in the Battle of Jutland and received six hits. In 1923 he was on the "Courageous" as a lieutenant.

He also travelled extensively, although perhaps not always in a ship of the Royal Navy. For example, on 23 March 1929 he arrived in London when aged 31 years, on a P&O ship having boarded in Hong Kong, and is described under occupation as "Royal Navy". There are other naval records of him, one being when he arrived in London from Brisbane on 25 May 1932 travelling to Addingham and still a Lieutenant.

Harold settled in Addingham after retiring from the Navy and is listed on the Electoral Roll at 7 Bolton Road from 1938 and later went to live at "Marshfield", Leeds Road, Ilkley from 1949. He does not appear to have married and died in Wharfedale in 1968 aged 70 years.

At least 34 older men born in 1879 or earlier served. Many were volunteers and some were conscripted when the maximum age was raised to 41 years. Some were Regulars or Reservists and most served for the duration of the war when many were in their 40s. A few of the early volunteers are:-

- **Harry Horsman** born in 1877. The publication "Craven's Part in the Great War" lists Corporal H Horsman of Addingham serving in West Riding Regiment *(Ilkley Pals)* awarded a DCM. The citation for this appears in the London Gazette for 30 March 1916 Ref 9/12944, serving in 9th Battalion of Duke of Wellington's West Riding Regiment. It reads:-

  "For conspicuous gallantry and devotion to duty during operations. He directed his stretcher bearers under fire and continued to tend the wounded after the dressing station had received two direct hits"

  His medal card indicates that he was in France from 14 July 1915 and so must have enlisted in late 1914. At that time he would have been 38 years of age. Service number 12944, and later when he served as Sergeant in the Labour Corps, service number 512342.

  Harry was married in 1899. Both he and his wife Charlotte were born in Addingham. As newly-weds they lived at 10 School Lane. In 1911, living at 52 Main Street, Harry was a cotton warp dresser. His son Clifford also served. Harry died locally in 1945 aged 68 years.

- **George Rishworth Snowden** who enlisted in May 1915 was the oldest man to serve, and also a volunteer. Aged 48 years he should not have been accepted for service. Men over the normal recruitment age were sometimes accepted if they had special skills urgently needed by the military and they met the medical requirements. There is no evidence that George had special skills. In 1911 he was a mason's labourer and earlier had been a farmer's son. He served from 8 May 1915 until 2 April 1919 when he was discharged as sick to Hudsons Yard, Addingham. During service he was sent overseas.

- **Sylvester Selby** born in 1877 was another older man. He married Martha Marshall at St Peter's Church in 1899 when a gardener. The couple were married for six years and had children, Doris born in 1902 and twin boys born in 1905. Martha died when she was aged 27 years.

It is possible that Sylvester had served in the army as a young man. He enlisted as a volunteer on 24 August 1915 in the Royal Engineers. This may have been a previous regiment as he went straight to the rank of Corporal and does not appear to have had any initial or basic training. At that time he was living at 29 Main Street. Within a month he was in a specialist unit, the Chemist Section, and had the rank of "Corporal Chemist" for which he received enhanced pay of 2s. 6d. per day and 6d. per day Corps pay. There is only one medal card in his name and it shows that he went to France on 20 September 1915 as a Corporal and was awarded the 1915 Star. The service numbers are 113294 and 25854.

The Chemist Section was responsible for handling gas which was transported to France from the manufacturing unit at Kestner-Kellner in Runcorn. From July 1915 volunteers and specially selected men were trained in the use and handling of gas and, from December 1915, phosgene *(carbonyl-chloride)* gas canisters. Gas was first used by the British against the German army at the Battle of Loos in September 1915. The British development of chemical warfare was in response to the gas attacks by the Germans at Ypres in April 1915. The training was done at the huge Royal Engineers' base at Longmoor in Hampshire. Also developed and tested there were the early prototype "gas defenders" to help troops combat the effects of gas and gas attacks. Initially these gas masks were both primitive and of little value. The first effective ones were introduced in mid 1917.

A Chemist Corporal would receive gas handling training and it was a small unit, initially two companies of 34 sections of 28 men. The complement was doubled in August 1915, which was when Sylvester joined, giving around 1,800 men to cover the whole of the Western Front. Once in the field the men would be required to fire gas shells from 4-inch Stokes guns, to handle gas discharges and to be in charge of flame projection devices.

Sylvester carried out this dangerous and highly stressful work in the field in France, then on 31 August 1917, now 40 years of age and following a letter to his captain, he was transferred at his own request to the Pioneer Corps and had the rank of Lance Corporal. This letter to Captain Slater dated 4 June 1917 reads:-

"On account of ill health and age, I desire your permission to revert from rank of Corporal in the Special Company of Royal Engineers to that of Lance Corporal in the Pioneers. In my opinion my retaining such rank prevents other men who are more competent than myself from attaining such rank"

Once in the Pioneer Corps, Sylvester would have been doing the essential work of the army such as ditch digging, road making and loading and unloading of supplies, as well as more skilled tasks. Pioneer Corps sometimes trained others in these skills. There are other notes on his service record which may give an indication of Selby's character. For example:-

10 October 1915 – reprimanded for irregular conduct whilst on guard duty in France
9 September 1916 – failing to salute
4 January 1917 – absent 24 hours from duty
23 June 1918 – absent from roll call in the field at 9 p.m. Reported at 9.23 p.m. Claimed illness.

Also on his file is a Certificate of Proficiency as a road foreman dated 8 July 1918 with enhanced pay.

On 25 August 1916, when Sylvester had been at the front for a year, he sent a letter to the Craven Herald about so called patriotic people not pulling their weight at home while on the front men are fighting to prevent tyrants being resident in England. The Herald describe him as an "Addingham Horticulturalist at the Front" and said he had interesting views on the war and other problems. His rank was Corporal Selby with 1st Battalion, Section 2, "A" Company Royal Engineers. In a letter of 21 September 1917 he feels that the way to victory is to carry on and prepare for a few more years of war. "We will achieve victory because our Empire and Government is based on justice, freedom and liberty and this is what we fight for". Clearly a man of opinion.

In early 1919 Sylvester sustained an injury and was transferred to England from France with a dislocated and fractured jaw on 2 February, and to hospital. A note on file asks if the injury required investigation and the curt message in reply from his commanding officer was "No!". Sylvester was demobbed "sick and wounded" and he returned home on 9 May 1919. He died in 1932.

The Lord Derby Scheme, introduced in late 1915 to stimulate volunteering for the army, was popular with Addingham men and from service records they can be identified. There were at least 22 and most volunteered in the last few weeks of the scheme in December 1915. All appear to have "attested", in that they agreed to be available for military service when called up. Most were called up in mid 1916.

- **John Gill Lowcock** born in Addingham in 1890 worked in a cotton mill in Skipton and went to France in December 1916. John served in the York and Lancaster Regiment and the Northumberland Fusiliers. In May 1918 he was severely wounded but returned to the front a few months later only to be killed in October near Ypres

- **Alfred Midwood** hailed from Whitby but settled in Addingham, later marrying a local girl in 1913. At 5ft. 2in. he was in a Reserve battalion but later volunteered for the Machine Gun Corps where he trained as a driver. He lived at 7 Bolton Road and in Church Street

- Brothers **Hedley** and **William Richardson** volunteered under the scheme on the same day as each other. Hedley was mobilised on 17 February 1916 whilst William was in Reserve. Hedley was killed on 4 July 1916, before William was mobilised on 3 November 1916. William survived

- **John Lister** was one of two Addingham men of this name to be killed. Born in 1889, John lived at 4 The Green when he enlisted.

John was the only son of Henry and Amelia who in 1891 farmed at Small Banks. By 1911 Amelia was a widow "of private means" living at 4 The Green. John lived with her, working as a chairmaker's labourer. His service record says he enlisted on 10 December 1915 when aged 26 years and 137 days. At only 5ft. 1 in. John was too short to serve in the infantry and was in the West Yorkshire Reserve Battalion.

At some time, possibly on 15 June 1916, he went to France and when in France he was called before a Court of Inquiry. This was on 5 August 1916 and it investigated the injuries of two men including John Lister of the 1st East Yorkshires, formerly the West Yorkshires. Unfortunately the rest of the details of the tribunal are illegible. John was reported accidentally wounded in the field on 30 July 1916 and it is likely that this is the incident which the court investigated. The injuries were gunshot wounds to scalp, arm and forearm and John was in hospital, possibly until 17 September 1916. Because of his height he would most likely have been serving behind the lines, possibly at a headquarters so gunshot wounds would not have happened during combat. Indeed on 17 June 1916 he was recorded as joining the depot at Etaples. According to his record there is no evidence that John was admonished or punished in any way.

After the gunshot incident, John was re-admitted to hospital with low back pain and did not re-join his unit in Etaples until 29 September 1916. In 1917 John did see action, as on 2 July 1917 he was wounded, although he may have been in the field in a support role. The record is unclear but he may have been hospitalised in England and later returned to France.

He was killed in action on 26 August 1918 aged 29 years when serving as Private 31193 when in the 1st Battalion, East Yorkshire Regiment. John had previously served in 19th West Yorkshire Regiment as number 25956. Commemorated on the memorial at Vis-en-Artois, John has no known grave.

Medals

Every man and woman on active service in a "theatre of war" qualified for a medal. Those who served in UK based volunteer units, fire, ambulance, or doing essential work such as mining, munitions or farming, did not qualify. The medals awarded for service were:-

The British War Medal: approved in 1919 and covered service to 1920

The Victory Medal: An oak leaf was authorised to be worn on the ribbon if a person had been Mentioned in Despatches

The Territorial Forces Medal: For all members of the TF including nursing sisters who were in the TF on 4 August 1914 or former TFs who had completed four years if they had re-joined before 30 September 1914 and served years of service overseas

The 1914 Star: Awarded to all men and officers who had served with the British Expeditionary Forces in France or Belgium between 5 August and 22 November 1915

The 1914-15 Star: In 1919 King George approved a version of the 1914 Star for those who similarly served but up to the end of December 1915

Medals for those who were killed were awarded to next-of-kin. All were inscribed with name, number, rank and regiment.

Next of kin of men who were killed received a circular commemorative bronze plaque about 4 inches in circumference.

A Silver War Badge was issued for the more than 2,000,000 who were discharged from service as a result of being wounded or from sickness. This was authorised by King George in September 1916 to honour all personnel who had served either at home or overseas from 4 August 1914 and up to 31 December 1919.

There were several awards for conspicuous gallantry or service. The hierarchy is:-

- Victoria Cross *(VC)*

- Distinguished Service Order *(DSO)* and Bar

- The Order of St Michael and St George

- Order of the British Empire *(OBE)*

- Military Cross *(MC)* and Bar

- Distinguished Conduct Medal *(DCM)*

- Military Medal *(MM)*

- Meritorious Service Medal *(MSM)*

In addition there were special bravery awards in other services, such as the Royal Air Force and British Navy.

Other governments awarded medals to foreign service personnel in recognition of particular service to their nationals. For example, the French Croix-de-Guerre and Médaille Militaire and the Belgian Chevalier de l'Ordre de Léopold II.

A man could also have been Mentioned in Despatches, awarded a Distinguished Service Certificate or a Gallantry Card.

The Military Medal was instituted by Royal Warrant on 25 March 1916 for "acts of gallantry and devotion to duty performed by non-commissioned officers and men of our army in the field".

The London Gazette published the names of recipients but not the citation. No full list of citations remains.

Several Addingham men received honours and decorations for bravery. Most received the Military Medal *(MM)* or the Distinguished Conduct Medal *(DCM)*. James and Arthur Hillbeck were brothers as were Arthur and Frederick Holmes.

Sergeant Major J Kettlewell	DCM and MM
Corporal Horsman	DCM, "Ilkley Pals"
Corporal L Baul	MM, 5th Yorkshires
Corporal J Hillbeck	MM, Royal Engineers
Private A Hillbeck	MM, Royal Field Artillery
Corporal A Holmes	MM, Royal Engineers
Private A Jacobs	MM, Northampton Regiment
Corporal Lawrence	MM, Machine Gun Corps
Lance Corporal G Strickland	MM, West Yorkshire Rgmt.

Private J H Thompson   MM, H.Q. Staff

Private P Holmes   MM, Royal Berkshire Rgmt.

Corporal A Holmes   Belgian Croix de Guerre and
possibly MM

Sergeant F K Holmes   Mentioned in Despatches and
MSM

Sergeant Quartermaster John McRink Mentioned in Despatches

Sergeant Major Jack Kettlewell received both the Military Medal
and the Distinguished Conduct Medal.

John was born 3 August 1892 in Addingham and our most highly
decorated Addingham son. Always known as Jack, his parents were
Thomas, a quarryman, and Anne.

He arrived in France on 15 July 1915 and was with the 9th West
Riding Regiment number 12854. A medal card confirms his awards.
It reads:-

"West Riding Regiment 12654
France 15 July 1915
15 Star, MM and DCM
Rank W.O.2 *(Sergeant Major)*
To "Z" class *(demobbed)* 1 March 1919"

Jack's citation for the DCM in the London Gazette on 2 December
1919 reads:-

"for fine courage and leadership during an attack on Putoy on 4
November 1918. After two of the officers in the company had
become casualties, he led half the company with great boldness,
capturing several prisoners himself. Later he was severely wounded
in the right leg but hearing that all officers in the company were
casualties he took command of the company and refused to leave
until the final objective was reached and the position consolidated.
He then came back to headquarters with prisoners and gave a
valuable report of the situation"

A family source connects Jack with Mount Hermon Sunday School,
and that he was a champion boxer for the regiment, later running a
boxing club in Addingham before emigrating to Australia. Jack did

return at least once and this was in December 1927 when he arrived in Hull from Brisbane on the Largs Bay and a 35 year old spinner whose destination was Addingham.

When Jack left the army in March 1919 he was still only 26 years of age and had served overseas for four years. Achieving the rank of Sergeant Major was also remarkable at such a young age but his earlier Territorial service may have contributed to his skills.

Where servicemen lived

An analysis of addresses shows that around one fifth of homes in the outlying areas had someone serving and there is a similar pattern in the village with, on average, one quarter of homes. In some streets the actual number was higher.

Southfield Terrace had 30 men from 18 of the 26 houses of which 7 lost their lives, Cragg View had 9 men serving from 5 of the 12 houses, and Bolton Road had 23 men serving of which 2 never returned.

The addresses given below are those in the 1911 census, the serviceman voters list of 1918 and the address given on enlistment. The man may have lived there for many years. Other men who served and who lived in these streets when they were children or after the war are not included.

	House Number	Year
Cragg View		
William Hall	2	1918
Allan Holmes	No number	1911
Arthur Holmes	No number	1911
Fred Holmes	No number	1911
Harry Horsman	2	1915
Donald Brear	4	1911-1918
Hedley Cooper	6	1891-1911
Harry Dickinson	12	1911-1919
Stephen Dickinson	12	1911
Southfield Terrace		
William Townson	1 and 7	1911-1919
George Gale	3	1911-1919
William Gale	3	1911-1915
Anton Wynn	5	1911-1919

Bernard Wynn	5	1911-1919
James Wynn	5	1911-1919
Alfred Townson	7	1911-1919
James Townson	7	1911-1916
Alex Sutherland	No number	1911
Wilfred Holmes	15	1911
Archie Watts	15	1914-1918
Fred Watts	15	1914-1918
Wilfred Holmes	21	1911-1917
Irwin Topham	23	1911
John Topham	23	1911
Lewis Topham	23	1911
Stanley Topham	23	1911
Herbert Wilkinson	23	1918
Thomas Ward	27	1917-1920
Edwin Lister	27	1911
Frank Schofield	29	1918
William Dixon	29	1914-1917
William Horsman	31	1911-1917
James Longbottom	33	1918
John Appleyard	39	1911-1920
Ellis Hartley	41	1918
Harold Hillbeck	49	1911-1919
Joseph Pass	49	1911-1919
James Harrison	51	1911-1918
Percy Bromilow	No number	1914

The houses in Bolton Road include what is now called the Rookery. In some records these are classed as Bolton Road and in some The Rookery. The odd numbers were mostly demolished later and were behind Mount Hermon Chapel.

Bolton Road

William Hood	4	1918
Joseph Bell	4	1911
Percy Jones	6	1918
James Holmes	10	1918-1920
Mitchell Storey	14	1911-1918
Marmaduke Storey	14	1911-1918
Wilfred Ettenfield	18	1918
Francis Spencer	20	1911
Harry Spencer	20	1911-1918

Harry Russell	24	1918-1921
John McRink	38 and 42	1901 and 1911
Laurence McRink	38 and 1	1911 and 1918
Bernard McRink	38	1911
William Pease	38 and 16	1918 and 1920
James Hillbeck	5	1901
William Whitaker	7	1901
Alfred Midwood	7	1915
George Craven	13	1911
William Ettenfield	13	1911
George Fisher	21	1911
Fred Fisher	21	1911
James Fisher	21	1911
John Fisher	21	1911
Fred Ideson	No number	1911

George Fisher enlisted as a Regular soldier on the same date and in the same regiment as John McRink. They were neighbours and probably friends.

News from the front

News about the men in the services arrived in many forms. Families would receive pre-printed postcards with multi-choice options, sent when their loved one was unable to write a letter. Ornate postcards, often handmade, with embroidered flowers and lace could be purchased in French towns and were sent as birthday or Christmas greetings. Postcards from the Red Cross were sent out in thousands, often in response to requests for information where families had had no news for a while.

Newspapers received lists of the dead and wounded and printed these. Later in the war there were newsreels.

As we have seen, men wrote letters home and, where they could not, comrades, nurses, padres would do this for them. The most dreaded letters were those informing families of a death and were usually sent by an officer. Some were brief and factual whilst others tried to give grieving relatives some comfort and some idea of how the young man died.

The **Ellis** family of Cragg House have preserved letters sent on the deaths of brothers Charles and James:-

- **Charles** died on 24 May 1915 and was a Trooper in the Yorkshire Hussars, who joined up in September 1914. The first letter, a handwritten one from Major Lane-Fox Squadron Command 'A' Squadron, written on the same day that Charles was killed:-

> 24 May, 1915
>
> Madam,
> I am sorry to have to send you very sad news and I wish I knew how I could convey it to you less abruptly than by letter. But this I fear impossible.
>
> Your son, C. Ellis, who was doing so well, and earning the high opinion of all who saw his work with this Squadron, was I am sorry to say killed in the trenches near Ypres yesterday – Whit-Monday. He was killed instantaneously, shot through the head by a piece of high percussion shell.
>
> We were under fire from 3 a.m. till evening.
>
> I am very sorry to lose so good a young soldier from my Squadron, and I can realise what a loss his death will mean to you, but he has died for his country and what better death can one wish for those that one is fond of.
>
> Yours truly,
>
> G. R. LANE-FOX
> Major

A second letter, handwritten, was from a comrade who was standing next to Charles when he was killed:-

> Wednesday, 26 May, 1915
>
> Dear Madam,
>
> You may have heard that 'A' Squadron, Yorks. Hussars was in action May 22–24. It is with great sorrow that I have to tell you of your son, Charles Ellis. On Monday,

24 May, we were in the trenches and subjected to a very heavy shell fire for over 15 hours and about 4.30 a.m. on that day your son was within 4 feet of me in the trench.

We received an order to move further down the line and at that moment a shell burst over our heads and I picked up your son who had just fallen, but he had already passed away, and the end must have been absolutely instantaneous.

Your son was in my Troop and has from the very first been all that one could wish a soldier to be, quietly and thoroughly doing his work. He met his death like a brave man and we are all proud of him.

I believe Major Lane-Fox intended to write to you also, and he may be unable to use his hand for a bit, and he is in hospital.

I express my great sympathy with you and your family.

The personal effects will be forwarded through the proper quarter.

I may add that we buried your son before we were relieved.

Yours truly
(no legible name)

This letter tells of the burial but, although the grave would have been marked at the time, subsequent heavy fighting and shelling meant that Charles had "no known grave" and was recorded on the Menin Gate at Ypres.

The Secretary of State sent a very formal, pre-printed letter.

The family received letters of condolence, including one in July 1915 to Mrs Ellis from the Reverend Bateson, Secretary of the Wesleyan Army and Navy Board. The Ellis family were Wesleyans.

Possibly following an interview with Mr and Mrs Ellis the Ilkley

Gazette printed an Obituary on 5 June 1915:-

Yorkshire Hussars in Action
Trouper Ellis one of the Slain
Major Lane-Fox slightly wounded

Quite a number of Ilkley men are attached to the Yorkshire Hussars and during the Whitsuntide holidays while people in Ilkley were getting as much enjoyment out of life as possible, the Hussars were having a particularly unpleasant taste of shell fire at the hands of the Germans and several Hussars were either killed or wounded. One of those killed was Trooper Charlie Ellis, Crag House Farm, Addingham Moorside. Trooper Ellis was 29 years of age and joined the Yorkshire Hussars in September last. His regiment had only been at the front a few weeks, and this was their first experience of work in the trenches. Trooper Ellis before joining the Hussars worked for Mr W Wood, Butcher, Church Street, Ilkley, and was particularly well known in Ilkley and district, indeed he was one of those steady, good natured, straight going young fellows who makes friends everywhere. The Reverend Joseph Dawson referred to the death of Trooper Ellis before commencing his sermon at the Ilkley Wesleyan Church on Sunday morning and reference was also made to the sad event in the evening by the Reverend H C J Sidnell. Mr and Mrs Ellis were first notified of their son's death in a letter received from Major G R Lane-Fox on Friday morning dated 25 May. Major Lane-Fox is in command of 'A' Squadron to which Trooper Ellis was attached

- **William James** (Jimmy) died on 10 November 1918. Jimmy was wounded early in November 1918 and sent a standard postcard to his family indicating "I am wounded and have been admitted to hospital". He died of wounds three days later but the official notification did not arrive until after the Armistice. It was written on 19 November 1918 and sent from York. The family were told that Jimmy died of wounds at 19th Casualty Clearing Station but it was not until 29 April 1919 that they were officially notified where he had been buried. A Wesleyan

Chaplain wrote a compassionate letter to Mrs Ellis on 10 November 1918 from the 19th Station:-

10 November 1918

Dear Mrs Ellis,

I am exceedingly grieved to tell you that your dear boy was severely wounded in the recent fighting, and has since died in this hospital. Everything was done for him that medical skill could devise, but gangrene had already set in, and every effort to save your loved one was unavailable.

I saw him last night in the ward, and we had a nice long talk together. He was very bright and looked exceedingly bonny. It made my heart bleed to see the poor boy and to know there was no chance of his recovery.

We talked of prayer and looking up to God in time of need, and he said he prayed every night. He assured me he was leaving himself in our Father's hands, and was still hoping to get better and come home to see you. He sent his best love to you all at home, to his sweetheart Clarcie, and to his Uncle.

When I went to the ward today I was told he had passed away peacefully an hour or two after I left him in the night.

I expect to bury him tomorrow in the Soldiers' Cemetery at Caudry near Cambrai and a cross will mark his last resting place.

May I say how greatly I sympathise with you in your great sorrow. God be very near to you and comfort you, and may you be sustained by the wonderful hope of seeing your loved one in the grand Resurrection morning when God's people shall be gathered.
It may console you to know that your dear boy did not appear to suffer very much.

With kind regards,

Yours sincerely,

W A PARROTT, Wesleyan Chaplain

(Note: his sweetheart was Clarice not Clarcie)

Cecil Ellis received a letter from Ronald Brear:-
29 November 1918

Dear Cecil,

Just a line from your old chum to try and cheer you by the way, as I know how hard it will be. Believe me, Cecil, I have not yet conceived that I will not see him (Jimmy) again; the dear lad; the best friend a lad ever had was Jimmy, and you know it.

I feel sure you know what friends we were, and we must believe it was God's Will to call him while in the prime of life.

We must help each other to be as bright and cheerful as possible even though it is hard, and makes life seem scarcely worth living, but we must trust Him who loves us and cares for us at all times; one who neither slumbers nor sleeps and is ever-willing to help us.

With deepest sympathy and best wishes

Your ever sincere

RONNY

The letters are reproduced here by kind permission of the Ellis family.
Local newspapers, the Craven Herald, Ilkley Gazette and West Yorkshire Pioneers, published extracts from letters sent by servicemen. Extracts selected by the newspapers would have to meet the censorship code laid down by the Government and may, therefore, have been taken out of

context. No doubt the proud families wanted to share the news from the front. Here are some of the more detailed extracts; for clarification some words have been added or changed:-

October 1914   Private Hanson Binns says that he is under incredible shell fire in the trenches but he is in the best of health and spirits even though his boots are worn out *(he had been at the front for six weeks)*

November 1914   Private Walter Emmott is fit and well, he has received no letters for a long time but sent six parcels, letters and postcards. He had captained Addingham football team and was serving in 3rd Duke of Wellington's West Riding Regiment

                    Private Williams sent a postcard to say that he was wounded but okay in hospital and hopefully would soon be discharged back to the front, but hopes to get furlough first. "The hospital is in a big French hotel and the nurses are splendid"

February 1915   Private Clifford Fawcett with the East Lancashire Regiment said he sailed to Le Havre then was in action at Ligny on 25 August 1914 with 150 men killed, wounded and missing. Under heavy shrapnel fire from 5 a.m. to 6 p.m. and fighting rear-guard actions up to Le Fort village where the Colonel was killed. "Now we are up to our knees ladling water day and night"

May 1915   Bombardier Fred Hall of 4th West Riding Howitzer Brigade wrote to Mr Shuttleworth at the Sailor, "The beer is poor quality, I could drink a whole brewery and not get intoxicated"

4 June 1915   Private W Wall 6th Duke of Wellington's. "Two weeks ago the Germans shelled us out of our billets. Three were hit – two killed and one wounded – I had twelve to fifteen days in the trenches but have not seen a German. The Germans keep well below the parapet and shoot from loopholes. The "stay at homes" should see the damage out here – many villages are totally in ruins"

June 1915   Private Harold Redshaw of Yorkshire Hussars in France. "Five men have been killed and four and our Major wounded. Lots of our chaps are laid up with gas, its awful stuff and not fair play. It's about time some of the chaps at home stirred themselves up, it's not fair to those out here"

Gunner Leonard Wall. "Gassed very badly on Whit Monday *(my)* eyes not the same since. A few killed and a lot wounded. I'm in a very hot *(dangerous?)* place right in the front. The weather is so hot we can hardly stand it"

July 1915   Gunner Keighley with 4th West Riding Howitzers. "Please can you send two balls and two bats as it's fairly quiet so cricket helps relieve the monotony. If the single ones at home could get a glimpse of ruined homes, church site, they would not hesitate to come forward. We are all well and hope to be home for Christmas". *(note – the bats and balls were sent out)*

August 1915   Private Percy Hustwick; "I came across Ted Hudson at the front the other day, we had a long chat together and dinner with him. I am writing this from our dug-out. Three of us take it in turn to do telephone duty. Sometimes up to our knees in mud but it dries quickly and it's quite sunny now. Germans send over Black Marias, coal boxes, aerial torpedoes, trench mortars and gas shells. Gas shells make our eyes smart and fetch water out of them like coming out of a tap"

Private Archie Watts acknowledges receipt of a parcel and thanked Addingham people who had contributed. His job was to go up the line for the wounded, fetch them down to the first dressing station then forward to base, about six miles.

October 1915   Private John Baul serving with his brother Corporal Lawrence Baul. "My brother and I are keeping fit. Neither of us has been hit by any of the Kaiser's ammunition though our comrades have fallen around us week   by   week.   When   in

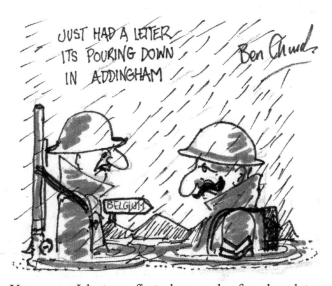

the Ypres area I lost my first chum and a few days later his successor in my affections departed wounded to a probable destination in England. However, amidst all the shot and shell and uncertainty of life day by day the knowledge that our dear ones in the old country are safe and our hearths and homes not devastated gives us good heart to keep us cheerful. If you are proud of the boys who do things, we are proud to fight for our women and children and all those who have perforce to remain in Albion keeping the flag flying there, our commerce going and turning our common fodder for us and our allies in arms. I doubt whether many people at home realise the enormous expenditure of shell and small arms ammunitions in this world war. Although there is a great deal of deliberate shooting by machine guns as with rifles yet at a moment's notice, these deadly weapons will spit fire to the tune of 500 to 700 rounds per minute. This is a manly game, yet such is war in all its nakedness that one cannot help but feel the horror and degradation of the whole thing. However we have a saying 'stick it if it kills you'

Private John H Baul was the brother of Corporal L Baul 5th Yorkshire Regiment machine gun section who won the Military Medal

November 1915   Private W Dove. "About a week ago I had the pleasure of meeting my two brothers and about half a dozen Addingham lads, and it was a treat to talk about old times. I am glad to say they all looked fit and well after their four months on the continent. The other night the Germans played a dirty trick shelling us out of bed about midnight. At the time we were billeted in tents about three miles behind the front line, and as canvas makes very poor cover for shell fire we had to make a bee line for some trenches that had been dug for that purpose. It was rather amusing to see some of the lads doing record time with nothing but their great coats on"

Corporal Sylvester Selby writes that two Irishmen were carrying stew rations and tipped the whole amount over as they went up an incline into the trenches. They slipped on the mud and cursed both the Kaiser and the weather.

Private G Foster observed that every time the men leave the trenches they come out a few short and this increases the number of little white crosses. "However we are winning but very slowly"

December 1915   Miss Lucy Wade of Addingham has received a letter from the trenches from an Addingham soldier A Watts, thanking her for the work she is doing on behalf of the soldiers from the village. He goes on to give a description of moving the wounded at night. "It is frightful work in this weather," he says, "the nights are black as ink, and we have to take the poor lads through mud feet deep, sometimes having to take them all out so as to get the car out of the shell holes, at other times we have to wait behind what was once a lovely dwelling house until the shells stop for a few minutes". After describing what was once a beautiful town but is now a ruin he says, "It makes you think what would be the result if the Germans got the chance to get to England, but I am thankful to say they never will. I don't know if you have got any slackers at home or not, but if you have tell them from me to put their shoulder to the wheel and come and do their bit one way or the other"

February 1916   Private J Oldfield wrote that he was pleased to read reports of us *(Addingham men)* and "that you have a better opinion of us than some of the Ilkley people who have friends in the Dukes and who run the good old "Howtys" down *(Howitzers)*. We have read various skits which certain Ilkley persons sent to the Ilkley papers, but I think he will look a bit small when he reads of the distinctions that the good old 11th Battery have earned in the firing line. We have three DCMs, two MCs, and a few more recommended so I think we have done very well"

March 1916   Private P Hudson writes thanking Mr Flint for the parcel which is the first he has received since being in the front line. He was under fire and described the Germans firing mortars. "When you see them coming they just look like a 4lb syrup tin and when they burst it's awful"

May 1916   Private A Watts writes from France that he should have been coming home next week but all leave had been stopped. He had been in France twelve months

June 1916   Private Carl Moulding. "We are out of the trenches now and back in the country. We had a good four days march to get here, not very pleasant, the weather being scorching hot. Eventually we arrived safe and sound and found ourselves practically in the same district we were in last January. We do not spend the whole day doing nothing out here, we get a lot of manoeuvring and such like but we are now out of danger and able to have a good night's sleep, which is a big consideration. I was sorry to hear about Fred Fisher, I saw him when he came down to the dressing station and a very nasty knock it was. He was very plucky and even walked down to the doctor, but I thought it would be touch and go whether he got over it or not. I have had ten days in hospital with German measles but feel alright again. J Lister went home on pass this morning so I expect he will be giving you all the latest news. When my turn is coming I don't know" *(Carl was killed on 22 September 1916)*

Wilfred Holmes in France. "We are having lovely weather out here and it makes a lot of difference. It is bad

165

enough being in the trenches when it is fine. I spent all my Easter above the knees in mud and water, quite a change from Egypt.

I called to see Jack England on my way to the trenches and back. He has not been in yet, but he has had a few shells burst near where he works the other day and he and Wilkinson were very lucky to escape. We have a fairly easy time when not in the trenches, we have a band concert every night and it just keeps us alive, but we cannot help feeling a bit fed up sometimes. I wish it would come to an end before many more lives are lost" *(Wilfred was killed on 1 July 1916)*

Private E Hudson was "having a fair time and hoped he could soon have a swim in a nearby river. There are plenty of rats and a fox terrier takes care of them. It is rather miserable and I had two narrow escapes recently"

October 1916   Private Wilfred Holmes of Addingham, before going to the Western Front, served with one of the West Riding Battalions at Suvla Bay. In a letter to his sister at Addingham he mentions that he had taken part in a good deal of fighting on the Somme and had experienced a terrible time. "When we got over the top of the parapet," he says, "it seemed impossible to live in such a fire but the few of us that did get through routed the Bosches out of their dug-outs. They were glad to be taken prisoner. I saw a couple of them get killed. They were chained to a machine gun" *(Wilfred was killed on 27 April 1917)*

January 1917   Reverend J Duncan Percy, serving as chaplain with the RAMC, wrote of spending Christmas and New Year at a lonely dressing station amid a wilderness of ruins. There he met Sergeant Holmes with the tunnelling company of the Royal Engineers who was in the best of health and the only Addingham lad he had met. He was having a pretty rough time, with mud knee deep and often waist deep in places. The men were cheerful in spite of the hardships. "Their good humour and endurance are wonderful"

(Tunnellers were generally given the rank of Sergeant, together with enhanced pay, because of the precise and

hazardous work they had to undertake)

February 1917 Private C Whitaker of the Cameron Highlanders wrote saying that the cigarettes came just in time as two Addingham lads, Town and Hudson, were going up the line and they had only the official issue which isn't much, so he gave them a few packets to keep them going. Ashton and Townson had also gone up the line. "If this weather continues for a while old Fritz will be a beaten man as he is near it now"

Private W Gale. "Lads at the front are very happy with the generosity of Addingham people who have provided us with so many articles. Ellis Kettlewell walked four miles to pay us a visit the other day and I've seen J Pass, C England, G Sutcliffe, A Wynn, young Fisher and Alf Tiffany"

(Many of the men mention friends they have seen and the servicemen seemed to share information from home with each other)

March 1917 Sergeant Hustwick said that in a three mile race he came first out of 240 runners in the brigade sports, the first in their battalion. He was third home, and first in his battalion in the divisional sports four mile race out of 800 runners. He remarked that he had had a "good share of war since July and now deserved a rest"

April 1917 Private Stocks wrote that he had "just come out of the trenches after six days and it was good to have a strip and a wash". He was concerned about the potato situation at home and the amount of land being taken for growing them, but as long as a few Addingham farmers keep growing turnips "I don't think people will pine"
Private Hedley Cooper. "Villages and towns under the Huns hell for three years are just heaps of bricks. For pure unadulterated vandalism it would be impossible to imagine anything more thorough than the Hun"

August 1917 Driver Lister Foster said "the last six months had been the grimmest of his life" and he had mainly been on the

Somme. He had "rarely been in bed for three nights in any nine and the Germans were as strong as ever and very cunning"

September 1917   Stoker Barnes on HMS Superb said the sweets were very handy as when he was down in the stokehold they helped to keep down the coal dust very well

January 1918   Corporal F Hartley of the Dukes *(Duke of Wellington's West Riding Regiment)* wrote to say that he had been wounded when out on a bombing raid. He was hit in the head but not to worry as he was able to walk and quite cheerful. "Coming out of the trenches we looked more like lumps of clay than soldiers". Got fourteen days special leave for taking a strong point *(heavily defended post)*. Sixteen had made the attack". He was getting extra rations

April 1918   Private J Bickle was involved in a big push on 21 March when the "Huns came over in huge numbers only to be gunned down by our men on open ground. We have the enemy checked and reinforcements will make our task easier"

The writer and broadcaster J B Priestley served from 1914 in the 10th Battalion of the Duke of Wellington's, West Riding Regiment – part of Kitchener's new army, formed in August 1914 in Halifax. Addingham man John Scott was there when Priestley was buried alive and helped to dig him out.

Priestley writes of his first few weeks in France in late August 1916 that his unit was living in and around a partly ruined farmhouse all huddled together on the stone floor. In two weeks he had not had his trousers off and asked his family to send vermin powder and soap. A few days later he described marching on cobbled roads which caused agony to his feet with choking dust from passing convoys, constantly on the move. Priestley, in the front line in the disastrous Battle of Loos on 25 September 1915, said that in full kit and so weighed down with extra cartridges and bombs the men could hardly move.

Some of the worst nights in winter 1915/16 were spent carrying heavy coils of barbed wire up communication trenches, knee deep in water and sometimes under shell fire, constantly slipping and being pinned down and cut by the coils of wire. "I saw men, no weaklings but powerful fellows, break down and weep". He observed that the conditions in which the lower ranks of the infantry were condemned to exist month after month "drained away health, energy and spirit".

Moving from one sector to another involved very long marches or in cattle trucks by rail, often with no proper rations. He tells of arriving in one unknown French town with nobody to report to, no food, no money and having to barter and sell kit to obtain food. In May 1916, his battalion was returning from a "stand down" by train. The train was just steaming into a station when the Germans started shelling the station. Enormous 12-inch shells dropped around them and the engine driver fled leaving the train like a sitting duck. Fortunately they were not hit.

In June 1916 Priestley says that his luck finally ran out. As Lance Corporal his job was to allocate the rations which had been brought up to his section and he stood in a shallow dug-out to do this. "Everything went black". A shell had landed only a few yards away and without the protection of the dug-out he would have been killed. The blast buried him alive and the surviving men began to dig him out, fortunately before he suffocated. John Scott was one of them. Priestley was in hospital for many weeks. His battalion, including John Scott, was in the Battle of the Somme, which began a few days later.

The Parish Church of St. Peter

6. WE WHO SERVED

List of All the Addingham Men who served

To be included in this list the men had to be born in the parish, lived here for a time before 1920, been recorded on one of the war memorials or the Scroll of Honour, or in any record or newspaper as being "of Addingham", or any combination of these. On occasions the connection is tenuous, but the man has been included in the list to ensure that his name is not forgotten.

The information has been obtained from:-

- St Peter's Parish Church records

- War memorials and Scroll of Honour

- Electoral Rolls for 1918 to 1920 which list absent servicemen voters at their home address

- Census records for 1891 to 1911

- Medal cards for serving soldiers

- Naval record sheets for seamen

- Service records for men who served from 1914 to 1920. This is an incomplete series as over half were destroyed by fire in the London blitz

- Wills, probate records and family recollections

- Newspapers for the war years

The total number of men recorded here is 414.

The Scroll of Honour in St Peter's Church records 265 men who served and returned. The war memorials record the names of 65 men who died, giving a total of 330. The actual number of men who died is 83 and some will be recorded on war memorials elsewhere.

As a guide to the list:-

- All men were born in Addingham unless otherwise stated

- All men who survived are on the Scroll of Honour unless otherwise stated

- All men who were killed are on the village memorials unless otherwise stated

- There is a parish address given for every man where one is known

ADAMS: Ernest

Born 1885 and the son of Joseph and Agnes of 126-128 Main Street where Joseph was a retail tobacconist. By 1911 Joseph is a watch and clock dealer at the same address.

ADAMS: Frederick

Born in 1886 at Beamsley and the son of James Leenie Adams and Gertrude. James and Frederick were both lithographic artists. Frederick returned to live in Addingham with his widowed mother at 1 Bolton Road and later at 1 High Mill Lane. In 1920 he married Madge Rishworth and lived at Walker Fold and Springfield.

Frederick enlisted in the Royal Garrison Artillery on 19 November 1915 when aged 30 years. He served in Sierra Leone, West Africa, being based in Freetown, arriving there on 10 June 1918. Sierra Leone had two German colonies as neighbours. Service Number 127362. In 1919 he returned to the UK on compassionate grounds as his mother had died. Demobbed on 10 June 1919 on medical grounds, he received an interim disability pension of 8s. a week for 20% disability.

AKERS: Robert William

Born 1875 at Kirby Wiske, Yorkshire. Employed as a gardener when he attested on 6 November 1915 aged 39 years and 11 months. At only 4 ft. 11 in. tall he was A1 fit but too short for full front line infantry service.

Assigned to the 261 Infantry Battalion from 7 November 1915 Service Number 25481, Robert transferred to the Leicestershire Regiment on 1 December 1917 and did not serve abroad. He was promoted to Lance Corporal on 14 March 1916 and to Sergeant on 30 May 1916. Demobbed on 20 February 1919 to 114 Main Street, Addingham.

Not on the Scroll of Honour.

ANDERSON: Percy

In January 1919 Percy, who had served with the 2nd Duke of Wellington's West Riding Regiment, returned home to Church Street after being a POW in Germany since May 1917. In 1918 his address was 6 Church Street. Born in Helmsley in 1897, Percy married Martha Clegg in 1925 at St Peter's Church when he was a watch and clock repairer.

APPLEYARD: John

Born 1879. John was a plasterer and by 1911 had been married for seven years to Cecelia. They had three children and lived at 39 Southfield Terrace. His parents were John and Rose Ann née Sutcliffe.

ASHBY: Edgar

Born Scarborough. Served as Medical Officer to the 3rd West Riding Regiment and held the rank of Captain. Married Mary Thompson, daughter of the former Rector of Addingham in 1907 at St Peter's Church. At outbreak of war he travelled to France with his regiment. Mary and her three children then lived with her mother at The Old Rectory. She carried out voluntary work locally. Edgar's brothers both served, one as a doctor and one as a chaplain.

Not on the Scroll of Honour.

ASHTON: Richard

Born 1900 and the son of James Ellis Ashton, a 41 year old beef butcher trading at 139 Main Street, Addingham. In 1925 Richard married Ethel Clarkson in Silsden and he was an electrical engineer. Brother Thomas also served.

ASHTON: Thomas

Service Number 28050 as a Private in the 6th Battalion Border Regiment, and before that the Service Number 3230 with Westmorland and Cumberland Yeomanry. Killed in action on 4 October 1917 in France and is buried at Cement House Cemetery, Langemark, Belgium, Grave reference Sp. Mem. B1.

Born in 1897 and the son of butcher James Ellis Ashton, who by 1918 was living at 14 James Street, Earby. Brother to Richard who also served.

ATACK: Frederick Wyndham

Born 11 June 1881 in Earls Heaton, Yorkshire. Frederick's brother James Edward Atack was a grocer and Parish Councillor. The two brothers were in partnership in Addingham for several years as grocers but during the war Frederick's wife moved to Litchfield. A report in the Craven Herald indicates that Frederick joined the Army Ordnance Corps in November 1915; however, his medal card shows him to be a Corporal in the Lancashire Fusiliers by the end of the war. Service Number 51928.

Not on the Scroll of Honour

ATKINSON: Brumfitt

Born 30 January 1878 and served in the Royal Garrison Artillery, Service Number 280568.

Read his story in "For King and Country"

ATKINSON: Charles J

Charles, born in 1896, died on 18 August 1916 when serving in the Duke of Wellington's West Riding Regiment, 1st/6th Territorials, with the rank of Corporal Service Number 6/4546. Buried at Authville in Lonsdale Cemetery Ref. VII. F. 7. on the Somme, 5 km north of the strategic town of Albert and near to Thiepval.

In 1911 Charles was a 15 year old railway porter for the Midland Railway and lived at 96 Main Street with his parents, grocer Barnet and Edith. Brother to Francis who also served.

ATKINSON: Francis

Born 1897 and known as Frank. In 1918 he was living with his parents in Barnoldswick. Brother to Charles who also served.

Frank served in the Navy and in early 1917 was off Africa serving on

HMS Astrea. From January 1917 to July 1919 the "Astrea" was servicing British stations in West and South Africa and as far as Kenya to support troops fighting the Germans on several fronts in Africa. It is not known when Frank joined the ship but when war was declared the "Astrea" was serving off Zanzibar and in late 1914 it bombarded Dar-Es-Salaam in German East Africa. One of the ship's officers was Harold Owen, brother of war poet Wilfred Owen.

Not on the Addingham Scroll of Honour.

ATTWOOD: Wyndham Joyce

In 1916 Wyndham *(who was known as Joyce)* was lodging at the Craven Heifer, Addingham, and worked as a salesman. Born in Exeter in 1885, he married Florence Carline in 1912. Florence died in 1915. After the war he married Catherine Carline in 1922.

Enlisted in the East Yorkshire Regiment on 22 February 1916 and in Reserve until 2 June 1916 and in France from 21 April 1917. Service Numbers 24669, 99297 and 41233. Promoted to Lance Corporal 5 May 1917, in August 1917 he received gunshot wounds which kept him in hospital for over three months. At some stage he was posted to the Durham Light Infantry and to the East Lancashire Regiment. Returned to France on 5 May 1918.

International Red Cross POW records indicate he was captured on 7 September 1918, "Nieppe" Number 41233, and held prisoner at Stendal, a large registration camp in Saxony, 90 km west of Berlin. Repatriated on 20 December 1918, it would be a further nine months before Joyce was discharged from military service.

BAILEY: George

George died of wounds in France on 6 August 1916 when serving in the Duke of Wellington's West Riding Regiment 9th Battalion. Buried at Quarry Cemetery at Montauban, which is 10 km to the east of the town of Albert and the scene of heavy and prolonged fighting. Grave Ref. VI. J. 2. A letter reported in the Craven Herald said that George had been seriously injured when a shell landed on a wheeled tanker and blew it to bits. Another report said that his leg had been blown off.

In 1911 George, born in 1887, was the unmarried son of Thomas Bailey, a widower of 4 George Street. Both men were labourers and part of a large extended family living in five rooms.

Brother John also served.

BAILEY: John

In 1911 John, born in 1897, was 32 years, single and lived with his widowed father Thomas. His mother Hannah was born in Addingham as were all John's nine siblings. Father Thomas, an overlooker in a silk factory, came as a young man from Macclesfield which was a major silk manufacturing centre.

BARBER: Arthur Douglas

Born 1887, the son of gardener William and Emma and known as Douglas. In 1901 the family lived at 4 High Mill Lane. On 9 October 1909 he married Lotty Rishworth at St Peter's Church when he was a labourer.

BARNES: Benjamin Clifford

Born in 18 February 1899, the son of Thomas and Lucy Ann who in 1911 lived at 38 Main Street. Ben was then a newspaper boy and Thomas a limestone quarryman working for J Green and Sons.

Ben served in the Royal Navy from 1917, possibly as soon as he became eighteen. A newspaper report on 21 September 1917 lists him as Stoker Barnes on HMS Superb and there is a record for him held in the National Archives to confirm this. His Service Number was K 41510.

HMS Superb, at the time Ben may have joined her crew, was at Scapa Flow. Earlier she had taken part in the Battle of Jutland on 31 May 1916, receiving no hits. She remained at Scapa Flow until October 1918 when sent to reinforce the British Eastern Mediterranean Squadron and a month later was the flagship which led the combined Franco-British force through the Dardanelles to receive the Turkish surrender. She sailed for England in April 1919.

BATES: William Noel

William enlisted aged 21 when living at "Fernhill", Ilkley. He joined Royal Engineers on 24 February 1915 when an engineering student.

Service Number 32307. Appointed Lance Corporal on 24 February 1915 and Corporal on 1 August 1915. Discharged "on 7 August 1916 for the purpose of being appointed to a commission", as noted in a War Department letter dated 19 August 1916.

The son of Dr William Richard Bates who, for a time, was General Practitioner and Surgeon in Addingham, and campaigned for the opening of the Coronation Hospital in Ilkley. Father William died in 1929 when living at Potters Hall in Addingham and there is a plaque to him inside St Peter's Church.

Born in 1894 William became a Chartered Engineer in 1923 with references from F Purcell Barnes DSO, OBE of Aldershot. At the time he applied, William was at Fuller Barracks, Aldershot. His education was listed as:

- Prep School Ilkley, the Royal School Armagh

- 1913 to 1915 Leeds University

- 1911 to 1912 Hunslet Engineering Company

- 1915 to 1916 HM Forces. Despatch rider for the Royal Engineers in France

- 1917 to 1922 Commission in Infantry. Served East Africa, Mesopotamia and Ireland

- 1922 to 1923 Commission in R.A.S.C. as Acting Adjutant 385 M.T. Company in Cologne

Not on the Scroll of Honour.

BAUL: John Horace

Born Newburgh, Nr Ormskirk on 19 May 1889 and known as Horace. Son of William John and Catherine of Highfield House, Turner Lane.

In February 1915 he was employed as a clerk at the Old Infirmary, Newcastle-on-Tyne; however, he must have already been in the army as by 18 April 1915 he was serving in France for which he was awarded the 1915 Star medal. He served in the Yorkshire Regiment as Private 2031, then later as Sergeant. In a letter home reported in Ilkley Gazette on 23 September 1915, Horace says that he is in the same unit as his brother Corporal L Baul. They went to France on the same day.

Horace is not listed on the Scroll of Honour. However, there is a Maurice Baul listed on it for whom I can find no trace in any available record, so I suspect that as Horace and Maurice sound similar a mistake has been made. It is also clear that John Horace did serve and it would be unusual for him not to be included on the Scroll of Honour as are his brothers.

BAUL: Richard Lawrence

Born in 1894 at Newburgh, he lived with parents William and Catherine at Highfield House, Turner Lane, and was a mill clerk. Father William was a farmer and butcher. Brothers John Horace and William Reginald also served.

Known as Lawrence, he served in the Yorkshire Regiment, Machine Gun Corps. Service Numbers 2077 and 23526. Went to France on 18 April 1915. Reported missing on 27 May 1918 it is likely that he was a prisoner of war. Lawrence received the Military Medal for bravery and the 1915 Star.

BAUL: William Reginald

Brother to Richard and John. He was a dairyman at 2 Westville Avenue, Ilkley, in 1911. Born on 19 May 1889 in Newburgh.

William served in the Royal Field Artillery and was a Corporal for a time. Service Number 111911. His medal card has a note, "reverted to Bombardier on admission to hospital on 23 April 1918".

BECK: Norman Winterburn

Born 1898 in Guiseley, Norman was killed in action on 14 June 1918 when serving with 2nd South Staffordshire Regiment. Service Number 42112. Buried in Bienvillers Military Cemetery about 25 miles from Bapaume. Norman is believed to have enlisted whilst under age, at Keighley in case his age was discovered. At that time he lived in Addingham and probably enlisted in the first year of the war.

The son of Florence Beck, formerly Kershaw, and the grandson of Elizabeth Ann Clarke of 50 Main Street.

BECKWITH: James

Born in 1875 in Liverpool, James enlisted in the Royal Army Medical Corps aged 43, when he lived in Liverpool and worked as a dock labourer. There is a note on file indicating that he should never be medically higher than B1 because he enlisted over the age of 40 years. This is dated 18 April 1918. James served at home from 22 June 1918 to 7 November 1918 and then in France from 8 November 1918 to 25 November 1918 when he embarked for Salonika, and served until 23 May 1919.

James married Mary Yeadon in 1900 when she lived in Main Street with her grandfather Adam Yeadon a retired grocer. The couple lived in Addingham for at least four years as daughters Jane and Doris were born in the village.

Not on the Scroll of Honour.

BELL: Ernest

Born 1 December 1886, in 1911 Ernest was an unmarried baker living with his parents at 113 Main Street, Addingham. Father Henry was in business as a draper.

BELL: Frederick William

Frederick was officially presumed killed in action on 3 September 1916. He died on the Somme and is recorded on the Thiepval Memorial.

Served in the 1/5th Duke of Wellington's, West Riding Regiment and the 1/6th West Yorkshire Regiment, Prince of Wales Own. Service Number 2 41236.

Brother Norman also died in the war.

BELL: Joseph

Born in Brighton in 1885, Joseph lived at 4 Bolton Road and was a house painter. Married Alice, née Dickinson in Addingham sometime between 1901 and 1909.

A local newspaper reports in July 1918 that he was in the Lancashire Fusiliers and a prisoner of war in Germany. An International Red Cross record shows that a Private 36596 J Bell arrived in Dover on 28 November 1918 after being repatriated. Joseph served with the 11th Lancs Fusiliers.

BELL: John William

John, born in 1881 and known as Willie, was the son of coachman John and Alice who in 1881 lived at Barnes Buildings, Addingham. By 1901 William was married to Eliza and a carter. By 1911 the couple lived in East Morton, near Bingley.

BELL: Norman Francis

Born at Draughton in 1893, Norman served in the Royal Navy as an Ordinary Seaman and was on the HMS Glasgow when he died on 22 November 1917 aged 24 years. His death was following an appendix operation and he is buried at the British Cemetery in Rio de Janeiro. Grave reference Section AA. Row 2. GRI. Service Number J/59740.

In 1917 the "Glasgow" was patrolling the Brazilian coast searching for German raiders and until then had been part of the Mediterranean fleet following her actions in the Battle of the Falklands in December 1914. The ship had a mascot which was a pig which the crew found at sea. They named it Terpitz.

At the time he died, Norman was married to Edith and they lived at 17 Wharfedale View. Parents William and Mary lived at Back Beck.

Brother Frederick was killed.

BELLERBY: Harry

Born 1897, Harry was killed in action in France on 21 March 1918. He had enlisted at Keighley and served in the Machine Gun Corps, Service Number 103569 and before that was a Private 7643 in the Highland Light Infantry. Recorded on Poziers Memorial on the Somme.

There is a note on his medal card for 10 June 1922 requesting permission from the Machine Gun Corps to dispose of his medals, presumably because they were not claimed by the family.

In 1911 Harry was an errand boy living at 10 Brewery Road, Ilkley, with parents William and Annie. William worked as a carter for the District Council, and their three eldest children were born in Addingham where they lived until around 1904.

Brother Percy also served.

Not on the Addingham War Memorial.

BELLERBY: Percy

The son of William and Annie, Percy was born on 27 June 1894. He married Kathleen Doris West at Ilkley on 9 August 1919.

Served in the East Yorkshire Regiment, Service Number 13162 and the Lancashire Fusiliers Service Number 67316. His unit was in France from 14 July 1915. Awarded the 1915 Star medal.

Brother Harry also served.

BENSON: Bernard

Born 1894 in Johannesburg, Transvaal, Bernard was the son of Wesleyan Minister Joseph Benson who was in Addingham during the war years. Father Joseph had married Jessie, who was born in Cape Town, whilst he was in the ministry there in 1887. The family lived at Springfield Mount.

Brother Harold W also served.

BENSON: Emanuel

Emanuel was the son of William and Margaret who farmed at Lobwood House, Farfield for many years as had several generations before that. Emanuel was born in 1880 on the farm of 280 acres and spent some time in his childhood in Durham where his mother was born.

He served in 1/6th Duke of Wellington's West Riding Regiment.

Further details in "For King and Country"

BENSON: Harold Washington

Born 1889 in Pretoria, South Africa and the son of Wesleyan Minister Joseph and Jessie.

Harold enlisted in August 1915 aged 26 years in the Royal Engineers when living in Dublin and an art student. Service Number 73137. Posted to the Signal Depot as a Pioneer on 9 August 1915 and promoted to Lance Corporal on 10 August 1915. Harold served in Egypt during 1915/1916 and then in Basra from 24 March 1916. He was admitted to hospital several times during his short service in Basra and invalided to India on 6 June 1916 after only three months in Basra. By March 1918 he was medically unfit and allocated Medical B3. He joined the Signals Depot at Poona in India on 16 December 1918 and left Bombay on 8 February 1919 for the UK.

A note on his service record says "art master" and his address as Springfield, Addingham.

Brother Bernard also served.

BENSON: Robert

Born in1881, Robert was the son of William and Margaret who farmed at Lobwood House. In 1911 he was a single man, living with his parents at Brockabank on the Moorside and employed as a gardener.

Brother to Emanuel who also served.

BICKLE: Joseph

Joseph was a grocer working for Mr Atack in Main Street, before he attested on 5 November 1915 when aged 22 years. His next of kin was mother Sarah of Wakefield.

Served with the Yorkshire Regiment, Service Number 24188 and later 26454 when in the Machine Gun Corps. In France for 2 years 54 days, from 22 May 1916. Wounded on 7 July 1916 and again on 8 July 1918. In 1918 he spent time in hospital at Boulogne then at Chelmsford for 31 days. As a result of injuries he was left with a disability in his right wrist. In a letter to Mr Atack earlier in 1918 Joseph said that he had been part of the Big Push.

Not on the Scroll of Honour.

BIDGOOD: David

Born in 1887 to Thomas, a stone mason, and Ann, David was their only child. By 1911 the family lived in Bradford and 23 year old David, a dyer, supported his parents. He married Mary Palmer in 1913.

David served as Private 241251 and 619157 in the West Yorkshire Regiment and the Labour Corps, and is believed to have enlisted in December 1914 serving until 27 June 1919.

In 1921 David and his family sailed from London to Wellington, New Zealand. He is believed to have been a tram conductor with Wellington

City Council. Died in New Zealand in 1962.

Not on the Scroll of Honour.

BINNS: Hanson

Hanson, born in 1893, was the son of farmer Hanson and Sarah Jane née Holmes.

Joined the Scots Guards and in 1911 in Egypt. His medal card indicated that he was in the First Scots Guards and had Service Numbers 2689 as a Private and 7548 as a Lance Corporal. Went to France with his unit on 13 August 1914, participated in the Battle of Mons and the subsequent retreat to the Marne, Aisne and first Battle of Ypres in 1915. Hanson's unit was in all major battles on the Western Front until 1918. Awarded the 1914 Star.

On 20 February 1919 Hanson married Betty Lister, daughter of Bramley Lister, when he was still a serving soldier. In 1918 he lived at Croft House, Addingham.

Brother Henry also served.

BINNS: Henry

Born 1892 he was the son of Hanson and Sarah J living at Oliver Farm, Nesfield, and a joiner.

Enlisted in the Royal Engineers on 12 April 1915 at Liverpool when aged 23 years, Service Number 35903, as a skilled carpenter. Went to France on 6 October 1915 and was awarded Superior Skills enhancement on 13 May 1916 whilst serving there. Appointed 2nd Corporal on 31 March 1918, he was wounded the same day with gunshot wounds to his right arm. He was awarded the 1915 Star.

BINNS: John William

Born 10 January 1898, the son of Jonathan, a quarry man, and Emma, who lived in Addingham from around 1895 to 1900. John William was a frame tenter.

Served in the Royal Naval Reserve from at least 1917 to 1919.

BLACKBURN: Wilfred

Wilfred was killed in action on 29 July 1916 aged 23 years when serving in France with the Duke of Wellington's West Riding Regiment 10th Battalion as Acting Sergeant with Service Number 13716. Recorded on the Thiepval Memorial Pier and Face 6A and 6B. Wilfred died when his unit was fighting on the Somme following the offensive of 1 July 1916. A letter to his uncle of 11 August said Wilfred was killed when his unit halted an advance.

Lived with his uncle, Thomas Blackburn, at West Hall in Nesfield and worked as a farm servant. Wilfred was born in 1894 at Barrowford, near Nelson.

BLAKEY: James Alfred

Born 1898, in 1911 James lived with father Fred at 8 Chapel Street. Fred was a grinder and he and all three children were born in Addingham. Their mother Beatrice had died in 1907 when only 35 years old. James worked in textiles. Later lived at 3 Railway View.

BRAYSHAW: Miles Hanson

Born 1886 and the son of plasterer Robert and Esther who in 1901 lived at "Hunterlands", Turner Lane. In 1911 Miles was a 24 year old single labourer living with his sister, now Mrs James W Ettenfield, at 8 Adelaide Terrace. Shortly after in July 1911 Miles married Annie Espin from Thirsk.

There is a medal card for a Myles Brayshaw but not for a Miles. This person served in Royal Engineers and in Egypt from 29 December 1915. Sapper Service Number 98635, and awarded the 1915 Star. I believe this is the correct person.

Miles died in Thirsk in 1949.

BREAR: Benjamin

Born in 1878, the son of William, a timber merchant of the Saw Mills, Addingham. Benjamin was an architect and in 1911 lodged in Sussex as he worked as a civil engineer for a cement company, living with the proprietor's family. He went to South Africa, returning from Durban to London, arriving on 4 November 1914.

Within four months of his return from South Africa, Benjamin enlisted on 22 March 1915 in the Royal Engineers, and served in 211th Field Company as a Sapper Service Number 83977. With his educational background it would have been possible for him to train as an officer but he appears to have remained a Sapper throughout his service. Benjamin went to Egypt in November 1915 where he stayed until March 1916. His unit embarked for France in March 1916 and the rest of his active service was in France. Granted a furlough in late 1917 he overstayed his leave from December 1917 to 3 January 1918. His address on demobilisation on 15 March 1919 was The Saw Mills, Addingham.

He travelled extensively as a civil engineer when he lived at Low House, Addingham, including to the Gilbert Islands, Australia, Canada and America.

BREAR: Ronald

Born 17 April 1897, son of Edward and Mary Jane. At aged 13 Ronald was already a chair maker working with his father at the English Timber Company. The family lived at 4 Cragg View.

Served in the Royal Naval Voluntary Reserve based at Tyneside, Service Number TZ/11090. Ronald's medical card also indicated that he served in the Fleet Arm Service Division. There are no details of his service.

BRIGG: John Haggas

Born 1891 in Luton. In 1911 he was a 20 year old architect and pupil living near Luton with parents Thomas and Helen. The family had several servants.

Served in the Territorial Forces, joining the 4th Bedford Yeomanry in 1911 when aged 19 years. Before that, whilst a pupil at Malvern College, he had been a cadet. He was mobilised on the first day of the war, serving at home until 6 February 1916 when his unit was posted overseas.

John married 24 year old Doris Smith in Keighley in September 1919 when a 28 year old Captain in the Bedfordshire Yeomanry and living at High House, Addingham. Her father was Prince Smith, gentleman.

BROMILOW: Percy Winton

Born 1889 at New Cross, London, and served in the Royal Army Service

Corps in Mechanical Transport, 694th Company, as a Private Service Number 285392.

Percy lived at Beacon Cottage, Southfield Lane Row *(sic)* and attested on 10 December 1915 when he was a travelling salesman. Served 2½years of which 15 months was in India and a note on file says "unfit to spend another spell of hot weather in India". This was from the M.O.H. at Station Hospital, Peshawar *(undated)*. When discharged he accepted 52s. 6d. in lieu of a plain suit of clothing.

Not on the Scroll of Honour.

BROWN: Henry

Probably Harry Brown, born 23 October 1895 in Addingham. Baptised at St Peter's Church on 15 December 1895 as Harry, he was the son of John and Eleanor and John worked in the saw mill. In 1901 the family lived at Druggist Lane and all were born in Addingham. By 1911 the family were living in Keighley and Harry, now aged 15 years, was an iron turner.

BROWN: John Henry

 John was killed in action on 13 March 1917 aged 26 years serving as a Territorial in the Wharfedale Howitzers. Service Number 785991. John served in the Royal Horse Artillery and the Royal Field Artillery and was a Sergeant in "D" Battery of the 312th Brigade. Buried at Queens Cemetery, Bucquoy Grave Reference I.J.4. The cemetery is 15 km south of Arras.

He was a Corporal by 20 November 1914 when a newspaper report mentions that he was a member of Addingham football team.

Born in Addingham in 1890 and the son of Thomas and Eliza Ann of 42 Main Street.

Brothers Philip and Willie also served.

BROWN: Philip

Philip was born in Addingham in 1895 and died of wounds in France on 11 May 1917 when aged 22 years. His brother John had died two months

earlier also in France. Philip was serving in the Territorial Forces in the Royal Field Artillery and possibly, like his brother, he was part of the Wharfedale Howitzer Brigade. Service Number 781190. At the time he was wounded, Philip was in "D" Battery of the 311th Field Artillery. He is buried at Etaples Cemetery Part II Graves A-C. His record says son of Thomas and Eliza Ann. Native of Addingham.

BROWN: William

Born in 1897. In 1911 Willie was the 14 year old son of widower Thomas Brown of 42 Main Street, Addingham.

Brother to John Henry and Philip who were both killed.

BUCKLE: Herbert Gladstone

The first record of Herbert in Addingham is in the 1919 Electoral Roll as a serviceman living at 147 Main Street. Born in 1881 in Wortley, Yorkshire, he was a confectioner.

It is not known where Herbert served but there is one medal card for a Herbert G Buckle serving as a Gunner in the Royal Garrison Artillery. Service Number 99758.

Herbert died in 1945 when he lived at 142 Main Street, leaving a widow Evelyn Maude.

BURKE: Charles

Born 1887 in Leeds and the eldest of six serving sons of Annie and quarryman Charles Burke. Charles was married to Sarah and a daughter Ada Marion was born in September 1914 when they lived at 7 Main Street, Addingham.

Enlisted at Colne on 3 March 1916 when one day short of his 28th birthday. At the time he was a platelayer for the Midland Railway Company living at Gate House, Slipper Lane, Colne. Appointed to "A" Company Railway Troops Depot as Assistant Ganger. Service Number 157312. His service record is faded but he did serve overseas in Egypt and in France. A local newspaper says he was serving in Egypt in 1917. Charles served until 21 August 1919.

BURKE: Edward

Edward served in the Northamptonshire Fusiliers as a Sergeant and in France from 24 July 1915. Wounded in November 1917 and in September 1918. In a letter home Edward said that his overcoat and oilskin saved him from further injury, although he had a bullet wound in his thigh.

Born in 1893 in Addingham, the son of widow Annie Burke, he had five brothers serving. Edward married Sarah A Burnell in September 1913 when aged 20 years.

Possibly in the Royal Flying Corps and the Lancashire Fusiliers. Service Numbers 2158, 50364 and 57192. Awarded 1915 Star.

BURKE: Ernest

Born 1900 and son of widow Annie Burke of 13 Jubilee Terrace.

No military records of his service have been identified.

BURKE: Frank

Frank enlisted on 14 September 1914 aged 20 years and 11 months. He served in West Riding Regiment, Service Number 12807; however, he was discharged with defective vision during his initial training.

Born in 1894 Frank, a weaving overlooker, was one of the six serving sons of widow Annie Burke.

BURKE: Frederick

Born 1899 Frederick was the son of Michael and Jane-Anne of 10 School Lane. A quarryman and cousin to the six Burke brothers.

BURKE: John

Born 1896, one of the six brothers to serve.

A local newspaper reported him wounded in 1916 and in a letter home in July 1916 he said that he had lost his left eye and thought "his head had gone west". This happened when he had only been in the trenches for one hour.

BURKE: Joseph

Born 1878 Joseph was killed in action on 12 October 1916 when serving in the 2nd Battalion of the Duke of Wellington's West Riding Regiment. His name is recorded on the Thiepval Memorial Pier and Face 6A and 6B.

Joseph attested on 4 December 1915 when aged 37 years and 11 months. He then lived at 15 Keighley Road, Skipton, and was a weaver. In France from 30 August 1916.

His next of kin was his mother Mary Burke of 15 Keighley Road, Skipton. Mary, like her husband John, was born in Ireland and they lived in Addingham until at least 1900 and four children were born here.

Not on Addingham War Memorial.

BURKE: Walter

Born 1892. One of the six serving sons of widow Annie of Jubilee Terrace and in 1918 at 13 Chapel Street.

CARLINE: Frederick Greaves

Frederick was the son of George Carline, landlord at the Craven Heifer, probably from around 1917. His mother was Mary, and he was born in 1885 in Matlock, Derbyshire. Before taking the Craven Heifer his father was the Baths Manager at Harrogate and in 1911 Frederick was an Assistant Rate Collector.

Frederick enlisted in November 1916. Served in the 15th London Regiment. Service Number 534515. Wounded in late 1917 when with the heavy gun section. Wounded again in April 1918, his injuries were from shell fire and gunshot wounds to legs and knee and he may have had a knee-cap removed. His service record shows he embarked for France on 10 May 1917. On 4 January 1918 he joined the Anti-Aircraft School for training. The injuries received on 7 April 1918 resulted in a transfer to Leeds Military Hospital. He was discharged from there in January 1919 and from military service one month later having been on active service just over two years.

Brother-in-law to Wyndham Joyce Attwood who also served.

Not on the Scroll of Honour.

CHAMBERS: Harry

Born 1879 Harry was killed in action on 5 May 1915 when serving with the 2nd Battalion Duke of Wellington's West Riding Regiment, Service Number 14603. He was 36 years of age and is recorded on the Ypres Memorial the Menin Gate, panel 20.

Harry, a stone hewer, enlisted at Bradford where he lived with wife Bertha. Brought up in Addingham and lived with his parents Thomas and Rebecca at Main Street, Addingham.

Not on the Addingham War Memorial.

CHAPLIN: Fred

Born 1890. Fred appears in records in Addingham for the first time in March 1914 when he married Ellen Tiffany at St Peter's Church and was a 24 year old labourer. In 1918 he lived at 8 Rose Terrace.

CLARKE: Charles Prior

Born in Skipton in 1882. Charles was killed in action at the Battle of Coronel. His body was not recovered for burial.

Read his story in "For King and Country".

CLARKE: John

Born 1879 and the son of William and Ellen Clarke. In 1901 John was living at 21 Main Street and nephew of George and Jane Foster. Brother to Charles who was killed.

Believed to be Lance-Sergeant 8840 in 2nd Battalion of King's Own Yorkshire Light Infantry and a Regular soldier who enlisted at Batley and was killed on 26 August 1914 in the retreat to the Marne. Buried at La Ferté-sous-Jouarre Memorial Ground. The death record says that this person was born in Darjeeling, India. 'Craven's Part in the Great War' notes that he is not proven to be the John Clarke on the Addingham Memorial. However, I am unable to find another.

CLARKE: John

Born 1890, probably in Silsden. John was killed in action or died as a result of enemy conflict on 18 September 1917 when serving as an Ordinary Seaman in the Royal Navy on HMS Stonecrop. Official

Number J 66434. His body was not recovered for burial.

John was the son of Joseph and Selina Clarke. Date of Birth in naval records is 23 October 1890. John was married and his wife Mary lived at 114a Main Street, Addingham.

Not on the Addingham War Memorial.

CLAYTON: George N M

Born 1881 George was a Regular soldier, signing on at Halifax on 19 November 1908 for six years when he was aged 27 years. His six years would not have been completed before war was declared and there is a form on his service record dated 1919 indicating that he served throughout the war; signing on for continuous service from 1916. His service was with the West Yorkshire Regiment, Reserve Battalion. Service Number 9277.

When he enlisted in 1908, the Reverend Hall, Rector of Addingham, gave George a reference saying he believed him to be honest but out of employment.

George, a silk spinner, lived in Addingham with his grandparents from at least 1891, at Stockinger Lane and later at 3 George Street.

Not on the Scroll of Honour

CLAYTON: Sydney

Born 1897 in Carleton, the son of coachman James and Agnes who in 1911 lived at 10 Adelaide Terrace. A mill worker, Sydney married Florence Bedford of Ilkley. In 1918 Sydney lived at 10 Ilkley Road. Brother Walter also served.

CLAYTON: Walter

Born in Carleton in 1899 Walter was the son of James and Agnes. In 1918 Walter lived at 10 Ilkley Road, Addingham.

Brother Sydney also served.

CLEGG: Maurice

Born in October 1894 and son of Arthur and Fanny of 1 Railway View. Arthur was a stone quarryman and all the family were born in

Addingham.

Enlisted on 29 February 1916 when aged 22 years and 274 days and living at 22 Main Street. Maurice at 5ft. ½in. tall was allocated service in the 87th Training Division as he was well under minimum height for infantry service. Service Number 70474. In August 1917 he was assessed as no longer physically fit with "bad physical development not caused by active service". An enquiry was to be carried out as he was deemed to be "improperly enlisted". He was discharged on 31 July 1917 and awarded £7 10s. compensation. His height may have been re-assessed in July 1917 as 4ft. 11in.

COCKSHOTT: Thomas

Born 1885 and the son of Thomas and Ann who for over 20 years farmed at Low Sanfitt. In 1911 Thomas junior worked on the farm. His sister Emily was a schoolteacher in the village.

It is not known where Thomas served but there are two medals:-

Gunner in the Royal Garrison Artillery Service Number 99843
Corporal in the Machine Gun Corps Service Number 88747

COOK: Alfred

Probably born 1888 in Bingley, he was the son of Samuel and Eliza who, in 1901, lived in Bingley. By 1911 Alfred was a gardener at Farfield Hall, and he married Clara L Brown on 17 April 1911.

Alfred attested on 9 December 1915 when aged 28 years and was held in Reserve until 30 May 1916. At that time he lived at Wellhouse, Addingham and was still a gardener. Assigned to the Durham Light Infantry Service Number 32968. In France with his unit from 6 November 1916 until 19 May 1918. Alfred was wounded in April 1917 and transferred to the UK on 20 May 1917 for medical treatment. His medal card shows he also served in the Labour Corps as 554602, probably after discharge from hospital.

In 1918 he lived at 59 Main Street, Addingham.

COOPER: Hedley

Hedley, born 1886, was the youngest son of Edward and Martha. Edward was a chair and cabinet maker and the family lived at Cragg View. In

1911 Hedley was a railway clerk and brother Herbert a music teacher. It is believed that Hedley joined the Royal Flying Corps in November 1915 and became a radio operator.

Hedley became a naturalised United States Citizen in 1926 and married Alice, probably in the United States. They travelled together in 1924 and later Hedley travelled to England on 26 July 1927 with daughter Barbara who was born in Dallas. Their onward address was Cragg View. Both returned to New York on 10 September 1927 when Hedley was 41 years old and a violinist.

COTTOM: Frederick

Fred was the son of Sarah and John a carter. In 1911 the family lived at 1 George Street and 31 year old Fred was a single general labourer, lodging with his sister's family with several of his siblings. There were thirteen people in this extended family living in a two bedroom house. In 1918 he lived at 12 Rose Terrace.

Brother to James and Thomas who also served.

COTTOM: James

Born on 21 August 1888, the son of John and Sarah E. In 1901 James lived at 2 Church Street. Father John was born in Belmont, Lancashire. All their five children were born in Addingham. In 1911 James lived with married sister Jane Ellen Lodge at 1 George Street. In 1918 he lived at 12 Rose Terrace.

Brother to Fred and Thomas who also served.

COTTOM: Thomas

Born 1892 and brother to Frederick and James who also served.

A newspaper report for November 1915 states that Tom Cottom had joined the Royal Garrison Artillery at Woolwich.

A Thomas Cottom of the RGA/RFA was awarded a Silver War Badge and discharged with wounds on 15 February 1919, having served overseas. Service Number 680486 and this may be him.

Thomas is not on the Scroll of Honour, although he was living at 12 Rose Terrace in 1918.

There is no evidence of his military service other than the report in the newspaper. However, a Thomas Cottom born 1892 was buried at St Peter's Church on 20 June 1921 aged 29 years and he may have died of illness or wounds as a result of military service but is not on the Addingham War Memorial.

CRAVEN: George Edwin

Born in 1879 his parents were James and Margaret and in 1891 they lived in North Street with three of their surviving children. James was a silk card grinder. In March 1910 George, a silk weaver, married Alice Alenton and they lived at 13 Bolton Road and later at 38 Main Street.

A local paper records that G E Craven was wounded in October 1917 and had been serving since early 1917.

Brother Herbert also served.

CRAVEN: Herbert

Born 1895 and the son of James and Margaret of 2 George Street. In their thirty two years of marriage the couple had twelve children of which eight had died. Thankfully both Herbert and George, their two surviving sons, returned after the war. In 1918 Herbert lived at 39 Main Street.

A Private H Craven served in the 1/6th Duke of Wellington's West Riding Regiment as a Territorial and went to France on 14th April 1915

CRESSWELL: Alfred

Born in 1895. Killed in action on 23 July 1918 in France and buried at Raperie British Cemetery at Villemontoire Grave Reference IIIA.E.6. The cemetery is close to Reims and Aisne.

Alfred had enlisted in the Manchester Regiment on 16 April 1915 at Manchester, when he was aged 20 years and 8 months. Service Number 18405. A grocer's assistant he lived in Morecambe at the time. Posted to the 26th Reserve and served in Egypt during 1917. Appointed Corporal on 26 March 1917 whilst in Cairo and served there until 18 May 1918 when, with his unit, he left from Port Said in 1918 bound for Marseilles. At some stage after this he was posted to the Loyal North Lancashire Regiment 2nd Battalion as Lance Corporal, Service Number 40164.

The son of railway signalman James W and Mary Jane. The family lived in a different town in each census. Mary Jane née Smith was born in Addingham and the couple married in 1892 at St Peter's Church.

Not on any Addingham memorial.

CUNLIFFE: John Reynold Pickersgill *(Pickersgill-Cunliffe in some records)*

Born in 1895 at Saffron Walden in Essex and was killed in action on 14 September 1914 in France aged 19 years, nine months before his cousin, also John, was killed. Served in the Grenadier Guards and embarked for France on 12 August 1914 when his address was Beaufort Gardens, Kensington. He had been a Cadet Officer whilst at public school.

Sophia Pickersgill née Cunliffe was his great-grandmother and the extended family held land and property in Addingham for several decades. His parents Henry Pickersgill-Cunliffe and his wife Arlette née Reynolds had a country estate and a London house and John was their only son and heir.

Recorded on the memorial plaque inside St Peter's Church but not on the village war memorial.

His cousin, John Cunliffe Pickersgill Cunliffe *(Pickersgill-Cunliffe in some records)* was born 1884 in Oxted, the son of Charles and Evelyn Pickersgill-Cunliffe. The family were bankers, with a house in London and an estate in Surrey. Both were great-grandsons of Sophia Cunliffe who is buried in Addingham as Sophia Pickersgill. He was a career soldier and a Captain in the Worcester Regiment and was killed in action on 4 June 1915 at Gallipoli. His younger brother, Evelyn, emigrated to Canada, arriving there around 1902, and returned to fight in France with the Canadian Forces. He is not recorded on the Addingham War Memorial inside Addingham Church.

DEAN: THOMAS

Born 1 September 1887 and son of warehouseman Francis and Sarah.

Enlisted on 16 January 1918 aged 30 years and served in Duke of Wellington's West Riding Regiment as Service Numbers 5352 and 53025. In France from 21 November 1918 until 13 September 1919.

Thomas, a warehouseman, married Arabella Waite in 1913. Lived at 19

Low Mill Lane with wife Arabella and his widowed mother.

DEWHIRST: Abraham

Born 1886 and the son of Richard and Hannah of 11 Victoria Terrace. In 1911 Abraham a house painter was married to Ethel and son-in-law to Benjamin Mortimer of 101 Main Street.

Enlisted on 11 December 1915 and served in the Northumberland Fusiliers in France as a Private 35960. Discharged on 8 July 1918 severely injured and died five years later as a result of the wounds he received. Awarded the Silver War Badge.

Brother Richard also served.

DEWHIRST: Richard Taylor

Brother to Abraham who served, Richard was born in 1898. In 1901 he was living with his uncle John Whitaker at Cross Ends. By 1911 Richard was a single ironmonger's assistant of 72 Main Street.

DICKENSON: Harry

Born 1892 and the son of Samuel and Harriett. In 1911 he lived with widowed mother Harriett at 12 Cragg View.

Served as an Engine Room Artificer on destroyer HMS Swift and involved in a battle on 20-21 April 1917 with six enemy destroyers off Dover. His ship was hit. The ship later saw action in spring 1918 in the First Ostend Raid although its main duties were as a front line naval defence for the channel and southern coastline guarding the passage of cross-channel troop and supply ships.

Brother Stephen also served.

DICKENSON: Stephen

Born 1883, Stephen was the son of stationary engine driver Samuel and Harriett. All of their many children were born in Addingham and in 1891 they all lived at Wesleyan Terrace. In 1910 Stephen married Celia Foster.

Served in the Army Service Corps and attained the rank of Corporal, Service Number M2/052331.

In 1918 at 7 High Mill Lane.

DICKSON: John

Born in 1898 at Conisborough, Yorkshire, his father Fred was a domestic chauffeur and worked for Mr George Douglas at Farfield Hall. The family probably came to Addingham around August 1916 when George Lester, the previous chauffeur to Mr Douglas, was called up for military service.

DIGBY: Thomas Alfred

Born 1891 at Hampton Court. Thomas arrived in Addingham with his family during the war years as both he and his father were in the service of the Pickersgill-Cunliffe family. In 1911 father Alfred was coachman/chauffeur living at The Stables, Northwood Park. This was the palatial home of John and Helen Pickersgill-Cunliffe and their very large family. Two of Helen's unmarried daughters, Mary and Gertrude, came to live in Addingham around 1916 at the family property of Holme House, bringing with them several servants, including the Digby family. Thomas worked as gardener, Alfred as chauffeur and his wife Eliza worked in the house. The family may have left Addingham with the two sisters as they do not appear in the Electoral Roll after the early 1920s.

Not on the Scroll of Honour.

DIXON: John

Born 1890 John married Edith Town in 1908 when 19 years of age. He worked as a butcher and a tanner. Their third child was born two months after John was called up for service.

Enlisted on 26 June 1916 and called up for active service in September 1917. At 5ft. 9in. tall, John was posted to the Grenadier Guards as a Private Service Number 30163. He was granted a few days leave in late 1917 and whilst at home his 5 year old daughter Ruth became ill. She died just after Christmas, a week after John returned to his unit, and there is a note on his service record that he was quarantined for a time from 28 December 1917 because he had been in contact with diphtheria.

In France from 22 April 1918 until late August when on 30 August 1918 when he received gunshot wounds to his upper legs and buttocks and spent two months in hospital.

Shortly after leaving hospital John received news that his younger brother William had been killed in Italy. John and William were the sons of William and Ruth Ann and in 1911 the family lived at 6 Ilkley Road. In 1918 he lived at 14 Victoria Terrace.

DIXON: William

 Born in 1896, William died of wounds on 28 October 1918 in Italy when serving in the Duke of Wellington's West Riding Regiment 10th Battalion as Corporal, Service Number 18739. Buried at Giavera British Cemetery, Arcade, Plot 1 Row H Grave 9. It is not known when William went to Italy but whilst serving in France in 1916 when aged 20 years, he had been wounded and sent a letter home in November 1916 to say he was convalescing in Rouen. In Italy William's unit was moved to the front line from Salletuol to Palazzon on the River Piave and there was heavy fighting in a battle known as the Passage of Piave which lasted from 23 October 1918 to 4 November 1918.

The son of William and Ruth Ann before he enlisted William, like his father, was a boot and shoe maker. Brother to John who also served. In 1918 William's address was 29 Southfield Terrace.

DOBSON: Mark

Born in 1868, Mark was too old to enlist for military service at the outbreak of war, so he must either have been a Regular soldier or have volunteered for a specialist service as it was possible to be accepted for service up to the age of 50 years and Mark was aged 46 years at the outbreak of war.

Killed six months into the war on 3 April 1915 in France when serving with 2nd Battalion Prince of Wales Own West Riding Regiment. Service Number 3/10012. His burial was at "Y" Farm Military Cemetery at Bois-Grenier, just south of Armentières. Grave Reference L38 and Mark was one of the first burials here. In France from 5 November 1914. Awarded 1914 Star.

Son of Francis and Mary Ann who in 1871 were living at the Oddfellows' Hall, Lodge Hill. Francis, a retired coach proprietor, was 79 years of age and Mary Ann was aged 29 years. By 1881 Mary Ann was a widow living in Huddersfield with her two children and had several boarders.

Not on the Addingham War Memorial.

DOVE: James

Born in 1894 James was killed in action on 8 August 1916 aged 22 years. As a Private, Service Number 15707, James served in the Northumberland Fusiliers 9th Battalion in France from 15 July 1915. Buried at Dantzig Alley British Cemetery at Mametz. Grave Reference I.C.39. The cemetery is about 8 km east of Albert and it was opened in July 1916 after the Battle of the Somme.

James enlisted on the same day as his brother Matthias and in the same regiment. Matthias was killed two months after James.

The burial record says "son of Thomas and Frances Dove of 49 High Street, Steeton". However, Thomas had died several years earlier. In 1901 the couple were publicans at The Swan in Addingham and all their children were born in Addingham.

Brothers Matthias and William also served.

DOVE: Matthias

Born 1892, Matthias was killed in action on 4 October 1916 aged 25 years, just two months after his brother James was also killed in France. He is buried at Warlencourt British Cemetery close to Bapaume. Grave VIII. K.40. Matthias served in the Northumberland Fusiliers. He was in the 10th Battalion Service Number 15706 when he died. Both went to France on the same day in 1915.

In 1911 mother Frances was a widow living near Sedgefield, County Durham with her also widowed sister Dorothy. Matthias and his brother James were working underground at a colliery as breaksmen. Clearly fallen on hard times the extended family of ten people lived in four rooms in a colliery house. However, Fanny returned to Yorkshire at some time between 1911 and 1915 as she was living at 49 High Street, Steeton, when her sons enlisted.

Brothers James and William also served.

DOVE: William

Born 1890 in November 1912 William married Muriel Waterhouse at Steeton. His father is given as Thomas Dove, deceased. In 1911 William was visiting an Appleyard family in Elmsley Street, Steeton, and is described as a coal miner working underground. It seems likely that he, like his two younger brothers, was living with mother Fanny in Sedgefield. He lived in Steeton after marriage.

William was a Territorial serving in 1915 in the 1/6th Duke of Wellington's West Riding Regiment Service Number 1984 and in France from 14 April 1915. Later he was posted to the North Staffordshire Regiment as Private 242065. William returned home on 11 April 1919.

In November 1915 William sent a letter of thanks to Mr Flint for the food parcel and mentions meeting up with his two brothers, both being in France for four months.

DRIVER: Harry

Born in 1890 in Halifax, Harry was a Regular soldier and served for ten years enlisting on 16 February 1909 when aged 19 years. In 1911 he was serving in Hong Kong in the 88th Company Royal Garrison Artillery. Before 1917 he was posted to 5th Battalion in the same regiment and later to the Labour Corps. Service Numbers 9671, 31534 and 439427. It seems likely that Harry was wounded or had a debilitating illness as he was awarded the Silver War Badge and finally discharged on 12 February 1919. His other medals were not issued until 1933, no doubt because he did not apply for them at the end of the war.

 Harry may have spent little time in Addingham as his parents Joseph and Mary are not recorded in the village until the 1911 census when they lived at Marchup. Joseph was a polisher at a chair works. The family were still in Addingham in 1917 as a newspaper reports that in a letter to his father Harry says that they are "holding their own against the Germans".

Not on the Scroll of Honour.

DUNN: Alexander

Born on 19 November 1898, Alexander lived with parents, weaving overlooker James A and Mary, at 10 Cragg View and later at 7 Jubilee

Terrace. In 1918 Alexander lived at 23 Chapel Street.

ELLIS: Charles

Born 1886 in Ilkley, Charles had been in France for only a few weeks when he was killed. The son of Lister and Margaret of Cragg House Farm and a butcher. In 1901 the family had farmed at Lumb Gill and before that at a farm on the Moorside but in Ilkley parish. Lister and Margaret had six children of which four were sons. Charles and brother William James both died in the war.

Read their stories in "For King and Country".

ELLIS: Harry

Born 1888, Harry was a gardener and in 1911 lived with his wife Eleanor and baby Lucy at 5 Parkinson Fold. The youngest of the five children of George and Mary Jane, Harry spent his early years at 2 Parkinson Fold. His father was a general labourer and Harry worked in textiles.

ELLIS: William James

Known as James, and born in 1897 in Ilkley, James died of wounds on 10 November 1918, just one day before the Armistice. He is buried at Caudry British Cemetery, Grave Reference I.B.5. Caudry, east of Cambrai, was taken by the 38th Division in October 1918. As a Private Service Number 47052 James served in 15th Battalion of the Durham Light Infantry, and before that he had enlisted in Skipton in the West Yorkshire Regiment, Service Number 76298.

The son of Lister and Margaret, of Cragg House. James was aged 18 years when his brother Charles was killed.

Read more in "For King and Country".

EMMOTT: Ambrose

Born on 30 August 1884 at Beamsley, Ambrose had served for 17 years in the Royal Marines as Private CH/13074. Wounded in 1916 and again in March 1917 and by that time had already served in the Dardanelles in 1915. He died aged 35 years on 25 March 1918. Recorded on the Arras Memorial at Faubourg d'Amiens Cemetery.

The son of James and Ellen who in 1891 lived at High Mill, Addingham. James was born in Beamsley and a joiner. Ambrose enlisted in 1901. Based at Chatham he married Daisy Simpson in 1906 when he was described as a soldier.

Brother Walter was also killed.

EMMOTT: Harold

Born in 1892, his mother was Selina and his step-father, George Rishworth Snowden, a farmer at Causeyfoot House. Harold emigrated to Australia as a young man, possibly in 1913 when he was 21 years old.

He enlisted in the Anzac forces and was in the Dardanelles in 1915 serving with the 11th Battery. Following the evacuation of troops from Gallipoli he served in France.

As Harold Snowden, he wrote many letters to his mother detailing his army life, including one before he embarked for the Dardanelles in which he expressed a hope that he would get some UK leave.

After the war Harold returned to England. His marriage banns were read in Addingham in 1920 but because neither he nor his future bride were resident the marriage was conducted in Guiseley. Harold, then a 27 year old mechanic, married Mary Kirk. He then returned to Australia with his young family in 1927 on the "Baradine". Harold was employed as a carpenter.

Died in 1977 at Coonabarabran, New South Wales.

Step-father George also served.

EMMOTT: Walter

Born in 1892, Water was killed in action on 20 March 1915 when serving in 2nd Battalion, Duke of Wellington's West Riding Regiment as a Lance Corporal 3/9406. A former Regular soldier, he was a Reservist recalled to his unit at outbreak of war on 5 August 1914. Buried at Comines-Warneton, Hainault, Belgium. He was stretching after sleeping when shot. His nickname was "Pont".

His parents were James and Ellen Emmott of 6 Bolton Road. Walter married Florence Watts in September 1913 when he was a 21 year old labourer. His widowed mother lost two of her sons as his brother

Ambrose was killed in 1918.

ENGLAND: Charles

Born 12 June 1892 and the son of Jonathan, a joiner, and Mary. In 1911 the family lived at 2 Adelaide Terrace and Charles was an office boy. In 1918 the family lived at 2 Ilkley Road.

Brother Sydney also served.

ENGLAND: Edgar

Born 16 May 1877, Edgar was the son of Abraham and Ann and in 1881 the family lived in Parkinson Fold. Abraham was a journeyman joiner and by 1891 he was living in Barrowford and had re-married. In 1899 Edgar married in Nelson. His wife was Alice May Nicholson.

Enlisted on 9 January 1915 aged 37 years and served in Royal Artillery, Service Number 75096. At home until 14 February 1917 then in France until 22 April 1919.

Whilst serving in France his acknowledged son, Cyril Nicholson, was killed in France on 31 December 1917 aged 19 years. He was in the East Lancashire Regiment, Service Number 32262 but had formerly been 030476 in the Royal Army Service Corps.

Edgar was not discharged until 31 March 1920 when his fitness was B2 and he was almost 47 years of age. Served for 5 years and 33 days he was granted an enhanced pension for 7 years' service.

ENGLAND: John

Born 31 March 1896, John was the son of Arthur and Ann England. Arthur was a butcher in Main Street but some time before the 1911 census the family moved to Aintree, Liverpool. When John married Gladys in 1917 father Arthur was a farmer.

Brother Thomas and William also served.

ENGLAND: John

Born 1875 and known as Jack. He was one of the nine children of John and Phoebe and John was a land agent. John junior married Louisa Holmes on 26 December 1900 when he was a farmer. In 1901 the couple lived at 4 Ilkley Road, Addingham, and were related to the England family living next door, two of whom, Charles and Sydney, also served. In the census John junior is described as a musician. In 1911 lived at 3 Church Street and John junior is a joiner.

He sent a letter home saying he "can't imagine why there should be strikes in England in the light of the serious escalation of the fighting".

ENGLAND: Sydney

Born 11 August 1883, Sydney, according to a newspaper report, enlisted in 1916 and in September of that year was wounded in the left thigh by shrapnel.

Father Jonathan was, in 1901, a farmer and "horse carter" and the family then lived at 2 Ilkley Road. In 1911 Sydney was unmarried and a cotton weaver living with parents Jonathan and Mary at 2 Adelaide Terrace.

Brother Charles also served.

ENGLAND: Thomas

Known as Tom and born 11 April 1900. Thomas did not attain 18 years until April 1918 and would not have been eligible for overseas service until after the war was over.

The son of Arthur Widdop England and Ann, he moved to Aintree with his family as a child. In 1911 Arthur, who had been a butcher in Addingham, was now a dairyman and cow keeper on his own account.

Brother to John and William who also served.

ENGLAND: William

Born in October 1891 as William Summerscales England, son of Arthur and Anne E. The family had moved to Aintree, Liverpool, by 1911 when Arthur was in business as a dairyman. William married in December 1919 at Liverpool.

William enlisted in 1914 when a schoolmaster with Liverpool Education Authority and he worked in the Infantry Records Office. Saw service in France from 27 March 1915, and served with Reserve Battalion (Scottish), the King's (Liverpool) Regiment and the Royal Army Service Corps, Service Numbers 3609 and S/246551. Held the rank of Lance Corporal and later Staff Sergeant.

Brother John and Thomas also served.

ETTENFIELD: Wilfred

Born 1896 and the son of Richard and Sarah and brother to William who also served. A local newspaper reports that Wilf Ettenfield joined the Royal Engineers in 1915 and there is only one medal card for a Wilfred Ettenfield. He was a Driver, Service Number 84185, in the Royal Engineers serving in Egypt from 21 December 1915 and awarded the 1915 Star Medal.

Wilfred may have married Miranda Hodgson in 1919 and in the 1918 Electoral Roll lived at 18 Bolton Road.

ETTENFIELD: William

There is only one medal card in this name and this is for a William who served in the Northumberland Fusiliers and the Royal Highlanders with Service Numbers 5344 and S 27560.

Born 1892, William was one of the five children of Richard and Sarah, all born in the village. In 1901 the family lived at "Printers or Painters Shop", which was close to the Rookery on Bolton Road, and father Richard was a journeyman painter. William became a mill overlooker and in 1911 lived with his now widowed mother at 13 Rookery.

Brother Wilfred also served.

FAWCETT: Clifford

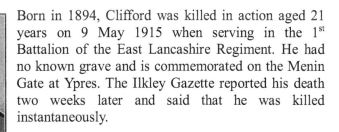

Born in 1894, Clifford was killed in action aged 21 years on 9 May 1915 when serving in the 1st Battalion of the East Lancashire Regiment. He had no known grave and is commemorated on the Menin Gate at Ypres. The Ilkley Gazette reported his death two weeks later and said that he was killed instantaneously.

Clifford lived with his family in Nelson with four siblings and father Joseph and all the children were textile workers. Clifford's mother was Anne Louisa and the daughter of Mr and Mrs T Myers of Main Street, Addingham. Clifford's only known address in Addingham is Wharfedale View.

Not on the Addingham War Memorial.

Brother John also served.

FAWCETT: John

Born in 1896 and son of Joseph and Anne, John enlisted aged 19 years at Colne on 18 September 1914. Serving in the Royal Engineers, Service Number 52519, on 7 October 1914 he joined the 80th Field Company as a Driver and later was posted to other companies. His work as a Driver was with horses as there are several references to stables. In 1915, when aged 19 years, John requested leave as his parents had not seen him for over a year and he was granted a pass for October 1915. He was absent from his unit by one day, following the expiry of his leave, but returned "sober and properly dressed". John was then serving with the 5th Bridging Train. File says "case dismissed" and "under punishment".

Three months later he was "absent" for 1 hour 20 minutes and fined four days' pay. Two weeks later on 17 March 1916 at about 9.00 a.m., when on duty, he boarded a troop train at Plymouth and woke up to find himself in Salisbury. The railway officials there told him to apply to Radnor House for a travel warrant to go back to Plymouth and then he was conducted to Salisbury Police Station where he was detained awaiting further orders. In the same year there was a charge of "inattention on a march" for which he was confined to barracks for two days.

Either ill or injured, John spent time in hospital in June and July 1918. He was in the 5th General Hospital and later a Red Cross hospital. John served until 7 June 1919 and was discharged to his parents' address in Nelson, from the 106th Field Company serving at Cambrai.

Not on the Scroll of Honour.

Brother Clifford was killed in May 1915.

FISHER: Fred

Born on 4 June 1894, Fred died of wounds on 5 May 1916. He was gassed in early 1916 and it is not clear if it was the effects of gas which killed him. In a letter recorded in the Ilkley Gazette for June 1916 another soldier, Private Moulding, said that while in a Dressing Station, he saw Fred Fisher who was wounded.

Fred was an early recruit into the New Army, enlisting at Ilkley in early September 1914. A Private in the 9th Battalion Duke of Wellington's West Riding Regiment, Service Number 12947, he served in France from 15 July 1915 and was awarded the 1915 Star.

Four Fisher brothers served, Fred, George, James and John. Parents David and Ellen had seven children, all sons and in 1911 the family lived at 21 Bolton Road, Addingham.

FISHER: George

George was a Regular soldier who enlisted on the same day as John McRink as the two have consecutive service numbers and were in the same regiment. In 1911 George was serving in the Hussars at Ailwal Barracks, South Tedworth, Andover. A single man and aged 21 years, he had enlisted aged 18 years on 19 April 1909. His medal card indicates that he was in the 10th Hussars, Service Number 4264, and went to France on 6 October 1914 for which he was awarded the 1914 Star.

Born 6 January 1890, his parents were David and Ellen, and in 1918 George lived at 21 Bolton Road

One of four brothers to serve.

FISHER: James

Born on 3 February 1897. His parents David and Ellen had lived in Addingham since the 1880s. All seven children were born in Addingham.

His three brothers also served.

FISHER: John W

Born on 24 February 1892 and the son of David, a general labourer and Ellen.

John was a gardener and enlisted as a volunteer and a newspaper report of February 1916 said that he had just returned to the front after home leave.

One of four brothers to serve.

FLESHER: Henry

Born 26 July 1896 in Ben Rhydding, and the only son of James Hugh Flesher and Margaret née Cockshott. Margaret had been brought up on the Cockshott family farm on the Moorside, where in 1881 her father John farmed. Although still described as a farmer in 1911 James Flesher, Margaret and children lived at 30 Victoria Terrace, Addingham, where Henry, aged 14 years, was a scholar.

In 1918 lived at Turner Lane with his parents.

FLINT: Christopher

Born in 1880 in Leeds. In 1901 he was a tea salesman, described as an employer and lodging in Keighley. In 1904 he married Nellie Varley who helped run her family grocery shop at 127 Main Street, Addingham. By 1911 Christopher was a grocer.

Early in the war Christopher took on the role of organising comforts, pen pals and food parcels for Addingham lads in the forces. There are many letters of thanks to him on records. In 1916 Christopher was conscripted and a presentation, arranged by the Parish Council, was made to him as thanks for all the money he had raised and the sterling work which he had done for the community.

Christopher served in France as a Gunner in the Royal Garrison Artillery, Service Number 177064.

FOSTER: Arthur

Born in 1882, he died of wounds on 31 December 1917 aged 38 years when serving as a Territorial in the 1/6th Duke of Wellington's West Riding Regiment. Buried at Lijssenthoek Military Cemetery Grave XXVI.D.4. near Ypres. Arthur is recorded as the son of M E Foster and husband to Edith of 10a School Bridge, Addingham.

In the early years of their marriage Arthur and Edith lived at Cockshott Place and Arthur was a carter.

FOSTER: George

Born on 3 January 1884, George, named after his father, was one of thirteen children, eight of which were sons. Four served in the forces, George, Lister, Thom and William.

The son of George, a farm labourer, and Sarah Ann. This large family occupied both 6 and 7 High Mill Lane. Father George died in 1902 and his family continued to live in the same houses. George junior was a bricklayer's labourer.

FOSTER: Lister

Born on 26 September 1887 in Silsden. Son of George and Sarah Ann née Lister. By 1911 Lister, a labourer, was married to Maggie and lived at Bark Hill, Addingham.

Serving in the Royal Garrison Artillery in 1917 when aged 30 years, Service Number 103768.

FOSTER: Thom

Born in 1897/1898 and son of George and Sarah Ann. Thomas was killed in action on 14 April 1918 when serving at the Ypres Salient. He is recorded on the Ploegsteert Memorial at Comines-Warneton which is south of Ypres and close to Messines.

Thom may have been under age when he enlisted as in 1901 he was aged 3 *(born 1898)* and a newspaper indicated that in November 1915 he went to Inverness to join the Highlanders. Thom *(as Tom)* did serve in the Gordon Highlanders, Service Numbers 12792 and 266657, but his death record indicates he joined in Leeds. By November 1916 he was wounded in France and again in August 1917.

One of four brothers to serve.

FOSTER: William

Born 1891, William was one of the four sons of George and Sarah to serve. In 1911, when living at 6-7 High Mill Lane, he was a single, cotton weaver.

FYNN: Thomas

Born 1888 and son of William and Martha of Smithy Yard. Thomas married Annie Kendall in Bradford on 4 May 1910 and he had a son, also Thomas, born on 21 August 1914.

Thomas was 26 years old when he was called up on 5 August 1914 and this was two weeks before his son was born. However, Thomas had no choice in the matter as he was a former Regular and now a Reservist serving in a Territorial unit. On the first day of war he would have been mobilised.

He certainly served in France with the 6th West Yorkshire, Service Numbers 240298 and 523092, and was in France from 16 April 1915 and awarded 1915 Star. His previous Service Number 1765 was for service with Prince of Wales Own West Yorkshire Regiment.

On 21 November 1918 Thomas was admitted to No.13 Stationary Hospital in Boulogne with rheumatism. He was then a Lance Corporal. Thomas returned to England from France on 10 December 1918 and he served until 11 October 1919. He finished service as a Sergeant and was granted a pension.

Not on the Scroll of Honour.

GALE: Albert

Born on 11 January 1897, named Albert Edward, and the son of Albert and Margaret of 1 Plum Tree Hill. In 1911 they were at Brockabank and Albert senior was a mason's labourer.

It is believed that Albert served in the Royal Garrison Artillery.

GALE: George

Born in Keighley on 14 March 1896 to James, a mill hand, and Charlotte. In 1911 George, a silk worker, lived with parents at 3 Southfield Terrace. George married Annie Hanson in 1920 and was then a painter living with his family at 20 Jane Street, Saltaire. Father James was an overlooker, presumably at Salt's Mill as Jane Street was a mill house.

Brother to William who was killed.

GALE: William

Born in 1887 and he was the son of James Leonard and Charlotte Gale.

William was killed in action on 1 October 1918 when aged 31 years and serving as a Territorial with the Royal Field Artillery, Service Number

786017, with the rank of Staff Sergeant. He was buried at Fifteen Ravine  British Cemetery at Villiers-Plouich, about 12 miles from Cambrai. Grave VII.E.10. William enlisted in June 1915 and went to France in 1917.

William married Alice Cousins whose father, Albert Cousins was publican at the Swan Inn. In 1918 he lived at The Swan, Addingham.

Brother George also served.

GEARY: Alfred Thomas

Alfred served in Yorkshire and Lancashire Regiment as Private 5346. Enlisted on 5 June 1916 aged 36 years. Mobilised on 21 July 1917. Discharged from service in December 1918. He may not have served overseas.

Born 1879 in Haynes, Bedfordshire, a farm labourer and cowman, his only recorded connection to Addingham is the birth of a son Percy in 1906 in Addingham as listed on Alfred's badly damaged army service record. Percy's birth was registered at Skipton. Alfred and his wife Fanny, née Bell, seem to have lived in several places.

Not on the Scroll of Honour.

GILL: Casson

Born 1886 and the son of John, a mason, and Ellen who, in 1891 lived at Sugar Hill. In 1901 the family lived in Silsden. Casson married in June 1916 when he was a boot and shoe maker of Agnes Street, Beechcliffe, Keighley.

A Corporal in the Labour Corps from 1917, he enlisted on 19 April 1916 aged 20 years, and served until 17 January 1920. Service Number 125610. Before serving in the Labour Corps he was with the Royal Engineers.

Not on the Scroll of Honour.

GILL: Henry

Born on 20 August 1899, Henry was the son of warp dresser Henry and Sophia who in 1901 lived at 25 Main Street. The couple had four children but one died in childhood leaving three boys, two of whom served in the forces.

Bother Lister also served.

GILL: Lister Cockshott

Born 1895 and the son of Henry and Sophia of 25 Main Street.

Attested on 2 November 1916 at Ripon when aged 21 years and 219 days and a clerk, joining the Royal Garrison Artillery and initially based in Perth, Scotland. Service Numbers 127206 and 301905. The Territorial Force is mentioned twice on his service record and on his medal card, so it is likely that he served in a Territorial battalion of the R.G.A.

There is a discrepancy in his record as it indicates he spent time in hospital in Peshawar, India, from 24 October 1916 to 21 December 1916, which was before he enlisted!

Lister suffered an attack of malaria in June 1917 and spent time in Colaba War Hospital in Bombay in May 1918 with a skin condition. His unit, in 1919, and possibly until he was discharged in January 1920, was at the No 8 Mountain Battery, based in India. Lister applied for a disability pension in 1920 because of the malaria but his request was refused.

Brother Henry also served.

GORDON: Harold Sommerville

Born 1893 at Heaton, Bradford, and the youngest son of William Bonnalie Gordon, a solicitor, and Maude née Bacchus. From 1902 to at least 1908 the family lived at Hallcroft Hall and William practised in Ilkley.

Harold served in the 2/8th Gurkha Rifles, joining as a Lieutenant, possibly before the start of the war. He later became a Captain and after the war became a career soldier, eventually retiring with the rank of Brigadier.

His mother Maud died in 1907 and is buried at St Peter's Church as are two of her children, including Marjorie who married Captain and later Major Richard Alexander Fawcett of 1/6th Duke of Wellington's Territorials who served in France. She died aged 27 years in 1914. Also buried there is brother William Bonnalie Gordon junior who died November 1919 at Howden Isolation Hospital aged 30 years. He, in 1911, was a medical student. It is not known if he served in the war.

Not on the Scroll of Honour.

GOULDING: John W

Born in 1885 at Brampton in Westmorland. John was killed in action on 21 August 1915 in the Dardanelles and is recorded on Helles Memorial, panels 117 to 119. As Private 14319 in the 8th Battalion of the Duke of Wellington's West Riding Regiment, John landed at Suvla Bay on 7 August 1915 and was killed exactly two weeks later. The son of George and Margaret, by 1901, aged 15 years, John was a weaver in an Addingham silk mill and living at 12 Victoria Terrace with 40 year old widowed father George who was a railway plater. John enlisted at Ilkley early in the war.

Brother Richard also served.

GOULDING: Richard

Born in 1887 at Long Marten, Westmorland, the son of George and Margaret and brother to John who was killed. In 1901 the family lived at 12 Victoria Terrace. In 1915 father George lived at Head Farm, Barden. A third brother, Thomas, lived in Addingham and worked as a farm servant at Street Farm for a Rishworth family. Richard married Ann Ideson at Barden Wesleyan Chapel in October 1916.

At the time he enlisted at Skipton on 8 December 1915, Richard was a 27 year old shepherd at High Gamsworth, Barden. Richard was mobilised at Halifax on 22 January 1917. His service record is badly damaged. He was posted to the 3rd Battalion of the Machine Gun Corps and at this time his Service Number was probably 90569. Richard served in France from 20 July 1917 to 5 February 1919 and he was demobbed from his unit at Ripon on 8 March 1919.

Not on the Scroll of Honour.

GRAY: James

Born 1877. In 1891 he was the 14 year old son of Isaac, a silk spinner, born Nesfield, and Mary of Adelaide Terrace. By 1901 James was recently married to Annie née Haigh and lived at 11 Parkinson Fold.

James enlisted at Ilkley on 1 September 1916 when he would have been 39 years old; however, his age is given as 34 years 10 months. He lived at 1 Sunset, Ben Rhydding, and was a gardener. James joined the West Riding Regiment, Service Number 12783, but was later discharged as unfit for further service.

GRAY: John William

Born 1887, John was the son of William Henry and Annie Gray *(Grey in some records)*. Although John, like his father, was born in Addingham, by the time he was a four year old the family were living in Skipton.

John was a Territorial and joined in 1908 when he was aged 21 years, lived at Bunkers Hill, Skipton, and worked for the railway company. Service Number 697. John's service record is badly damaged but he appears to have signed on again with the regiment. There is no war service recorded but the record is incomplete.

Not on the Scroll of Honour.

GREEN: William

Born in Bradford in 1878 William served in the 12th Service Battalion of the King's Own Yorkshire Regiment and enlisted aged 39 years in 1915 as Private 1378. Also served in King's Own Yorkshire Light Infantry, joined the Lancashire Regiment on 5 May 1916 and may have also served with the "Miners Pioneers". He was demobbed on 2 May 1919.

William married Amy Freckleton and in 1901 the couple and one month old Martha were living at 77 Main Street, Addingham. A son Thomas was also born in the village. William was a roofer and slater.

Not recorded on the Scroll of Honour.

HADLEY: Arthur

Born 12 March 1886 in Normanton, Yorkshire. Arthur was the son of Isaac and Harriett and living at 1 Brumfitt Hill in 1901. Harriett was a schoolmistress and Isaac was the Addingham Cooperative Store Manager. The couple had a daughter, also Harriett, who married Thomas England born Addingham, an engineer and surveyor. In 1911 Arthur is an assistant surveyor, aged 24 years, living in Borham Woods, Herts, with them.

Later in 1911 it is believed that Arthur emigrated to Canada, travelling to Montreal on the "Laurentic" and arriving on 23 September 1911. Served with the Canadian Expeditionary Forces.

HADLEY: James

Born 26 March 1899 in Keighley. James was the son of Sydney Charles Hadley and Isabella. Father Sydney came to Addingham between 1901 and 1910 to take up the post of stationmaster at Addingham and the family lived at the stationmaster's house. Isabella died when James was 10 years old. Sydney was born in Australia and one of a large family who emigrated first to New Zealand, then Australia and then returned to England. Sydney continued to live at Station House and remarried in 1915 and was stationmaster throughout the war years. In 1918 recorded at 123 Main Street. Brother Sydney also served.

HADLEY: Sydney Kitching

Born 5 February 1895 at Halton, Lancashire. Sydney was killed on 18 October 1917, aged 22 years, when serving with the Canadian Forces in France. He served with the Canadian Infantry as Private 681303 in the 116th Battalion. Sydney is buried at Etaples Military Cemetery in the Canadian Sector. Grave Reference XXX.E.12A.

By 1914 Sydney was living in Canada and at the time he enlisted he lived at the West End YMCA, Toronto. In 1911 before emigrating he worked as a clerk in an estate office whilst his father, also Sydney, was stationmaster at Addingham.

Brother James also served.

HALL: Clifford Whalley

Born 3 July 1891 at Leeds. Clifford was one of the two sons of the Reverend Hall, Rector of Addingham, to serve. In 1911 Clifford was an assistant master at Milton Abbas School in Dorset, living with the headmaster, two other teachers and two servants.

Brother George also served.

HALL: Fred Kirk

Born 1880 in Pateley Bridge. Fred appears to have been a former Regular soldier and served in a Royal Field Artillery unit for four years before 1914. He also served for three years as a Territorial. It is likely that he went to war with the Territorials as he "enlisted" on 4 August 1914 when aged 34 years and embarked for France on 15 April 1915. At that time he was living at 3 Cockshott Place, and worked for Henry Pease and Company. His Service Numbers are 758 as a Bombardier with the Royal Field Artillery and later 776126 when he held the rank of Corporal. Fred was wounded on 18 November 1917 and demobbed on 22 January 1919. He then applied to join the Regular army but this request was refused on medical grounds.

In 1921 Fred wrote saying that he believed he was entitled to the Territorial Efficiency Medal as he enlisted in 1909 in the 4th West Riding Howitzer Brigade of the Royal Field Artillery and was on active service from 4 August 1914, serving until 22 January 1919, making a total service of 12 years and 2 months of which 3 years 9 months was overseas service. This was signed 776126 Corporal F K Hall D/245 Brigade RFA. A letter from a Major in RFA 276th West Riding Battalion in Ilkley confirms his continuous service. There are several letters on file regarding this medal and it appears that he was successful in the application. Fred was also awarded the 1915 Star.

In 1919 when living at 1 Plum Tree Hill, Fred was awarded a pension of 8s. 8d. and 7s. for his wife and four children. This from 23 March 1920 then in 1921 extra money for another child.

A quarryman, married to Annie and for a time lived at 8 School Lane, Addingham. In 1918 recorded at 3 Cockshott Place.

HALL: George Roland *(Reverend)*

Born 1876 in Leeds. George was a Clerk in Holy Orders and by 1911 a Church of England clergyman in Bradford. George married in 1918 at Girlington Church, Bradford. His wife was 25 year old Annie Smith and he was a 32 year old widower. The Reverend Joseph Hall, George's father and Rector of St Peter's Church, Addingham, married them.

Served as Chaplain to the Forces and on 27 November 1918 was based at North Camp, Ripon. As this date was after the Armistice he may have earlier served overseas.

Brother Clifford also served.

HALL: William

In both the 1918 and 1919 Electoral Roll William is a serviceman voter of 2 Cragg View, and lodging with Joseph and Isabella Horsman.

HARGRAVE: Edward

Born 1889 and the son of Frank and Mary Hargrave. In 1911 Edward was an engine cleaner for a railway company. Although father Frank was born in Ripon the family had by 1911 lived in Addingham for at least 26 years.

It is believed, but not proven, that Edward served in 6th King's Own Scottish Borderers which he joined on 5 July 1915. He was wounded and discharged as a result of those wounds in 1918 after serving overseas.

Brothers James, Frank and John also served.

HARGRAVE: Frank

Born 1885. Frank was the son of Frank and Mary who in 1918 lived in Stockinger Lane. Frank senior was a quarryman and his son a bricklayer's labourer.

Believed to have served in West Riding Regiment as Private 13641 and from 11 September 1914. A local newspaper reported Frank wounded on 8 September 1916 when serving in "West Ridings". There was a Silver War Badge issued to a Frank Hargrave who enlisted on 20 November 1914 and was discharged following wounds which made him unfit for service on 24 May 1917. He was Private 13641.

One of four brothers to serve.

HARGRAVE: James

Born 1892. In 1911 James lived with parents Frank and Mary at 5 Jubilee

Terrace and he was a bricklayer's labourer. In 1918 recorded at Stockinger Lane.

Three brothers also served.

HARGRAVE: John

Born 1877 in Bradley and the son of Frank and Mary. By 1901 John was married to Emma and living at 14 School Lane, Addingham, and was a waller. In 1911 lived at 1 Main Street and had five children under eight years of age. It appears that whilst John was in the forces Emma went to live with his parents at Stockinger Lane. John is listed at 2 Stockinger Lane in 1918 and 1919.

One of four brothers to serve.

HARGREAVES: Andrew

Born in 1899 in Skipton. In 1911 the family are listed as Haygreaves and living at 21 Main Street. Andrew was the son of Ernest Henry and Anna. Ernest was an artificial teeth maker. When Andrew married after the war, his father is given as Ernest, a dentist of 21 Main Street, Addingham.

Three brothers served.

HARGREAVES: James Ernest

Born in 1897 at Skipton. In 1911 James, known as Ernest in some records, was a 15 year old butcher living with parents Ernest and Anna at 21 Main Street.

One of three brothers to serve.

HARGREAVES: Thomas Philip Chabert

Born 1898 in Skipton. In 1911 he was the grocer son of Ernest and Hannah of 21 Main Street. On 17 April 1920 Thomas married Elsie McNicholl in Addingham. Thomas died in 1959 when he lived at Midway, Moor Lane. His wife and son, Kenneth McNicholl Hargreaves, a higher grade postman, were granted Probate. In 1918 recorded at 21 Main Street.

One of three brother to serve.

HARRISON: Ben

No local records except his name on the Scroll of Honour and a letter recorded in the Ilkley Gazette on 15 October 1915 saying that he was a Bombardier.

He wrote the poem on the back cover of this publication.

In the 1918 Electoral Roll, a Ben Harrison lived at Junction, but he was not registered as a serviceman voter.

HARRISON: James

The local paper reports that Sergeant James Harrison was wounded in May 1917. He was a Reservist recalled at outbreak of war and he was in a dugout at time of injury.

A James Harrison is in the 1918 and 1919 Electoral Roll as a serviceman living at 51 Southfield Terrace, and Annie Harrison is also living here.

HARTLEY: Ellis

Born 15 September 1883 and son of blacksmith George and Ellen of 4 Victoria Terrace. In 1918 recorded at 41 Southfield Terrace. Brother Frank also served.

A local paper reported Gunner E Hartley of the Royal Field Artillery ill from trench foot in 1917. There is only one medal card for this name and regiment. Service Number 174013.

HARTLEY: Frank

Born 27 April 1889, Frank was the son of George and Ellen. A railway porter he married Lily Lowcock at St Peter's Church on 31 December 1910 and shortly after was living with parents-in-law Joseph and Mary Lowcock at 32 Main Street. In 1918 lived at 95 Main Street.

A newspaper report in January 1918 says that Corporal Frank Hartley was shot in the head when out on a bombing raid. His wound was not serious. He was granted 14 days' special leave because he and his group of fifteen took a "strong point". It says that Frank joined Kitchener's Army in September 1914 and went with them to France in July 1915.

Of the seven medal cards in this name the one which is most likely is for Service Number 12814. Awarded 1915 Star and demobbed on 18 February 1919. In France from 15 July 1915.

Brother Ellis also served.

HATTON: Foster Bradley

Born 1881, Foster was one of the twin sons of William Hatton and Ann née Bradley.

When Foster enlisted on 2 August 1916 aged 35 years and 6 months, he and wife Annie née Dickinson lived at 4 Beacon Street. Foster described himself as a mason whereas in the 1911 census he was a bricklayer's labourer and lived at 12 Bolton Road. Foster is recorded in 1918 at 4 Beacon Street.

Called for active service on 22 January 1919. This may have been because in 1916 he was graded medically BII. It is not clear from his service record what regiment Foster joined but he was given Service Number 338552 as a Private and later as a Sapper when he had Service Number 341124. At that time he transferred from Ledbury to Ripon. It seems unlikely that he saw overseas service.

HAWKINS: Bertram Alfred

Born in 1898, possibly in Peckham, London. Parents were Albert, a butler, and Ada. It seems likely that father Albert came to work as a member of staff at Farfield Hall and clearly moved around as all his three children were born in different places.

When Bertram enlisted on 4 August 1916 aged 18 years and 1 month, he was a gardener living with his parents at Farfield Cottages. Served in the Royal Field Artillery Territorial Forces joining the 397th Battery on 12 December 1917 when he was of age to serve abroad, i.e. after his 19th birthday. Bertram was a driver with the unit and his Service Number probably 166723. On 24 August 1918 just after his 20th birthday, Bertram was gassed and wounded by shell. In hospital until 13 October he was then transferred back to Reserve. On active duties again by 2 April 1919 he saw service in Germany at Solingen where he served until 12 October 1919. Not demobbed until 1920.

In 1918 recorded at Farfield Cottages.

HAYNES: Charles Harry

Born 1882 in High Wycombe, Buckinghamshire. In 1901, aged 19 years, Charles worked with foxhounds at Birdsall Kennels and was a boarder. He and wife Lillie née Anderson were married in 1903 in Helmsley and at that time she was employed as a servant in Ilkley to a Holmes family. Charles had a rural background and his parents William and Jessie appeared to work on large country estates. By 1911 Charles and Lillie had six children with several places of birth indicating that Charles travelled for employment. A daughter May, born in Kineton, near Stratford-upon-Avon, was buried in Addingham aged 8 years in November 1916. In 1918 and 1919 the family lived at 11 Rose Terrace.

There is a death record for Charles Harry Haynes in Chelmsford in 1945 and a Probate for him granted to widow Lillie Haynes. Charles was "of Police Headquarters" and it is possible that he was a police officer when he lived in Addingham.

HELLEN: James Harrison

Born 1891 at Coniston, near Ulverston. James married Jane Gale in August 1915 at St Peter's Church, Addingham. His father Joseph was a copper miner and James a teamster living in Coniston. Jane's father Albert E Gale was a farmer at Brockabank. It appears that for a time the couple lived with him.

James joined the army in Lancaster on 12 July 1916 when his occupation was "timber leading". He was 5ft. 10in. and A1 fit. Served in several theatres of war with the Royal Garrison Artillery as Gunner 105969. Within his training period, James contracted pneumonia and was ill from 15 October 1916 to 2 December 1916.

In Italy from May to September 1917, he went to Egypt where he spent six months until March 1918, then, without a break, he was posted to Salonika and was there for nine months until December 1918. Whilst in Salonika, in August 1918, he contracted malaria and "debility" due to the climate, and spent time in the 28th General Hospital, Salonika. It would seem that James was in the front line of battle wherever he served; however, his service record does not indicate that he was wounded.

Discharged 29 February 1919 he planned to work for J Booth & Son of Silsden.

HEWERDINE: Harry

Born in 1887, Harry was the son of the Headteacher at the Wesleyan School and lived at Springfield Mount. By 1911 Harry junior was an assistant teacher, aged 23 years, in a secondary school at Southend-on-Sea, Essex.

It is possible that he served in the Army Service Corps as an Acting Sergeant, Service Number S4/125318.

HEWITT: William

Born on 12 June 1896, William and his twin sister Mary were the children of James and Annie Hewitt. James was a labourer and the family lived in Nesfield. After this the parents do not appear in any local records; however, in 1901 both children are boarders with widowed Sarah Holmes at 1 Wharfedale View. In 1911 both Willie and Mary worked as silk drawers and still boarded with Mrs Holmes.

HILL: Malcolm Walter

Born in 1891 in Allerton, Bradford, and the son of wool buyer John Thomas and Harriett née Illingworth. By 1911 father John was a gentleman farmer "on his own account" and living at Farfield. Malcolm now aged 19 lived at home and was an articled clerk to a solicitor. Father John died in 1916; however, the family continued to live at Farfield as Malcolm is registered there in 1918.

A newspaper reports him wounded in September 1916 when he may have had the rank of Lieutenant. At that time he had been at the front for thirteen months and enlisted in September 1914 in the West Yorkshire Regiment.

An old boy of Bradford Grammar School he worked for Messrs Wade, Tetley, Wade and Scott, Solicitors of Bradford, and he was a nephew of Alderman James Hill MD.

HILLBECK: Alfred

Born 1887 in Ulverston and awarded the Military Medal. Alfred was the son of James, a carter, and Rachel. Several members of the Hillbeck family lived in Addingham.

Alfred was killed in France on 18 April 1918 when serving as a driver in the Royal Horse and Royal Field Artillery. Service Number 2555 in "D" Battery 251 Brigade. He was buried at Chocques Military Cemetery. An article in the Westmorland Gazette of 27 April 1918 reported his death. It says Alfred was killed whilst asleep. It is believed that a shell hit the Battery and he and many others were killed in the impact.

He had been recommended for the Military Medal for gallantry on two occasions and had been in France since 22 August 1915. Before joining the colours he had been a carter.

Brothers Harold and James also served.

Not on the War Memorial.

HILLBECK: Harold Birkett

Born 29 June 1897 in Kendal. Harold lived for a number of years in Addingham with his older sister Mary and her husband Philip Pass. In 1911 he was a boarder with them at 49 Southfield Terrace until at least 1919.

Read more in "For King and Country".

HILLBECK: James

James was born in 1883 in Kendal to parents James and Rachel. One of four children of the couple to live in Addingham. In 1908 James married Nellie Pass when he was a limestone quarryman, and in 1911 they lived at 5 Bolton Road, Addingham. The couple continued to live in Addingham at 5 and later 11 Bolton Road.

Awarded the Military Medal, as was his brother Alfred. James served with the Royal Engineers in Egypt from 23 December 1915 as Lance Corporal 84028. He later became a Sergeant and was demobbed on 12 March 1919.

One of three brothers to serve.

HOBSON: Henry

Born in 1888 Henry enlisted at Crosshills. Whilst serving as Private 41486 in the 26th Battalion Northumberland Fusiliers, Henry was killed in action on 5 June 1917. Recorded on the Arras Memorial at Faubourg-d'Amiens Cemetery.

The 26th was known as the "Tyneside Irish". His earlier service had been in the West Riding Regiment, Service Number 19776.

Parents William, a stone mason, and Sarah Ann née Craven were from Bradford but lived in Addingham for at least 13 years. In the 1911 census Henry is a patient in the Skipton Workhouse Infirmary.

Not on the Scroll of Honour.

HODGSON: Benjamin

Born 1878 in Ilkley. In 1900 he was married to Addingham girl Hannah and the couple lived at Southfield Terrace. Hannah's mother Anne Wilkinson lived with them. Recorded in 1918 at 1 Brumfitt Hill.

Ben attested at Skipton on 11 December 1915 when aged 38 years and was in Reserve until 25 October 1916. Served in the Artillery Reserve Brigade then later the Border Regiment, Service Numbers 36983 and 33554. After only three months initial training he was posted to France on 5 January 1917.

HODGSON: Thomas

Born in 1883, Thomas enlisted at Nelson where his family then lived. Killed in action on 30 November 1917, aged 34, when with the King's Shropshire Light Infantry 6th Battalion as Private 32388. His name is recorded on the Cambrai Memorial panels 8 and 9.

Son of James and Annie, the family lived in Addingham for several years and four of their children were born here and Thomas was a grocer's assistant.

HOLGATE: Dennis Albert

Born 1897 in Draughton, he died of wounds on 17 May 1917 when aged 19 years and serving as a Gunner with the Royal Horse Artillery and Royal Field Artillery Territorial Unit "D" Battery 312th Brigade. Service

Number 786032. Dennis is buried at Achiet-le-Grand Cemetery fourteen miles south of Arras.

It is likely that he was under age as a local paper reports that Dennis joined the colours in April 1915 and was in France by December 1916.

The son of limestone quarryman Joseph and wife Elizabeth, the family in 1911 lived at Manor Row, Draughton. Brother Frederick also served.

HOLGATE: Frederick Welburg

Born in 1900 in Draughton, and the son of quarryman Joseph and Elizabeth.

Frederick would not have been eligible for military service until mid 1918. There is no service record for him and it is unlikely that he saw overseas service as he would not have completed initial training until, at the earliest, autumn 1918.

Brother to Dennis who was killed.

HOLMES: Allan

Born in 1886, Allan was the son of John W and Hannah and one of their four sons to serve. A weaver and single, Allan lived with his parents at Cragg View in 1911. Recorded in 1918 at 148 Main Street.

Brothers Arthur, Fred and George also served.

HOLMES: Arthur

During his military service with the Royal Engineers, Arthur was awarded the Military Medal, the French Croix de Guerre and the 1915 Star. He was a sapper and an Acting Corporal, Service Number 83901, and served in Egypt from 21 December 1915 and must also have served in France to be awarded the Croix de Guerre.

His parents, gardener John W and Hannah, had four sons serving, two of whom were awarded a Military Medal for gallantry. Arthur, a house painter, was born in 1890 and in 1901 lived with his parents at 12 Beacon Street. Recorded in 1918 at 148 Main Street.

Brothers Allan, Fred and George also served.

HOLMES: Edgar Harold

Born 1880 and one of the two sons of James and Elizabeth to serve. In 1911 Edgar and father James live with sister Louisa and her husband John England, a joiner, at 3 Church Street. In 1901 the family lived at Southfield House where father James was a farmer and tailor.

Edgar enlisted 4 November 1917 at Ripon aged 37 years when living at 31 Southview (sic) Addingham, and married to Betty. As Private 188023 he served in the Royal Regiment of Artillery as a Gunner in 198th Siege Battery. Injured after the Armistice on 9 December 1918 and in hospital until 18 December 1918. His injury was reported to be "self-inflicted" and a court enquiry was held. It was stated that he tripped over a wire when moving into post about 1200 hours, fracturing an arm and elbow. At the Court of Enquiry of the incident the soldier was deemed to be "not to blame". He was granted a temporary pension in 1919.

Registered in 1918 at 3 Church Street.

Brother to James who also served.

HOLMES: Frederick

Fred served in the 210th Field Company with the Royal Engineers, attaining the rank of Sergeant. He may have served in the tunnelling section of the RE in 1915 and 1916. Awarded the Military Medal, as was his brother Arthur.

According to the 1920 publication "Craven's Part in the Great War" a Sergeant F K Holmes was mentioned in despatches and as a separate entry a Sergeant F Holmes of the Royal Engineers was awarded the Military Medal. He was a motor cyclist with the Royal Engineers. It seems likely that these refer to the same man.

In 1911 Fred, born in 1883, was a domestic coachman living with parents John William and Hannah at Cragg View. In October 1913 he married Eva Harrison.

Brothers George and Allan also served.

HOLMES: George Francis

Born 5 January 1881 and one of the three sons of John W and Hannah to serve. George in 1911 lived with his brother-in-law Isaac Grey at 6

Stockinger Lane and had three children, Granville, Herbert and Edgar.

HOLMES: James A

Born 1882, the son of James and Elizabeth and brother to Edgar who also served. He married in 1908 and three years later was living at 10 Bolton Road with wife Minnie and son Eric.

HOLMES: John William

A John William Holmes was born in 1884 to farmers John and Elizabeth. There are no other records of him in Addingham until 1918 when he is recorded as a military voter at 148 Main Street and still there in 1919.

Not on the Scroll of Honour.

HOLMES: Norman

Norman was killed in action on 27 November 1917 when serving as a Sergeant in the 2/6th Battalion of the Duke of Wellington's West Riding Regiment, Service Number 265024. His name is recorded on the Cambrai Memorial at Pas-de-Calais.

Born 1891 he was the son of John, a groom and cabman, and Elizabeth A of Cockshott Place. Brother to Percy and possibly John William who also served.

HOLMES: Percy

Born on 28 August 1892 and son of John and Elizabeth Ann. By 1911 the family had moved from Cockshott Place and were living at 49 Westmorland Street, Skipton. Percy worked as a grocer's carter.

Joined the 6th West Riding Territorial Regiment when aged just 17 years and at that time worked as a bleacher at English Sewing Cotton in Skipton. Service Number 1136. Awarded the Military Medal and also eligible for the 1915 Star as, according to his medal card, he served in France from 7 September 1915. He does not appear to have gone with the Duke of Wellington's Regiment as his service on the medal card is with the 8th Royal Berkshire Regiment, Service Number 17311. Became a Lance Corporal and later Sergeant.

Brother Norman was killed.

HOLMES: Wilfred

Born 23 March 1888 and the son of Smith and Sarah Holmes who lived at 21 Southfield Terrace. Smith was a weaving overlooker and Wilfred a domestic groom living at home.

Killed when aged 28 years, on 1 July 1916, the first day of the Battle of the Somme.

Read more in "For King and Country".

HOLMES: Wilfred

Wilfred enlisted in Skipton when he lived at Barnoldswick. As Private 10900 he served in the Duke of Wellington's West Riding Regiment 8th Battalion. Killed in action on 27 April 1917 aged 20 years and buried at Hermies British Cemetery Plot D6. This is close to the Bapaume to Cambrai Road.

Born in 1897, Wilfred was the son of William, a stone mason, and Sarah Ann Elizabeth Holmes of Back Beck. In 1911, aged 14, Wilfred lived with his widowed mother and 5 siblings at 15 Southfield Terrace.

HOLT: John Bretherton

Born 1888 in Nelson and the son of Thomas and Isabella. Thomas was a cotton manufacturer and employer. In 1901 they lived in Barrowford and in 1914 John, a bank clerk, was living in Addingham and married to Florence née Hewerdine, a teacher.

John enlisted on 10 December 1916 and placed in Reserve, but was not called up for service until January 1917. His service was with the Royal Regiment of Artillery as Gunner 140887. John served for less than a year and was discharged on 10 December 1917 due to disability. This was not from wounds and was described as a "condition which had been aggravated by service".

His address on discharge was Springfield Mount, Addingham. This was the home of his wife's parents and his father-in-law was Headmaster of Addingham Elementary School. Described as being of "good character" and granted a weekly pension.

HOOD: Charles

Born 1894, Charles was one of three brothers to serve. Presumed killed on 3 September 1916 aged 22, when serving with the 1/5th Duke of Wellington's West Riding Regiment, 49th West Riding Division, Service Number 4886. Recorded on the Thiepval Memorial Pier and Face 6A and 6B. His death was reported in the Ilkley Gazette on 16 October 1916. Father Isaac then lived at Victoria Terrace.

In 1911 Isaac and his second wife Mary lived at 7 Moor Lane together with two of Charles' half brothers who also served. Isaac worked for the District Council. Unusually for a man so young, a will for Charles was filed. Probate was granted to father Isaac of 30 Victoria Terrace, Addingham, road foreman. Charles left £133 9s. 8d.

HOOD: Joseph Leslie

Born 21 May 1900 and the son of Isaac and his second wife Mary.

Joseph was not eligible for military service until his 18th birthday and would have completed his initial military training only weeks before the Armistice. He may not have seen active service or served overseas.

Brothers Charles and William also served.

HOOD: William

Born on 3 September 1898 to Isaac and Mary. Father Isaac was born in Warwick and Mary at Kirby Stephen. Mary was Isaac's second wife, they married in 1898 and by 1911 lived at 7 Moor.

Brothers Charles and Joseph also served.

HORSMAN: Clifford

Born 1899, the son of Harry and Charlotte of 52 Main Street. Clifford and his father both served.

Clifford was a Gunner in the Royal Field Artillery, Service Number 786376, and had served with them from 1915. This was likely to be the 4th Howitzers of the RFA which was the Ilkley Territorial unit and he would be only 16 years of age when he joined.

HORSMAN: Harry

Born 1877, Harry was awarded the Distinguished Conduct Medal in 1916 whilst in France.

His story is in "For King and Country".

HORSMAN: Harry Lister

Born 1899, Harry spent the first few years of his life in Addingham where his parents and all his siblings had been born. By 1911 the family were living in Skipton and father Joseph was an insurance agent, but they moved back to Addingham before 1915.

Harry enlisted in the Territorials on 26 April 1915 at Otley. This was the 4th West Riding Howitzer Brigade based in Ilkley. Service Number 1196. His next of kin was father Joseph and his address was 2 Cragg View. Applied to become a driver and gave his occupation as farmer.

Enlisting in Otley where he was not known may have been a deliberate move as Harry was sixteen years of age at the time. He gave his age as exactly 18 years and he was actually 17 years old when his deceit was discovered. By then Harry had served 108 days and he was discharged on 13 August 1915 "because of having made a mis-statement as to age on enlistment". It is possible that his true age came to light when he spent a week in an isolation camp at the end of July 1915 with scabies.

There is no record of any further service but it seems likely that he did serve later as he was described as A1 fit and of good character.

Not on the Scroll of Honour.

HORSMAN: William Adam

Willie was killed in action on 26 September 1917 when aged 19 years and 10 months when in the 2nd Battalion of the Royal Scots *(Lothian Regiment)*, Service Number 302016. His name is recorded on Tyne Cot Memorial at Ypres, Panels 11 to 14 and 162. William had been reported wounded on 1 September 1917 with many small wounds, so he may have died of these wounds.

Born in 1898, and the son of Arthur and Martha

who worked in local textile mills, and in 1901 lived at 14 Main Street. Grandfather William was a grocer in Main Street. By 1911 the family lived at 31 Southfield Terrace. Father Arthur and Harry Horsman were brothers making Clifford Horsman, who also served, cousin to Willie.

HOWELLS: Enoch

Enoch initially appears to have joined the 2/5th Highland Light Infantry as Private 5703 and may have been, at one time, a Regular soldier. He attested on 5 December 1915 and served in France from 3 July 1917 after being mobilised on 17 October 1916 when already 45 years of age. He had various postings and served in the 10th Royal Field Artillery and was transferred to the Labour Corps on 28 April 1917.

Born 1871 in Keighley, Enoch, a painter and decorator, lived at 15 Mount Street, Bingley. The only record of an Addingham connection is the birth of a child, Mary, recorded in the 1911 census as born in Addingham.

Not on the Scroll of Honour.

HUDSON: Edward

Born 5 April 1884. His parents were chair maker Stephen and Jane who lived for many years at 6 Church Street, and Edward became a cotton weaver.

Brother James also served.

HUDSON: Edward Amos

Born in 1879 in Ilkley, to Amos, a joiner, and Eliza. Edward lived in Ilkley until he married Mary E Ettenfield in June 1904. The couple lived for many years in Cockshott Place and it was at number 5 in 1918 that Edward was registered as a military voter.

HUDSON: Edward Charles

Born 1887 and chauffeur to Mr Dunlop at Hallcroft Hall. A Reservist who was captured at the Battle of Mons and remained a Prisoner of War for over 4 years.

Read his story in "For King and Country".

HUDSON: James Henry

This is probably the "Harry Hudson" reported in November 1915 in the Ilkley Gazette as going with several others to join the Cameron Highlanders and later, in 1917, that he was serving in the "Camerons".

There are three medal cards and the most likely is for H Hudson, Private 41919 in the Highland Light Infantry, enlisted 11 December 1915 and discharged *(no reason given)* on 21 September 1918.

Born 1893, James was the son of Stephen and Jane who in 1901 lived at 6 Church Street. In the 1911 census James is listed as Harry Hudson aged 17, son of Stephen. Brother to Edward who also served.

HUDSON: Percy

In July 1916 a newspaper reported that Percy Hudson aged 18 *(so born around 1898),* of Church Street, Addingham, who had joined the Duke of Wellington's Regiment, was in a military hospital. Before the war he had worked at Bolton Abbey quarries.

In July 1917 there is a second report indicating that he was now a prisoner of war and was in hospital in Hoan with a bullet wound to his upper arm. He asked for soap and some eggs as he had none for weeks and hoped to be in "Blighty" by Christmas.

Apart from the newspaper reports I can find no other local, or POW, record relating to Addingham for a Percy Hudson.

HUSTWICK: Ernest

Born 1885, Ernest was killed on 21 August 1915 in the Balkan theatre of war and was buried at Gallipoli. His name is recorded on the Helles Memorial.

A Territorial, he joined the Duke of Wellington's West Riding Regiment in April 1908 and signed for 4 years. He was then aged 23 years and worked for Messrs Summerscales of Sun Street, Keighley. Only his Territorial service record survives. However, his war service was with the 8th Battalion of the same regiment, Service Number 10993. They landed in Suvla Bay on 7 August 1915 and Ernest was killed two weeks after his unit landed.

Not on the Addingham War Memorial.

HUSTWICK: Horace

Born December 1886 to labourer Joseph and his wife Sarah. Horace married Lilian Price in October 1912 when he was aged 24 years. Brother Percy, who was killed in 1916, signed as witness to the marriage. By 1911 father Joseph was remarried and employed on the Broughton estate at Skipton as a woodsman. The two boys, Horace and Percy, were labourers in 1911, living with a cousin in Bradford.

There is only one medal card for Horace Hustwick. This is for Sergeant 1267 and 156580 of the West Yorkshire Regiment Machine Gun Corps.

The Ilkley Gazette reported in January 1917 that Mrs Hustwick was notified that her husband had been killed. This caused great distress as an error had been made by a Lieutenant. It is not known if any apology was sent!

Earlier, in August 1916, whilst a Corporal, Horace had written that he had a lucky escape when asleep as shrapnel hit his coat. He saw both his Sergeant and Lieutenant killed by a shell which also killed four others. As a result he was in charge of 50 men and despite shells overhead, he had the men dig in. As a result of this action he was awarded a Certificate of Merit.

HUSTWICK: Percy

Percy was killed in action on the first day of the Somme on 1 July 1916, aged 27 years, when serving as a Territorial and as Private 1155 in the 1/6th West Yorkshire Regiment Prince of Wales Own. Recorded on Thiepval Memorial Pier and Face 2a, 2c, 2d, he has no known grave. His unit arrived in France on 16 April 1915 and Percy was awarded the 1915 Star.

Born in 1889, Percy and brother Horace, who also served, lived with parents Joseph and Sarah at Sugar Hill. Joseph was then a mason's labourer.

IDESON: Alfred

Born in 1891, Alfred joined the Royal Regiment of Artillery on 21 August 1914 as Private 22155. A single man of 23 when he enlisted, Alfred was a weaver living with parents Charles and Margaret Ann at 67 Bolton Road. Alfred must have had leave in February 1916 as that was when he married Mary Jane Mason.

Served at home from August 1914 to July 1915 when he embarked with his unit for the Dardanelles. Wounded in September 1915, from there he went to hospital in Malta. Served at home from 23 September 1916 to 5 November 1917. During this period, in May 1917, he was appointed a "skilled fitter". Further overseas service began on 6 November 1917 when he arrived in France. Gunshot wounds to the shoulders in September 1918 had him hospitalised in Rouen for a time. Alfred's service in France ended on 28 May 1919 and he served at home until discharged to 7 Daisy Hill, Silsden, on 30 March 1920. Awarded 1914-15 Star.

Not on the Scroll of Honour.

JACOBS: Arthur

Born 1899 in Greengates, Arthur in 1911 lived at 10 Rose Terrace with mother Priscilla, a spinner. She had eight children, none born in Addingham, and it seems from the place of birth that the family travelled widely for work.

"Craven's Part in the Great War" lists Arthur as being awarded the Military Medal whilst with the Northampton Regiment and that he was "formerly of Addingham". There are 2 medal cards for this name and regiment but neither mentions a Military Medal.

JONES: Percy

The only intimation that Percy, born in Glusburn in 1899, lived in Addingham and served in the war is the 1918 Electoral Roll which lists him at 6 Bolton Road, and he is living with Joseph Clarkson Berry and Sarah E Berry.

Not on the Scroll of Honour.

KEIGHLEY: Francis Joseph

Born 1890 in Burra, South Australia, and Frank in some records. By 1911 Francis and his family were living in Addingham and Francis was an assistant in a small wares factory living with his parents Charles and Mary Jane. Charles was a tape manufacturer.

When Francis was mobilised on 5 August 1914 with the 4th West Riding Howitzer Territorial Brigade he was living at High Bank, a manufacturer and unmarried. Served as C/298 and 776166, he embarked on 15 April 1915 for Le Havre, and joined the 245th West Riding Brigade of the Royal Field Artillery in the field on 20 May 1914. Transferred to England on 11 July 1916, he was in hospital with gunshot wounds to his neck received on 6 July 1916.

Before mid 1918 he returned to France and was re-assessed there for fitness and classified as "A" on 9 August, and posted to the field on 17 August 1918. Left from Dunkirk for Ripon on 20 April 1919 and demobbed to High Bank, Addingham.

KENDALL: William Lambert

William was killed in action in France on 30 October 1918 when serving as Gunner 65890 in the Royal Garrison Artillery, with the 155th Siege Battery. His body had been exhumed after the war and re-buried at Wulverghem-Lindenhoek Road Cemetery Grave Number 11.E.30

Postman William enlisted on 10 November 1915 when he lived at 25 Church Street, Ilkley. He went to France on 23 February 1916. Wounded on 22 May 1916 by shell, he received treatment at 1st Birmingham War Hospital and returned to duty on 8 August 1916.

Born in Ilkley on 9 March 1894, William's only apparent connection with Addingham is when he gave The Slade on Moorside as his abode in 1918 as a military voter.

Not on the Scroll of Honour.

KETTLEWELL: Ellis

Ellis married Hannah Rishworth in 1901. Born in 1879 in Ilkley Ellis was the son of Thomas, a coachman and Elizabeth.

Ellis volunteered on 27 March 1915 when 35 years of age and served with the Royal Engineers in Egypt from December 1915 to March 1916 then to France, until bouts of trench fever caused heart problems and evacuated to England in June 1918 to Keighley War Hospital. Remained in England until discharged on 4 March 1919 as no longer fit for active service. His home address was 3 Rose Terrace.

Uncle to John *(Jack)* and Fred who also served.

KETTLEWELL: Fred

Born 1897 to Thomas and Ann. By 1911 Thomas, a limestone quarryman, at 43 years of age, was widowed and lived with his sons, 14 year old Fred and 18 year old Jack, at Back Beck.

Both sons served and Fred probably served in the West Yorkshire Regiment as Private 22668 and 63080.

KETTLEWELL: John *(Jack)*

Born on 3 August 1892 in Addingham and always known as Jack, he achieved the rank of Sergeant Major and was awarded the Distinguished Conduct Medal and the Military Medal.

For his full story see "For King and Country".

KIDD: Edward John Cecil

Edward was buried at St Peter's Church, Addingham, on 15 April 1918 in a military funeral. He was killed whilst serving in the Royal Air Force as an observer and this was possibly over Netheravon Airfield. The war grave gives his rank as 2nd Lieutenant and that he served in the West Yorkshire Regiment and the RAF and died on 10 April 1918 of injuries following an airplane accident. Aged 21 years, he was the son of the Headteacher at the National School, Mr W Kidd.

The medal card says he entered the war on 13 February 1917 and first served with the Territorial 1/5th West Yorkshire Regiment as 2nd Lieutenant. Then the Royal Flying Corps again as 2nd Lieutenant.

Edward, born on 23 December 1896, was the only son of William and Clara née England who, in 1911, lived at Lynholme, Addingham. Nephew of Rhodes Kidd who also served.

KIDD: Rhodes

Rhodes, born 1876, was the son of Walter Kidd, a draper in Addingham, formerly a mason's salesman, and Emma née Rhodes, who in 1881 lived at Harrison Green, Addingham. In 1911, still single and aged 35, Rhodes was living with his unmarried sisters Elizabeth Ann and Eliza in

Bradford. All worked in textiles.

Rhodes served in the West Riding Regiment as Private 268858 from 8 December 1915. Possibly injured at some time, he was awarded a Silver War Badge on 7 February 1919 when 43 years of age. The reason given was "sick".

LANCASTER: John Thomas

Born in 1871, John *(known as Tom)* would have been aged 43 years in 1914.

The Pioneer newspaper on 30 April 1915 recorded that Tom Lancaster was with "4th Howitzers". This was a Territorial unit and part of the Royal Field Artillery.

Tom, as John Thomas, in 1881 lived at the Moorside where father Emanuel was a farmer. In 1896 he married Sarah Cockshott and still lived as a farmer on the Moorside. In 1911, the farm address is given as Doublestones, in Silsden. Recorded in 1915 at 20 Victoria Terrace.

LAWRENCE:

"Craven's Part in the Great War" records a Military Medal for a Corporal Lawrence of the Machine Gun Corps of Addingham.

It seems likely that this was one of two Ilkley brothers who served, and are known to have lived in Addingham around 1920. Their parents met and married in America when both were working there.

The most likely is Corporal Franklin *(Frank)* Thomas Lawrence who enlisted in 1914 and served until 2 February 1919. He was in the 9th West Riding Regiment as 12893 and landed at Boulogne on 15 July 1915. Later in the Labour Corps as 24296. The family have a newspaper cutting which tells of Frank being one of 300 men saved from the hospital ship "Anglia" when it struck a mine off Folkestone. The implication here is that he was wounded and on the way to England for treatment.

Franklin was born in Blackpool in 1896 and married Evelyn Wilson in Ilkley in June 1916. They registered the birth of a child in early 1921 when living in Addingham. Franklin died at 6 North Street.

His older brother John, born in the USA, married at Ilkley in 1918 when a Private 19232 in the 10th Hussars and served abroad from 18 October 1915. John was wounded as he was awarded a Silver War Badge. Lived in Addingham from around 1921.

Both brothers had the 1915 Star.

Not on the Scroll of Honour.

LEACH: Harry

Harry died on 4 March 1916 when serving in the 9th Duke of Wellington's West Riding Regiment in France, Service Number 12817. Buried in Bedford House Cemetery at Ypres. Harry died of wounds and had served in France from 5 July 1915. A newspaper noted that he was the first man from Addingham to enlist in Kitchener's Army.

Harry was born in 1878 in Bradford and his parents, William and Ann, were living in Addingham as early as 1881 at Bland Fold off Bark Street. In 1911 he was a quarryman of 2 Druggist Lane.

LESTER: George Ernest

Born in Herringer in Suffolk in 1879, George came to Addingham as chauffeur to Mr Douglas of Farfield Hall.

George was called up in 1917 and there is a letter on his service record from his employer Mr Douglas highly praising George's skills as a driver. The letter, dated 27 April 1917, refers to George as "Class 42 Number 293 in Military Register". This is reference to the classification system following the compulsory registration in August 1915 of all men of military age. Class 32 was one of the later classes to be called under conscription. Mr Douglas makes reference to the cars, including a Rolls Royce, which George had driven and maintained whilst in his employ and suggested that George would be useful to the army employed in this capacity. That seems to be what happened, as George was in the Motor Transport Section of the Army Service Corps as Private 321459. His army record lists him as a "light car instructor" and based at the Driving School, Osterley Park. With some part of his service at Isleworth, he was demobbed in January 1919, and does not appear to have served overseas.

In September 1918 he had a week's leave at 1 Lodge Hill and had

Christmas leave the same year. His army testimonial says he was "reliable, intelligent and sober".

One of his daughters Dorothy *(Dolly),* when in her early teens, corresponded with servicemen as part of an Addingham scheme.

LISTER: Charles

The son of Bramley and Margaret and born on 11 April 1897, Charles was brother to Thomas *(Tom)* and William who also served. In 1911 the family farmed at Turner Lane Farm. Recorded in 1918 at Walker Acre and later lived at Town Head Farm.

LISTER: Edwin

Edwin, born 1882 in Ilkley, married Mary Ann Price in July 1904 and, like his father Henry, a joiner. In 1911 Edwin and Mary lived at 27 Southfield Terrace and had five children. Recorded in 1918 at 10 Victoria Terrace.

LISTER: James

One of the two men of this name from Addingham to serve.

James was born in 1888 and enlisted at Richmond, Yorkshire, in the Alexandra, Princess of Wales Own, West Yorkshire Regiment. As Private 7637 he served in the 2nd Battalion. James was a Reservist and joined the Regular army in 1903 as a 15 year old boy soldier. When war broke out in 1914 he was recalled to his unit which was based at Richmond.

Served from 1914 and killed in action on 2 April 1917 aged 29 years, he is commemorated on the Arras Memorial at Faubourg d'Amiens. A local newspaper reported that during his three years in France, James had been wounded three times before he was killed.

The son of James and Emma Louise of Smithy Yard his father was a stonebreaker. In 1908, when aged 20, James married Susannah and by 1911 he was a machine comber living at 32 Dale Street, Shipley. At the time of his death his parents were living at 8 Cragg View.

LISTER: James

Born in 1881 and one of two men with this name to serve.

In 1911 James lived with his widowed mother Ann at 4 School Lane, and a single bricklayer. His father was Edward who died in 1908.

Brother John also served.

LISTER: John

John died of wounds on 1 September 1918 aged 38 years. He served in France from 5 July 1915 as Private 12845 in "A" Company 9th Battalion of the Duke of Wellington's West Riding Regiment and was buried at Bagneux British Cemetery at Gezaincourt. This is close to Doullens on the Somme.

Born 2 March 1880 to quarryman Edward and Ann. In 1911 John was a bricklayer living with his mother at 4 School Lane.

LISTER: John

Born in 1889, and one of two men of this name to serve.

John enlisted at Skipton on 10 December 1915 and was killed on 26 August 1918.

Read his story in "For King and Country".

LISTER: Richard

Richard was brother to John and James who served and was born in 1888. They were the sons of Edward and Ann and in 1911 lived with now widowed Ann at 4 School Lane and Richard was a domestic gardener.

Volunteered on the 9 September 1914 when aged 26 years and 7 months, at Ilkley. As Private 13604 he was in the West Riding Regiment; however, discharged due to medical problems.

Not recorded on the Scroll of Honour.

LISTER: Thomas

Born 1889. In 1911 Tom lived with parents Bramley and Margaret at Turner House Farm where he worked on the farm. Brother to Charles who also served.

Thomas is registered in 1918 at Walker Acre.

LISTER: William

Born 1881, William was the eldest son of Bramley and Margaret who, in 1911 lived at Throstle Nest. William, a stone dresser, married Florence in 1901 and had a baby son Victor. In 1903 Florence died aged 27 years. They had lived at the family farm, Small Banks, where William made his living as a carter and farmer. By 1911 William had married Annie and they lived at Commercial Street, Skipton. Brother to Tom and Charles who also served. In 1918 he was living at the Post Office, Addingham. The post mistress at the time was a Miss Lister.

Brother Tom and Charles also served.

LODGE: Thomas

Thomas, Service Number 896, served in 4th West Riding Howitzer Brigade of the Royal Field Artillery from 1908. Promoted to Sergeant on 10 August 1914, now aged 35 years, volunteered for overseas service and served until 1919. Thomas, born in 1879 had married Jane Cottam in 1898 and lived at 1 George Street. Thomas and Jane lived at 12 Rose Terrace.

Served in France from 14 October 1916 with the 183 Field Battery. There were other transfers and then in December 1917 he spent 8 months in Italy. Transferred later to the Western Front.

Thomas also served in the Labour Corps in France, possibly from 8 October 1918 when 40 years of age and where he became Sergeant 399145 in the 242nd Employment Company. Left Cherbourg on 30 December 1918 and demobbed on 4 February 1919.

Brothers-in-law Fred and James Cottam also served.

LONGBOTTOM: James Messenger

Born 29 January 1880 in Cleckheaton and the son of Joshua and Ann. In 1911 James married Hannah Hill, the daughter of John and Harriett Hill, farmers of Far Field, Addingham. James was a traveller and his father was a maltster. Hanna and James lived at 33 Southfield Terrace until at least 1918.

May have served in the North Staffordshire Regiment, Service Number 32329.

Not on the Scroll of Honour.

LOWCOCK: Ernest

The son of farmer Thomas and Margaret he was born on 6 April 1884. In 1891 they farmed at Holme House and then later had the Junction Refreshment Rooms. This was also a hotel as in 1901 there were several lodgers and servants. By 1911 Ernest was living as a lodger at 19 Wesleyan Terrace and was a carting agent. Lived at 4 Wharfedale View and in 1918 at 9 Wharfedale View.

Enlisted on 17 July 1917, aged 39 years. Medically B1 fit and assigned to the Labour Corps as Private 327918. Prone to bronchitis, Ernest had several spells in hospital and, in February 1919, a hernia operation. He had been in Leeds War Hospital from 28 January 1919 and was discharged from there on 20 May 1919 as "permanently unfit". It is unlikely that he saw overseas service.

LOWCOCK: John Gill

John was killed in action on 13 October 1918 aged 28 years when serving in the 1/4th Hallamshire Territorial Battalion of the York and Lancaster Regiment, Service Number 58236. Buried at York Cemetery, Haspres, which is 15 km east of Cambrai.

Previously John had served as 4992 in the Northumberland Fusiliers and volunteered for service in December 1915. To France on 23 December 1916, having been in Reserve until 30 July 1916. On 25 May 1918 he was wounded in France with gunshot wounds to his thigh, back and buttocks and spent a few months in hospital before returning to the front.

Born in 1890, when aged one in 1891 he lived with grandmother Emilia Lowcock who was born in Germany. In 1911 John was living with step-father Albert Gill and mother Annie in Skipton.

Nephew Louis also served.

Not recorded on the Addingham War Memorial.

LOWCOCK: Louis Walter

Louis served in the Durham Light Infantry as Private 37744 and in the Labour Corps as Private 379847.

The son of Emilia Augusta née Knoblauch, who married Addingham man Walter Lowcock in 1863 in Bradford. By 1901 Emilia was a widow of 49 Main Street who worked as a charwoman and 21 year old Louis was a cotton weaver. Shortly after this in 1902 Louis, a silk weaver, married Ellen Thornton and by 1911 lived at 4 Cross End and in 1918 lived at 21 North Street.

Uncle to John Gill Lowcock who also served.

LOWCOCK: William

The 1918 Electoral Roll has a William registered at 32 Main Street and a serviceman voter. This, in 1911, was the home of a William, aged 27 and son of Mary and Joseph. Both men are labourers.

LOWIS: Clarence

Clarence served from 19 October 1918 to November 1919 in 5th Reserve Battalion of the Durham Light Infantry. His address was Station House, Woodlesford, where his father Christopher Lewis was Station Master. Christopher was married in Keighley in 1897 when he worked for the Midland Railway on the Worth Valley Line. Clarence born 1900-1901 in Altofts was a few months old when the family came to live in Addingham. It is not known how long they lived here but by 1911 Christopher was Station Master at Woodlesford.

Clarence is not in any local records.

McCARTHY: Cornelius

Born 1886 and the son of Michael and Catherine née Sutcliffe, who in 1901 lived at 9 North Street. She was a local girl and Michael was born in St Giles, London and a bricklayer. By 1911 Catherine was a widow and lived at 3 Clifton Terrace, Ilkley. Cornelius was a butcher at the same address.

Brothers John, Timothy and Michael also served.

Read his story in "For King and Country".

McCARTHY: John

Born 1884 and one of the four sons of Michael and Catherine to serve. In 1911 John was an unmarried domestic gardener living with his widowed mother at 3 Clifton Terrace, Ilkley. Father Michael had died in summer 1910 but the couple had been married for 33 years and lived in Addingham for over 30 years. All the children were born in Addingham.

McCARTHY: Timothy

Born in 1890, the son of Michael and Catherine, in 1901 Timothy lived with his parents at 9 North Street. By 1911, aged 21, he was an assistant in an asylum in Burley-in-Wharfedale and on the Electoral Roll for Otley in 1913 and 1914 at Scalebor Park Retreat.

One of four brothers who served.

McCARTHY: Michael

Born 1885, Michael enlisted on 11 December 1915 when a 30 year old journalist living at Warwick Road, Batley, and unmarried. His next of kin was mother Catherine McCarthy of 2 Clifton Terrace, Ilkley.

Read his story in "For King and Country".

McRINK: Bernard

Born in 1887 and one of the three sons of Stephen and Mary to serve. By 1911 Bernard was a Regular soldier with the 3rd Reserve Battalion of the Yorkshire Regiment based in Richmond, Yorkshire, Service Number T652.

Brother John and Lawrence also served.

Read his story in "For King and Country".

McRINK: John

Born 1890 and a Regular soldier from 1909. John enlisted with George Fisher as they have consecutive service numbers. A Hussar of the Line, John was in France in September 1914 and served until 1919.

Brothers Bernard and Lawrence also served.

Read his story in "For King and Country".

McRINK: Lawrence

Born in 1886, Lawrence, or Larry, died of wounds on 8 September 1918 aged 32 when serving in the Royal Horse and Royal Field Artillery as Sergeant 27240 in the 165th Brigade. A Farrier Sergeant, Larry was buried in Belgium at La Kreule Military Cemetery at Hazebrouck, Grave Reference III.D.6. At the time of his death he lived with widowed father Stephen at 1 Bolton Road and a few years earlier at 36 Bolton Road.

Brothers John and Bernard also served.

McSHEE: Patrick

Patrick was a Sapper in the 210th Field Company of the Royal Engineers, Number 83839, when killed in action aged 43 years on 30 March 1918. Buried at Bellacourt Military Cemetery at Rivière, South of Arras.

Born in 1875 in Keighley he married in 1904 and lived at 9 Parkinson Fold with wife Edith and son William. A stone mason and sometime bricklayer by trade, Patrick was also a notable local footballer and had played for the Addingham first team in his younger days.

MAUDSLEY-CLAYTON: George Nicholas

George was killed in action on 2 November 1914 when he was a 32 year old Private in the Alexandra, Princess of Wales Own Yorkshire Regiment 2nd Battalion. Recorded on Panel 33 of the Menin Gate at Ypres as George Maudsley Number 7651. George, as Clayton, joined the Reserve Battalion of the West Riding Regiment as Private 9277 in 1908 and signed on for 6 years when aged 27 years.

Sometimes known as Clayton and sometimes Maudsley, his birth as "George N M Clayton" was registered at Skipton in 1881. In the 1901 census George is living with grandparents Isaac and Mary Clayton at 3 George Street and worked in a silk mill.

MERRY: Joseph

Joseph was killed in action on 31 July 1916 when aged 20 years. As

Lance Corporal 35619 he served in 3rd Battalion of the Grenadier Guards and is recorded on the Menin Gate at Ypres, Panels 9 and 11.

Born on 10 March 1897 and was the son of Joseph A and Jane Lowcock Merry née Boit. In 1911 Joseph senior was a foreman at the Municipal Waterworks for Keighley Corporation. The family lived in Haworth in 1916 when Joseph was killed.

Not recorded on the Addingham War Memorial.

MIDWOOD: Alfred

Alfred, born in Whitby in 1889, married Emma Bushley in Addingham in May 1913 and he was employed as a gardener. Alfred followed his sister Florence from Whitby as she, in 1901, was working in one of the mills in Addingham as a weaver. Lived at Church Street in 1918.

On 4 December 1915 Alfred attested when he lived at 7 Bolton Road with wife Emma and a child of 18 months. He transferred to Reserve, then mobilised on 12 April 1916. Served in the 19th Reserve Brigade of the West Yorkshire Regiment. Later transferred to the Machine Gun Corps where he trained as a driver, serving in France for 2 years and later Germany.

There are a number of charges on his file including riding a cycle on a public footpath on 10 October 1916 at Grantham. He was fined 5s. Later he was fined 4 day's pay for having dirty equipment during the Commanding Officer's inspection on 25 February 1918. Alfred served until 24 August 1919.

MILLS: William H

In 1916 a Harry Mills of 9 Rose Terrace married Mary Rider. He was aged 25 years, born 1891 and a plumber living in Hebburn-on-Tyne.

A William Henry Mills appears on the Electoral Roll in 1920 at 96 Main Street, Addingham, and a Harry Mills of 9 Rose Terrace is in the Electoral Roll for 1919. Not proven, but this is likely to be the same man.

MOORE: Granville Robinson

Born in Dacre in 1898. When aged 21, he married Isabel Skurr in Addingham in September 1919 and lived at Linden House, Addingham.

There is only one medal in the name of Granville R Moore and he is Sergeant 266647 in the West Riding Regiment. Newspaper reports for 30 April 1915 note that Granville Moore had joined the 6th West Yorkshire. Wounded in August 1916. Granville wrote to Mr Flint to say that he had a 2-inch piece of shrapnel removed from his leg when in hospital in Northampton.

Granville would have been aged 17 years in 1915 and still too young for overseas service in 1916 when he was wounded. It is also remarkable that he was a Sergeant at 21 years of age and on his marriage certificate his occupation is Company Sergeant Major!

MOORE: Joseph Harry

Born 3 July 1895 in Wilsden, Joseph, an only child, worked on his parents' farm on the Moorside. In 1914, when aged 19 years, Joseph married Emily Jackson.

MORTIMER: Benjamin

Born 1881 in Birstall, Leeds.

Benjamin enlisted, aged 36 years, and served in the Durham Light Infantry attached to the Army Service Corps for "labour abroad", Service Number 105895. He was home from 24 February 1916 until 25 March 1917 then in France until 26 August 1917.

In 1911 he lived at 101 Main Street, Addingham, and was a shop assistant in a tea and coffee business. Benjamin married Tabitha Dewhirst in Addingham on 21 June 1910 when he was a commercial traveller.

Not recorded on the Scroll of Honour.

MOULDING: Carl Stephen

 Carl died on 3 August 1916 aged 22 years when serving as Private 12750 in the 9th Battalion of the Duke of Wellington's West Riding Regiment. Recorded on the Thiepval Memorial. In September 1916 the Ilkley Gazette reported that Carl had lost his life saving a wounded comrade. Had been in France since 15 July 1915.

Carl enlisted at Ilkley in 1914 when working as a railway booking clerk at Addingham and had been born in 1894 in Lazenby, Cumbria. His Schoolmaster father William and mother Christina lived at The Schoolhouse, Lazenby.

MUNTON: Arthur

In 1911, Arthur lived at 2 Cross End, Addingham, with his wife of one year, Florence née Anderson. He worked as a signalman for the Midland Railway and was born in either Great Ford or Gresford in Lincolnshire in 1888. The couple had two children whilst they lived in Addingham; the eldest Doris died aged 26 days in January 1911.

Arthur attested on 15 November 1915 and was in Reserve until 2 September 1918. Served in the King's Own Yorkshire Light Infantry.

Not on the Scroll of Honour.

NORRIS: ERNEST

Born 1882, in 1891 Ernest lived with his widowed grandfather George Norris, in North Street. In 1906 Ernest married Clara Elizabeth Rishworth at St Peter's Church. She was aged 24 years and the daughter of quarryman Thomas Rishworth of 153 Main Street.

Ernest enlisted as a Regular soldier in September 1902 at Keighley in the Royal Field Artillery when aged 20 years and 9 months and employed as a servant to a greengrocer at Mill Lane, Linton, where he lodged. At the time he was a bricklayer, 5ft. 7in. tall with blue eyes and a fresh complexion. Ernest travelled to Seaforth where he was posted to the 68th Battery as a Gunner, transferring to Reserve with the rank of Corporal on 23 September 1905, Service Number 272338. Before enlisting he had served as a part time soldier in the 2nd Volunteer Battalion of the West Yorkshire Regiment. It was noted on his file that Ernest was used to the care of horses. His expected place of residence was 12 Victoria Terrace.

Ernest reported to his unit at Preston on 5 August 1914 and joined the 16th Battery of the Royal Garrison Artillery and arrived in France with them on 16 August 1914. Within days Ernest was fighting in the Battle of Mons which was a major defeat for the British and French armies. From 22 to 24 August Mons was the first battle with Germany on the Western Front and forced an Allied retreat to the Marne.

Ernest remained with his Battery in France until 7 September 1915. He had stayed on there for one year longer than his allotted 12 years' service and was discharged on 28 September 1915. His service for pension purposes was reckoned at 13 years and 6 days.

OGDEN: William

William served in France in 1914 as a Regular soldier, and was killed on 26 September 1914.

Read his story in "For King and Country".

OLDFIELD: John

Born in 1893 John was a Territorial and served in the 4th *(Howitzer)* West Riding Brigade of the Royal Field Artillery as Trumpeter Number 576. Aged 19 years when he joined the company in June 1912, John was only 5ft. tall and of slight build. At that time he was a spinner for Lister & Company. His next of kin was mother Mary Oldfield of 5 Wharfedale View. From 1914 John was a driver and embarked for France with his unit on 15 April 1915 for Le Havre.

A newspaper report for July 1915 refers to Oldfield as having "cushy work" because he is "on telephone staff" which keeps communication between observation posts. Because of his height John would not have been required to carry out front line duties and was posted to the 11th Battery in France. Between April 1915 and July 1916 when he was transferred to England, John had scabies, was injured and possibly wounded. He returned to France and then was sent back to England on 27 October 1916 from the 245th Brigade "invalided from overseas". Then after a few days' furlough from Liverpool he was posted to Reserve at Ripon in November 1916.

John was granted a £15 bounty on 2 July 1917 under Army Order 209 of 1916. No reason was given. He was discharged on 15 April 1919 with "no disabilities".

OVERIN: Willie

Willie enlisted on 11 September 1914 aged 23 years and 10 months. He was a draper's assistant when he enlisted at Scarborough in the Yorkshire Regiment, the Green Howards, as Private 12890. Posted to the 9th Battalion at Ripon Willie was promoted to Lance Corporal on 16 January 1915 when still in initial training. He went to the front in August 1915. Promoted to Corporal and then posted as Corporal on 15 July 1916. A newspaper reported him wounded in July 1916 and recuperating in St Luke's Hospital, Bradford, with bullet wounds to arm and thigh. By October 1916 Willie was attached to "Train Reserve" and promoted to Sergeant on 2 February 1917. December 1917 he went to the 51st Battalion Leicestershire Regiment as Sergeant. Other postings followed until 9 February 1919 when Willie was transferred to Reserve.

Willie was born in 1890, the son of Wesley and Sarah at 65 Main Street, Addingham.

PACEY: William Dibb

In January 1911 William married Isabella Bell at Addingham and he became a porter at Addingham railway station. His eldest two children Beatrice and Arthur were born in Addingham.

When William, born in 1885, enlisted on 29 March 1915 he was a 30 year old platform porter living at Station House, South Mirfield. Serving in the Royal Garrison Artillery as Private 176023 William was mobilised on 8 August 1917. He was posted to the 532nd Siege Battery on 18 February 1918 as a Gunner 1st Class. William had two unauthorised periods of absence. The first for two days 19 December 1917 to 1 January 1918 and was fined four days' pay and the second, also fined four days' pay for being absent "from duty as officers orderly" on 18 November 1918. William was then serving as a Signaller at North Camp, Aldershot. On 20 December 1918 William was discharged as "no longer fit" because of recurring bronchitis caused by service. Served for 3 years and 22 days.

Not on the Scroll of Honour.

PARKINSON: James Carlton

Born in 1898 and the only son of quarryman Robert and Alice Parkinson of 12 Adelaide Terrace. In 1918 recorded at 12 Ilkley Road, Addingham.

In 1916 when he enlisted on 24 February aged 18 years and 7 months, James was an overlooker. Transferred initially to Reserve and mobilised and posted on 30 June 1916, James served in the 23rd Durham Light Infantry as Private 250875. At only 5ft. 1¾in. James would not have been expected to serve as an infantryman. He went to France on 14 November 1916. In 1917 he had been in hospital at Leith for two months and before that in hospital in Abbeville, Tréport and Southampton with trench foot. On 21 May 1917 James was transferred to a Reserve battalion of the Durham Light Infantry.

PARKINSON: John Wilfred

Born 15 March 1897 and the son of John and Sarah who in 1911 lived at 9 High Mill Lane. John was an apprentice joiner and his father a silk weaving overlooker.

On August 1917 a newspaper reported Pte John Parkinson, youngest son of John of High Mill, as wounded and in hospital in Scotland.

PASS: Benjamin

Born on 4 December 1894, Benjamin was one of the three sons of Doctor and Margaret to serve in the war. Doctor Pass *(first name, not title)* came from Macclesfield to work in the silk mills at Addingham, and married local girl Margaret Beanlands in 1881. By 1911 Doctor and Margaret were running a fish and chip shop in Colne and Benjamin assisted in the business.

Benjamin was most likely a Regular soldier serving in the 1ˢᵗ East Lancashire Regiment as he was in France with the British Expeditionary Force on 22 August 1914 when aged 20. Service Number 10562. He became a POW. Awarded the 1914 Star.

Brother to Charles and William and cousin to James and Joseph who also served.

PASS: Charles

The son of Doctor and Margaret Pass of 6 Kitty Fold and born 26 June 1884 in Addingham.

Charles served in the 1/6ᵗʰ Battalion of the Duke of Wellington's West Riding Regiment as a Territorial from 3 May 1910 as Private 1408. At that time, aged 25 years, he lived in Skipton and was employed as a dyer's labourer at the English Sewing Cotton Company there. Went to France with his Territorial unit on 14 April 1915. Wounded in France on 10 September 1915, he was treated on the hospital ship "Newhaven" for a head wound. Returned to service after convalescence. Charles was discharged from service as physically unfit on 5 May 1916 with a hernia, aged 31 years. The record states, "Six months ago in Flanders complained of groin pain. Not there at outset of service. Was in Transport Section. Thinks it caused by horse riding". Note says "truss would not be effective", "consider soldier not to blame". Awarded the Silver War Badge and 1915 Star.

Brothers Benjamin and William also served.

PASS: James

Born on 21 June 1898 James was the son of Squire *(first name not a title)* and Elizabeth Ann née Stirk. By 1911 the family were living at 13 Elmsley Street, Steeton, and James, at 12 years, worked part time as a doffer in a mill. Squire was a wool comber born in Bollington, Cheshire. James married Jennie Dallas in Keighley in 1922.

It is likely that James served in the West Yorkshire Regiment and enlisted on 5 March 1917 when 18 years of age. Private 52628, he served abroad, later wounded and discharged on 31 January 1919. Awarded the Silver War Badge.

PASS: Joseph

Born in 1891, Joseph, a gardener, was the son of Philip born in Macclesfield. In 1911 the family lived at 49 Southfield Terrace, Joseph's mother Jane had died and Philip was married to his second wife Mary.

Joseph was in the Duke of Wellington's West Riding Regiment, Service Number 267274. Wounded four times and in November 1917 was reported as "dangerously wounded in the head" when serving with the Machine Gun Section of the Duke of Wellington's Regiment. He was gassed and discharged from the army on 12 July 1918 as a result of his injuries. Awarded a Silver War Badge.

A relative Kasheen Hastings recalls as a child visiting Joseph and said that he had problems with his skin peeling and spent his life quietly.

PASS: William

William was the son of Doctor and Margaret née Beanlands. Doctor was a silk spinner born in Bollington, Cheshire, and in 1901 the family lived at 5 Kitty Fold. William was born on 12 March 1890 and became a house painter.

Served in the 1/6th Duke of Wellington's West Riding Regiment as a Territorial, attaining the rank of Sergeant, Service Number 6/1096. William was discharged on 29 April 1916 at the end of his term of engagement having been in France since 14 April 1915. His card indicated that William re-enlisted after his term of engagement ended. His final rank was Colour Sergeant in the West Riding Regiment. Awarded 1915 Star.

Brothers Charles and Benjamin also served.

PEASE: William Henry

A William Henry Pease was registered as a serviceman voter in 1918 at 38 Bolton Road, Addingham, then in 1920 at 16 Bolton Road.

In 1920 an Alice E J McGrath, born in 1898, married a William Henry Pease in Skipton.

A William H Pease died in Skipton aged 40 years in 1938, born 1898.

Not on the Scroll of Honour.

PENNY: John Jackson

John attested on 12 December 1915 when aged 23 years 4 months when employed as a Police Constable at Preston, Lancashire. Served in the Royal Garrison Artillery as Private 165511. A note on his service record indicated that he would be available for service "on receiving permission of my Chief Constable in accordance with Lord Derby's undertaking for attestation of police officers for the army".

Mobilised on 12 June 1917, John went to France on 13 November 1917 and was demobilised on 26 August 1919.

John was born in Ecclesfield in 1892 and the son of John Jackson Penny an insurance agent who lived at 38 Main Street, Addingham, from at least 1898.

Not on the Scroll of Honour.

PERCY: John Duncan *(Reverend)*

The Ilkley Gazette in January 1915 reported that the Reverend Percy had enlisted in the Royal Army Medical Corps Territorials. He was "of Addingham" and a minister in the Ilkley Wesleyan Circuit. The Reverend Percy said the "call of duty was imperative".

There is a medal card in his name as Number 291 in the RAMC and he served in the 1ˢᵗ Brigade Sanitary Company and as a Chaplain. The sanitary brigades were attached mainly to field ambulance and were responsible for hygiene including clean water, de-lousing and other means of preventing infections.

Born 1877 in Devon, John married Winifred Pullen at Huddersfield in June 1918 when he was a 41 year old Wesleyan Minister of Cark Road, Keighley.

Not on the Scroll of Honour.

POCKLINGTON: William

William, born in Leeds in 1894, lived in Addingham in 1912. A mill hand at Lister and Company, Addingham, he served in the Territorial 4ᵗʰ West Riding Howitzer Brigade of the Royal Field Artillery, Service Numbers 573 and 776225.

William went to France with his unit on 15 April 1915 where he joined the 11ᵗʰ Battery. He was on a charge, reported in the field on 20 May 1915 for "hesitating to obey an order of a superior officer". Given 21 days "field punishment". In December 1915 was treated for scabies. He joined the 245ᵗʰ West Riding Brigade of the RFA in the field on 20 May 1916. Later William committed a number of offences on the same day and these were leaving a horse unattended, being in an area without a pass and absent without leave. Two months later was granted 14 days home leave and embarked from Calais on 10 March 1918. On 25 January 1919 joined the D/345 Brigade of the RFA. Some of his service after this was spent in Germany. Demobbed on 28 August 1919. Recorded in 1918 at 5 Low Mill Lane.

REDSHAW: Harold

Although he was born 1893 in Whitehaven, and his family farmed in several places in the north of England as tenant farmers, Harold had Addingham connections and was a friend of Charlie Ellis with whom he served.

There is one medal card for a Harold Redshaw serving with the Yorkshire Hussars for Private 2725 and 330450 Alexandra, Princess of Wales Own Yorkshire Hussars. Harold went to France on 17 April 1915 and served until 12 March 1919.

RENTON: George Lister

Born 1885 at Bolton Abbey, George lived with his family at Ferry Cottage, Addingham, and his father, also George, was a Police Constable. George senior was born at Nesfield where his family were farmers.

George junior emigrated to New Zealand and served in France with the New Zealand Expeditionary Force. Killed in France, aged 31 years, on 17 September 1916 when in the 1st Battalion Wellington Regiment of the NZEF, Service Number 10/2745. Recorded on the Caterpillar Valley Memorial on the Somme.

Not on the Addingham War Memorial.

RICHARDSON: Hedley

 Hedley was killed in action on 4 July 1916 on the Somme and is recorded on the Thiepval Memorial. He was serving as Private 3835 in the 1/7th Battalion of the Duke of Wellington's West Riding Regiment Territorial Force. Mobilised on 17 February 1916 when an unmarried shop assistant. Went to France on 19 June 1916 and was killed two weeks later.

Born in 1891 in Addingham, in 1901 Hedley and his mother Leola were living at 100 Main Street, Addingham where she was a stationer.

Brother William also served.

RICHARDSON: William

Born in 1900 he lived at Linden House, Addingham, and later was a costing clerk. His next of kin was mother widow Leola Richardson of Farsley. Leola had a stationery business at 100 Main Street for many years.

William went to France on 23 January 1917 with the 3rd North Staffordshire Regiment, and served there for six months. He may have been wounded as on 21 June 1917 he was in England and there for a further six months until 22 December 1917. Shortly after he was discharged having served 2 years and 13 days and awarded a pension for 1 year and 38 days. Service Number 3/31736.

RISHWORTH: Geoffrey

Geoffrey Rishworth (seated) with Wilf Ettenfield

Born in 1892, Geoffrey enlisted on 5 December 1914 aged 22 years and 65 days. He was a single man, a mason, and lived at 2 Beacon Street. At the time of enlisting Geoffrey was working on building the school in Hellifield. He joined the West Riding Regiment and marched to Halifax on the same day in his civilian clothes with others who had enlisted. Joined the 2nd Battalion and went to France on 14 July 1915 where he joined the Machine Gun Corps on 3 September 1916 and was attached to the 282nd Army Troop of the Royal Engineers for a time. Transferred to Reserve on 1 February 1919 and was discharged on 31 March 1920 having served over four years. His Service Numbers were 70803 and 14936.

Awarded the 1914-15 Star.

Geoffrey was the son of George and Ada Rishworth and in 1921 he married Annie Thorpe at Addingham, when he was a 28 year old bricklayer of 2 High Mill Lane. His sister Madge had married Frederick Adams who also served and they lived at 1 High Mill Lane.

RISHWORTH: George Thomas

Born on 26 August 1898 and brother to James who served and son of Harry and Mary Francis Rishworth. It is not known where George served, but he is recorded as a serviceman voter in 1918 at 13 Rose Terrace.

Christmas Card to Geoffrey Rishworth 1915.
(This, and photograph opposite, reproduced by kind permission of
George Rishworth)

RISHWORTH: George

Born in 1899 and the son of Thomas and Jane Rishworth who, in 1911, lived in a large extended family at 10 Victoria Terrace with Jane's mother, Jane Metcalfe, as head of house.

George, a silk spinner, enlisted on 8 October 1917 aged 18 years and lived at 28 Victoria Terrace. Served in the 3rd Battalion of the Yorkshire Regiment as Private 43599. Initially in the Training Reserve, he went to France on 1 April 1918, barely 19 years of age. Wounded two weeks later on 15 April, and transferred to Ashhurst War Hospital at Littlemore where he stayed until 14 May 1919, with both gunshot wounds and neurasthenia *(weakness of the nervous system – or "shell shock")*. Discharged on 17 May 1919 after 1 year 222 days. Awarded the Silver War Badge and a pension of 3s. 6d. a week. He was 20 years old.

RISHWORTH: James

Born on 2 September 1895 to Harry and Mary Francis. In 1911 Harry was a "marine" dealer on his own account and the family lived at 1 Bolton Road. James was then employed as a piecer. Recorded in 1918 at 13 Rose Terrace.

Served in the Nottinghamshire and Derbyshire as Private 4924, then the Oxford and Buckinghamshire as Private 32659 and then the Royal Army Service Corps as M 377179.

A newspaper article of May 1917 reported that he had been wounded when serving in the Oxford Regiment. With gunshot wounds to his left foot it was unlikely he would be able to march again. This may be why he was transferred to the RASC from the infantry and he would probably have been able to carry out support duties.

Brother George Thomas also served.

RISHWORTH: Leslie

A Leslie Rishworth is listed as a serviceman voter in 1918 at Marchup. No further information has been found.

RISHWORTH: Norman

Born in Silsden in 1895, Norman, in 1911, lived with his parents Abraham and Martha at Cross Bank where they had farmed for over 10 years. Norman, aged 16 years, was a wheel tenter.

He served in the Royal Field Artillery as a driver, most likely working with the horses which pulled the gun carriages. Service Number 223129.

RISHWORTH: Tom

Born in 1895 to Thomas and Jane who, in 1911, lived at 1 Plum Tree Hill.

Believed to have served as a driver in the 2nd West Riding Brigade of the Royal Field Artillery, formed in May 1916 from other artillery units. The Craven Herald, on 5 April 1918, reported Tom was in a stationary hospital in France. He had joined up in February 1917.

Tom is probably on the Methodist Memorial as T Rishworth. Also on this memorial are F Rishworth, P Rishworth and W Rishworth; however, none of them are on the main Scroll of Honour, nor listed in the 1918 servicemen voters for the village, nor has any military record been identified for the latter three.

In 1911 all the brothers Tom, Fred, Percy and Willie lived at home but on that census their name is Rushworth.

ROBINSON: George

Born in 1893 at Bolton Abbey, in 1911 George was 18 year old, single, silk spinner living with his parents, farm labourer Joseph and Agnes at 5 Main Street. Recorded in 1918 at 27 Main Street.

George was a Territorial, and enlisted in 4th West Riding Brigade of the Royal Field Artillery on 12 June 1912, Service Number 776229, when he worked for Lister and Company in Addingham.

On 17 April 1919 George continued his service in the RFA by re-enlisting and signing on as a Regular for two years short service as Private 1034297. He embarked for Palestine on 11 July 1919 and served there until 20 December 1920. Discharged on 12 December 1919 his record states "former service in RFA is allowed to reckon to give full service of 6 years and 308 days".

ROBINSON: Joseph Currie

In 1901 Joseph was living with his father John T, a silk spinner born Langbar and his mother Elizabeth née Ryder who was born in Bishop Auckland. Joseph was born in 1899 in Bishop Auckland and their other child Arthur, who was five months old in 1901, was born in Addingham. John worked for Listers and the family lived at 8 Low Mill Street. By 1911 Joseph had joined his father in the mill and they lived at 25 Low

Mill. In 1927 Joseph married Evelyn Wright when he was a 27 year old motor driver of Low House Farm where his father John was a farmer. Recorded in 1918 at 1 Low Mill Lane.

Five of his uncles also served.

ROE: Ephraim

Ephraim, born in 1882, was the son of Joseph and Mary Roe who, in 1891, lived in Main Street, and Joseph was employed as a chair maker. Later Joseph took the tenancy at Nudge and became a farmer. In 1904 Ephraim married Minnie née Lister. By 1911 the couple had moved to Main Street and in 1922 lived at 120 Main Street.

There is only one medal card for an Ephraim Roe and he served in the West Riding Regiment as Private 32855.

Brother Stanley also served.

ROE: Percy Brown

The son of washerwoman Kate who in 1891 was a widow living in Main Street. Kate née Rawson had married Thomas Roe in spring 1883. Percy was born in 1890 and his father Thomas Roe, in 1881, was a Licensed General Dealer who probably travelled house to house buying and selling. He was registered under the Pedlars Act of 1871. Thomas died aged 33. In 1911 Percy is a Regular Soldier and in 1915 he married Alice Johnson in Todmorden. Percy died in Keighley in 1920 possibly as a result of war service, aged 30 years. All his three children pre-deceased him.

Served in the Durham Light Infantry and later the Royal Engineers, he was a Transport Sergeant on the railways and served overseas. Service Numbers were WR 125492, DLI – 10838, Royal Engineers 31991.

Not on the Scroll of Honour.

ROE: Stanley

Born 12 April 1900 and the son of greengrocer Joseph and his wife Anna of 69 Main Street.

Stanley was not eligible for military service until May 1918 and even if he was called up then he would have been unlikely to serve overseas until after the war had ended.

ROE: William EDWARD

Born in 1883 the son of Edward and Harriett. The family lived at the Star Yard, Ilkley, and Edward was an ostler, probably at the stables in the hotel yard. William married in 1907 and in 1911 he and wife Janet were living at 14 Main Street, Addingham, and he was a cotton weaver.

William enlisted in 1914, was wounded in mid 1916 when aged 38 years and treated at the Northampton War Hospital. Before enlisting he worked for Walton and Company, manufacturers of Addingham.

ROSE: Dennis

The son of Harry and Mary Jane, Dennis was born in 1895. The family lived in Addingham until around 1900, living in Leeds and in Morley when Dennis, aged 16 years, was employed as an underground coal miner pony driver. Harry at that time was a bricklayer.

There are two medal cards in the name of Dennis *(or Denis)* Rose. The most likely is for a Regular soldier who went to France with the BEF on 15 August 1914, serving in the Army Service Corps as CMT/3519.

A Dennis married Minnie Kellet at Gildersome in December 1920 when aged 24 years and a miner.

RUSSELL: Harry

Harry is recorded as a serviceman voter in both the 1918 and 1919 Electoral Rolls at 24 Bolton Road.

A Harry Russell married Rebecca Anderson in Darlington in 1919 and the births of several children are registered at Skipton from 1920 to 1930. One child Olga born in 1928 was buried at St Peter's Church in 1948 when she lived at The Bungalow, Nab End, Silsden.

There is a Harry Russell in the Regular army in 1914 and a service record for one born in Sculcoates near Hull, but neither can be linked to this Harry Russell.

Not on the Scroll of Honour.

RUSSELL: Herbert Ernest

Born 1881 in Ilkley, Herbert married Emily at Addingham in 1906. Her father was carpenter James Emmott of 149 Main Street.

There is an army pension record for Herbert which shows that he enlisted, aged 35 years, in 1916 when employed as a domestic gardener and living at Hollybrook Lodge, Ilkley. He initially served in the West Riding Regiment as 3/23293 but was attached to the 6th Seaforth Highlanders. It appears that there was a problem with his ears which may have caused deafness either during, or before service, and he was discharged after being graded medically CII. This was the lowest medical category and would render him unfit for military service.

Not on the Scroll of Honour.

RYAN: Timothy

Born in Latchford in Lancashire in 1893. Timothy came to Addingham as a small child with his parents Thomas and Margaret who lived here from at least 1895 when a daughter was born. In 1911 they were living at 23 North Street and Thomas and the older children worked in textiles.

RYDER: Arthur Preshous

Arthur lived in Addingham when he enlisted as a Regular soldier at Halifax. Killed at Mons on 24 August 1914 when 19 years of age. As Private 10524 in the 2nd Battalion of the Duke of Wellington's West Riding Regiment, he would have landed at Le Havre on 16 August 1914 after being with his unit in Dublin. Buried at Saint-Ghislain Cemetery in Hainault.

Born in Bishop Auckland in 1896 he was living at 2 Low Mill and a mill hand in 1911 with sister Elizabeth and brother-in-law John Thomas Robinson. Their son Joseph, born in 1899, would also serve in the war.

Arthur had four brothers who served.

RYDER: Frederick

Born 1889 in Bishop Auckland.

When he was killed in 1916, Frederick had been in the army for seven years, enlisting in 1909 as a Regular soldier when he was aged 20 years and he had served in India. Initially reported missing on 5 May 1916, Frederick was presumed dead but this was not confirmed until many months later. He served with the King's Royal Rifles as Rifleman 9268.

A newspaper report in 1916 stated that he was serving with the King's Own Yorkshire Light Infantry and before the war had served with His Majesties Forces in India.

Also serving were his brothers Arthur who was also killed, Norman who lived in Addingham, and John, William and Charles who did not live in Addingham.

RYDER: Norman

Born 1896 in Bishop Auckland, Norman was the brother of Elizabeth who married John T Robinson and lived in Addingham.

The Craven Herald for May 1918 reported that Gunner Norman Ryder was in hospital suffering from shell shock received during a bombardment.

SCHOFIELD: Frank

In 1911 Frank was a 25 year old single Police Officer boarding with Charles Prior at 28 Main Street and is recorded in the 1918 Electoral Roll as a military voter in 1918 at 29 Southfield Terrace.

Only Frank's Territorial record survives and is dated 1908. At that time he was aged 22 years and 11 months and in the employ of Earl Fitzwilliam at Greasborough, Yorkshire.

Born 1886 in Wombwell near Barnsley, Frank had signed on at Wentworth as a Gunner in the West Riding Brigade of the Royal Field Artillery and had Service Number 154. It is possible that Frank transferred to the 4th Howitzers in Ilkley which was part of the same unit.

Not on the Scroll of Honour.

SCOTT: John

John was born 1890 in Burnley. Parents William and Janet were from Scotland and William was a nail maker. By 1901 they lived at Higher Marchup and William was a clog iron maker on his own account. By 1911 John lived with his other siblings at Cragg View, Silsden, and worked as a clog iron maker. His oldest sister, 24 year old Marjorie, was head of house.

John served with the 10th Battalion of the West Yorkshire Regiment. There is only one John Scott in the 10th and he enlisted on 10 December 1915 and was discharged on 16 April 1919, Service Number 42324.

A family story told by Jane Scott says that John saved the life of the writer J B Priestley and that Priestley always acknowledged this.

Read the story in "For King and Country".

SELBY: Sylvester

Born in 1877 at Ilkley, Sylvester volunteered when aged 38 years on 24 August 1915. At that time he was a widower living at 29 Main Street, Addingham.

Read his story in "For King and Country".

SIMPSON: Douglas

Born on 8 February 1899 Douglas was the son of Alfred and Clara who had a draper's shop in Main Street. Alfred had worked as a shopkeeper here and later took on the shop himself.

SKIRROW: William Alfred Rhodes

William was killed in action on 17 April 1918 aged 23 years, when serving in France with the 1/4th Battalion of the Duke of Wellington's West Riding Regiment, a Territorial unit, Service Number 260009. He is buried at Zonnebeke, West Flanders, and his unit had been in France from April 1915.

Born in 1895 to parents Alfred Rhodes Skirrow and Harriett Ann. Father Alfred was an Addingham man and the Skirrows had a farm in Main Street and for a time Alfred had lived at Southfield House. In 1911 William was a schoolboy living with an uncle in Leeds. After William was killed in 1918 probate was applied for and his estate was valued at around £2,000.

Not on the Addingham War Memorial.

SMITH Brothers

Brothers Allan, Craven, Tom, Reuben, John and Willie served.

Read their stories in "For King and Country".

SMITH: Dale

Born on 22 July 1897 to parents John and Sarah M they lived at 92 Main Street. Both Dale and his father worked in textiles. Dale was cousin to the six sons of Fred Smith who served.

Served as a Driver in the Royal Field Artillery, Service Number 786366, and a newspaper of April 1915 reported that Dale had enlisted in the "Leeds Engineers, Howitzer Brigade".

SMITH: Ernest

Born 1899 in Baildon, Ernest lived with his parents George and Grace at 5 Stockinger Lane in 1901 and George was a general labourer. Ernest was their only child. George became a gardener at a "gentleman's home".

SMITH: Ernest

Born 1880. In 1911 he was a 31 year old labourer married to Mary Ann and living at 3 Stockinger Lane. Recorded in 1918 at 149 Main Street.

Believed to have enlisted in the army in May 1915.

SMITH: Frank

Frank was born in 1883, son of Joseph and Eliza. Joseph was from Skipton and worked as a painter. By 1901 Eliza had died and Joseph, now an employer, had a house painting business and two of his sons, including Frank, worked in the business at 69 Main Street. Frank later had his own business as a painter and decorator when he lived with his sister Nellie, now Mrs Demaine, at 74 Main Street. She was a confectioner. Recorded in 1918 at 141 Main Street.

SMITH: Henry

Henry's birth was registered at Skipton in spring 1887 but there is no trace of the family in Addingham. However, when Henry enlisted he gave his place of birth as Addingham. At that time, in September 1914, he was living in Accrington, possibly with brother Charles who is named as next of kin, at Dowry Street, Accrington.

Henry joined the Lancashire Fusiliers aged 27 years, and before 1914 had been in the Special Reserve, 3rd Militia of the East Lancashire Regiment as a Territorial for over four years until February 1910, as Private 2881. Before that he may have been a Regular soldier with three years general service. Henry was later diagnosed with heart disease and discharged from service.

SMITH: John W

Born 1873 in Stillingfleet, Yorkshire. By 1901 builder John was living in Addingham and recently married to Alice. In 1911 lived at 4 Cragg View. Recorded in 1918 at 69 Main Street.

In October 1915 John sent a letter from the front saying that he was having a tough time and had just come out of the trench lines after 13 days. Later he wrote that he had been wounded when at the front near Albert.

> "The shell that wounded me also wounded three others and made three or four landowners *(killed)*. One shell burst only ten yards away killing two of the Royal Engineers and wounded one of the stretcher bearers who was carrying me"

SMITH: Joseph

The son of Joseph and Sophia and born in Morecambe in 1872. By 1881 Sophia, now a widow, lived with her children at Barnes Buildings, Addingham. Ten years later Joseph was living at Main Street with uncle John Hartley who was a coal merchant. In 1899 labourer Joseph married Dinah and by 1911 they had four children including a son, Thomas, who also served in the war.

SMITH: Ralph

 Ralph died on 27 September 1916 aged 34 years, when serving in the Leeds Rifles. This was "D" Company of the 1/8th Battalion of the West Yorkshire Regiment, Service Number 2782, a Territorial unit which landed in Boulogne on 15 April 1915. Ralph is recorded on the Thiepval Memorial Pier and Face 2A, 2C and 3D.

Born 3 November 1881 and son of James and Priscilla of Main Street where James was an insurance agent. By 1911 Ralph was a 29 year old house painter living in Armley with wife Anne.

Brother Roy also served.

SMITH: Roy

Born in 1893, the son of insurance agent James and Priscilla.

In 1910 Roy joined the 4th Howitzer Brigade of the Royal Field Artillery as a Territorial, Service Number 518, later 790189. He signed on for four years, re-joined and went to France with them on 15 April 1915. In France he was posted to 49th Base Depot on 19 November 1916, then posted to Battery A on 12 December 1916. Wounded on 5 May 1918 with severe gunshot wounds to his head and had some fractures. Transferred on 23 May from Etaples to the UK to hospital. Unfit for further service, Roy was discharged on 7 September 1918 with a pension and awarded a Silver War Badge.

Brother Ralph was killed in 1916.

Not on the Scroll of Honour.

SMITH: Thomas

Born September 1900. He would not have been eligible for military service until September 1918 and was unlikely to have completed initial training by the Armistice in November 1918. This does not mean he was discharged in November as the Peace Treaty was not signed for a further seven months, although it is unlikely that Thomas served in combat.

His parents were Joseph and Dinah who, in 1911, lived at 24 Main Street. Joseph also served and may have been an early volunteer.

SNOWDEN: George Rishworth

Born on 29 January 1867, George was old to be a serving soldier but as there is no-one else of the same name he must have served. The Ilkley Gazette reported that he enlisted in May 1915. It is likely that George served as a Gunner in the Royal Garrison Artillery and may have had Territorial experience with the West Riding Brigade of the Royal Artillery. George's medal card indicates that he enlisted on 18 May 1915 and was discharged on 2 April 1919 as "sick". He served overseas and was awarded a Silver War Badge. His late discharge after the war had ended may be indicative of time in hospital and convalescence.

In 1894 George married Selina Emmott whose son served with Australian Forces.

George lived at several addresses in the village and helped his parents Joseph and Jane farm at High Hang Goose on Cringles, Gildersber and at Causeway Foot House in Addingham. In 1911 the couple lived at 9 Rose Terrace.

SPENCER: Francis Robert

Francis *(Frank)* died of wounds on 13 August 1915 aged 22 years, hit in the arm and chest by shrapnel. He is buried on the Somme at Etinehem Communal Cemetery.

As Private 14838 Frank, born in 1893, served in the 2nd Battalion Duke of Wellington's West Riding Regiment. On 27 August 1915, when reporting his death, the Ilkley Gazette said that he had been in France for three months. One of the twelve playing members of Addingham football team to serve.

Frank was the son of John and Elizabeth Spencer of 132a Main Street. Frank's brother Henry also served.

SPENCER: Henry

Henry *(Harry)* born 1896 and the son of John and Elizabeth who in 1911 lived in Bolton Road. Both their sons served. John was a labourer and born in Draughton. Recorded in 1918 at 20 Bolton Road.

Harry, a postman in Addingham, was gassed in early 1916 and was treated at Eden Hall, Kent. Aged 20 years, he had enlisted in 1914.

Brother Francis was killed.

SPENCER: John Hilton

Born 1892. In 1901 John was the nephew of Mary Spencer of 1 Lodge Hill. She was a single laundress and born in Draughton. Recorded in 1918 at 134 Main Street.

Cousin to the Spencer brothers who also served.

STAPLETON: Abraham

Abraham married Martha Moore in February 1916 when he was a 26 year old warp dresser. When Abraham was born in 1890, the Stapleton family farmed at Gildersber where his parents Matthew and Sarah lived for many years.

It is likely that Abraham served in the West Riding Regiment as Private 267255. Abraham was most likely discharged in 1917 as he was wounded in May of that year and his right hand was amputated. Awarded the Silver War Badge.

Brothers Matthew and Lister also served.

STAPLETON: Alfred Patrick

Alfred was born in 1886 and the son of Francis and Catherine who, in 1891, lived at Stockinger Lane. Francis was a spinner born in Ilkley. Alfred was known as Fred and a journalist. By 1911 he was aged 20 years, lived in Sheffield and was a sub-editor for a newspaper. Recorded in 1918 at 122 Main Street.

There is a medal card for Alfred P Stapleton in the Border Yeomanry,

Service Number 30682, although in July 1917 he was serving with the 7th Cameron Highlanders. In 1916 he was reported wounded and treated in hospital at Huddersfield. Fred was buried alive but dug out and had a small wound to his back. Wounded again in May 1917.

STAPLETON: Lister

Born 27 March 1900, Lister was one of the three sons of Matthew and Sarah of Gildersber to serve.

Lister would not have been eligible for military service until his 18th birthday in March 1918 and even if called up immediately would not have completed his initial training until October 1918. Served for a period after the war ended.

STAPLETON: Matthew

When Matthew married Clara Read in Silsden in March 1919 aged 25 years, his occupation was Sergeant in the Durham Light Infantry. He served in that regiment as Number 54102 and is reported in a local newspaper as being in the military in July 1917.

Matthew, born 1893, lived at Gildersber, the home of his parents Matthew and Sarah. By 1923 Matthew, aged 29 and a widower, married Lily Barker.

Brothers Abraham and Lister also served.

STEEL: John

John worked for the Midland Railway Company as a platelayer and it is likely that his occupation brought him to Addingham. He was born in 1881 at Long Preston. He and wife Louisa lived at 73 Main Street from at least 1910 to 1919.

STOCKS: Ernest

Ernest attested on 7 December 1915 when aged 36 years. Called up in August 1916. According to a newspaper report in 1918 Ernest was in the Trench Mortar Battalion. At 5ft 1in. tall he should not have been serving in front line infantry. Ernest served in the 3/6th West Riding Regiment and during basic training transferred to 2/4th Battalion which went to

France at the end of December 1916 and he would have been in this first wave.

By June 1918 Ernest was in hospital with influenza and in hospital again three times in the next four months. In September 1918 he suffered a gunshot wound in the leg which was treated at 45 Casualty Clearing. Discharged from hospital on 12 October, Ernest re-joined his unit until December 1918 when he had home leave.

Initially the leave period was extended but when Ernest failed to report, he was put on a charge and tried in his absence on 18 January 1919. Found guilty and sentenced to 14 days' imprisonment and forfeited pay for the four days he was absent. Confined to prison on his return to France and when released Ernest was returned to England for demobilisation on 22 February 1919. He was 40 years old.

Born in Wakefield in 1879, Ernest married Nancy *(or Annie)* née Lister in 1901 and worked as a bricklayer's labourer. In 1918 was recorded at Plumtree Terrace.

STOREY: Marmaduke

Born 1888 in Skyreholme, the son of David and Ann and brother to Mitchell who also served. In 1911 Marmaduke was a 22 year old single weaver living at 42 Bolton Road. Recorded in 1918 at 14 Bolton Road.

Attested on 8 December 1915 at Skipton. Initially transferred to Reserve, then mobilised on 27 May 1915, he was posted to the 20th West Yorkshire Regiment, then on 1 January 1916 to the 89th Training Battalion, then to the Lincolnshire Regiment in February 1917. Service Numbers 30428 and 28676. Went to France on 31 March 1917. At the time he was with the 12th Labour Company. Still in France Marmaduke did not have UK leave until April 1919, then again on 24 August 1919 for 14 days and must have returned to France because on 10 October 1919 he was returned to the UK for discharge.

STOREY: Mitchell

Mitchell served in the West Riding Regiment and the Labour Corps, Service Numbers 267737 and 580586.

In 1901 he was the 22 year old son of David and Ann of 4 George Street, a mason's labourer and born in Skyreholme in 1879. David was a carter at the saw mills. By 1911 Mitchell was married to Margaret Alice. Lived at 11 Main Street.

Brother Marmaduke also served.

STRICKLAND: George Henry

Born in Thirsk in 1888 and the son of Thomas Strickland who was farming at Highfield Farm in 1901 and 1911. By 1911 George aged 22 years was a boarder in Bradford and a mechanic's pattern maker.

George was awarded a Military Medal for gallantry when serving with the 1/7th West Yorkshire Regiment, Territorials. The report of his MM stated that he was a Bugler and had joined in 1914.

STYLES: Thomas

There is an entry in the National Archives for a Thomas Styles, born 28 June 1894, as serving in the Royal Naval Air Service as F 11554 and born in Addingham. This is the only intimation of service in the armed forces for someone of this name.

Thomas, born 1894, was the 16 year old son of John Francis and Eleanor Styles in 1911, and the only one of their several children to have been born in Addingham. In 1911 Thomas was a joiner's apprentice living at College Road, Harrogate, and his father was a joiner.

Not on the Scroll of Honour.

SUTCLIFFE: Edward

Born 28 July 1887, Edward was killed in Greece on 3 August 1918 and one of four sons of Benjamin and Sarah to serve.

Read his story in "For King and Country".

SUTCLIFFE: Frederic

Born in 1896, the son of labourer John and Mary of 1 North Street.

In September 1917 the Craven Herald reported a letter of thanks for a parcel from Air Mechanic F Sutcliffe.

Fred was brother to John W who also served and in 1918 was recorded at 2 Church Street.

SUTCLIFFE: Frederick W

Frederick enlisted on 5 May 1915 when aged 36 years, and served in the Royal Field Artillery as Gunner 18066. Before enlisting he had served in the 2nd West Yorkshire Voluntary Brigade Royal Engineers. Posted to "D" Battery as Gunner on 6 May 1916 in the 170th Brigade, Frederick had several other battery postings. There is no evidence on his record of any overseas service.

There are two disciplinary matters on his service record – he was absent without leave *(AWOL)* for two days in October 1915 and fined two days' pay and in May 1916 he was fined four days' pay for "insolence".

Born in 1879, Frederick married Sarah Ann England in 1906 in Addingham. By 1911 they were living in Chadderton and he was a cloth piecer. Earlier in 1901 Frederick had lived with his father William, a labourer at New Houses in Bolton Road, Addingham.

SUTCLIFFE: Gamwell

Born 2 November 1890, the son of Benjamin and Sarah and brother to Edward, Tom and Oliver who also served. When Gamwell died in May 1948 aged 58 years he lived at 17 Malt Kiln Yard, Addingham.

Read his story in "For King and Country".

SUTCLIFFE: JOHN W

Born 1899 in Addingham, brother to Fred who served and son of John and Mary who, in 1901, lived at 1 North Street. Recorded in 1918 at 2 Church Street.

SUTCLIFFE: Oliver

Born 1879, Oliver was a Regular soldier and served in the Boer War.

Read his story in "For King and Country".

SUTCLIFFE: Thomas

Born 1889, and brother to Edward, Gamwell and Oliver who also served.

Read his story in "For King and Country".

SUTHERLAND: Alexander

Alexander died in Dykebar War Hospital on 10 December 1918 when he was 35 years of age, and is buried at Skipton Walton Wrays Cemetery Grave D "U" 129.

Joined the Regular army in 1902 when aged 20 years and so, at the outbreak of war, was already time served. He re-enlisted in 1914 and went to France in December of that year. Alexander served in the Imperial Yeomanry Yorkshire Hussars and later in the Royal Army Service Corps. Service Number M1/08675. In February 1917 he joined the 31st Field Artillery, was appointed to Regional Establishment on 20 December 1917 and to Corporal on 13 March 1918. At the time of his death, Alexander had served 4 years and 43 days and was awarded the 1914 Star and the Meritorius Service Medal.

Born in 1882 he was the son of Addingham's Police Constable John Sutherland. In 1911 Alexander was a boarder at Southfield Terrace and employed as a domestic chauffeur. He married Edith Lambert in 1913 and at the time of his death they lived in Manningham, Bradford.

Not on the Addingham War Memorial.

SWALES: Charles

Charles was a Territorial with the West Riding Howitzer Brigade of the Royal Engineers "B" Company. At the outbreak of war he was living in Darlington and working there as a mechanic for H Pease and Company. Recalled to his unit, he volunteered for overseas service at Otley on 6 August 1914. His Territorial number was 753 and later became 781193 when he was a Bombardier. Charlie suffered from myalgia and had injuries to his feet and he was kept "in service" whilst recuperating in hospital. He was treated at Sheffield War Hospital, and seems to have been discharged on medical grounds and received a pension for 20% disability of 6s. per week. At that time he lived at 11 Keighley Road, Silsden.

Born 8 March 1892, in 1901 he lived with parents William and Phoebe at 5 North Street. Recorded in 1918 at 2 North Street.

TAYLOR: Arthur

According to a local newspaper in November 1915, Arthur, born in 1890, went with several other Addingham men to join the Cameron Highlanders Regiment.

Arthur's parents, silk weaver William and Sarah, lived in Addingham from around 1880 and in 1901 lived at 2 The Green.

Not on the Scroll of Honour.

THOMPSON: G H

The Ilkley Gazette reported that a G H Thompson was in Italy, enlisted in 1914 and was on Headquarters staff. He received the Military Medal for ensuring despatches whilst under fire and serving in France. The report, in January 1918, noted that he had been employed at Farfield Hall and was "of Addingham".

Not on any Addingham records.

THOMPSON: Harry

Harry and his widowed mother farmed at Small Banks in 1901 when he was aged 10 years and she aged 54 years. Described as a farmer on her own account, Elizabeth had two other children helping on the farm. Born in 1891, by 1911 Harry was newly married to Ellen and worked as a farm at Bradleys Both. The Thompsons were still farming at Small Banks in 1911. Recorded in 1918 and 1919 at Gildersber.

THOMPSON: William

William born in 1877 lived with his parents at the Old Rectory. The family remained there after the Reverend Thompson retired as it was their private residence. William married Annie Hirst in April 1906. He was then aged 28 years and his occupation was "gentleman". Annie lived at The Hall, Ilkley and her father was a merchant. There is a plaque in St Peter's Church, Addingham, to the memory of William Thompson, elder son of the Reverend William Coates Thompson. William was born 9 May 1877 and died at Beck House in Giggleswick on 14 July 1925 after many years of ill health.

He served in the Boer War 1899-1901 and in European War with the 16th Durham Light Infantry. This was the 16th Reserve Battalion formed in

Durham in October 1914. On 10th April 1915 it became the Reserve Battalion.

Not on the Scroll of Honour.

THROUP: Thomas Gordon

Thomas married Mary Ann Wells in 1904. Born in 1885 and the son of Joseph Laycock Throup and Emma who had a greengrocer's shop in Main Street, Addingham. Recorded in 1918 at 4 Rose Terrace.

As Corporal 84115 in the Royal Engineers, Thomas served in Egypt from 21 December 1915 and was awarded the 1915 Star.

TIFFANY: Alfred

Son of Benjamin and Maggie and born in 1879, Alfred was killed in action in France on 20 July 1918 when serving as a Lance Corporal in the King's Own Light Infantry 2/4th Battalion, Service Number 39368. Previously served in West Riding Regiment as Private 5149. Alfred is buried at Bouilly Crossroads Military Cemetery Reference I.D.33.

A Private A Tiffany is on the Nominal Roll of the 2/6th Duke of Wellington's West Riding Regiment, Territorials. This unit went to France in 1915. His medal card says "presumed dead" and a report in the Ilkley Gazette in September 1918 states that he had been missing since July 1918 having "joined" in 1915 and been wounded in May 1917.

In 1911 Alfred lived at 15 North Street and was a groom.

TIFFANY: Joseph Edward

Born 20 December 1883, he was the son of Benjamin and Margaret and brother to Alfred who was killed. The family lived at North Street and Benjamin was a jobber in a factory. Joseph married Mary Hudson in 1910. After the war the couple and their children lived in Hazlewood, Bolton Abbey.

The Ilkley Gazette reported in October 1916 that Private J Tiffany of the West Yorkshire Regiment was a prisoner of war.

Not on the Scroll of Honour.

TIGHE: Albert

Born in 1892 and the son of Addingham couple John R and Ruth, Albert enlisted in December 1908 in the Royal Regiment of Artillery for 12 years. Albert was an 18 year old labourer.

Still in his six years' active service at the outbreak of war and was one of the first to go to France. Served in the 59th Battery as a Driver and was wounded in 1918, just 3 weeks before the Armistice. Transferred to Reserve on 21 December 1919 and discharged on 3 December 1920 at the end of his 12 year contract. Awarded the 1914 Star. Signed on again on 18 April 1921 in the Royal Field Artillery Defence Force. He had three Service Numbers, 5327, 52694 and 100263. There is a note on his file from the Commanding Officer of the 69th Battery, "a good driver, works well but inclined to insubordination".

Brother Edwin also served.

Not on the Scroll of Honour.

TIGHE: Edwin E

Edwin was killed in action on 15 June 1915 when he was 27 years old. Served as Private 7780 in the Alexandra, Princess of Wales Own Yorkshire Regiment 2nd Battalion. This battalion was part of the Regular army but, as there is no service record for Edwin, it is not known if he was, like his brother Albert, a Regular soldier. Edwin is recorded on the Le Touret Memorial panel 12, at Pas de Calais.

Edwin, born in 1888, was the eldest son of John and Ruth.

Not on the Addingham War Memorial.

TODD: Ernest

The son of Joseph Henry and Alice, in 1901 the family lived at Moorside. Joseph was from Long Marston, Westmorland. Born in Addingham in 1896, by 1911 Ernest was working and living in a convalescent home as a "domestic porter". The home, Hill Top, West? Drive, Ilkley, had a matron, Miss Abbott, and was owned by Leeds City Council. Recorded in 1918 at Moorside.

Brother William also served.

TODD: William Emanuel

Born on 4 July 1899 to Joseph and Alice and one of their two sons to serve. William lived with his parents who farmed at Moorside.

TOPHAM: Godfrey Stanney

Son of butcher Alfred and his wife Grace and born on 24 November 1886. He married in Ilkley on 23 August 1917, aged 30 years, when his occupation was given as soldier and living in Aldershot.

Godfrey was most likely a Regular in the army as he was serving in France by 11 November 1914 as Private 3463 in the 1st Dragoon Guards. He also served as D 3463 and was awarded the 1914 Star.

Brother to William Throup Topham who was killed.

TOPHAM: Irwin

Born 6 February 1897 to Thomas and Sarah. In 1911 the family lived at 23 Southfield Terrace and Thomas was a coal carter, born Gargrave. He was now married to Annie. Thomas and first wife Sarah had six sons, all born in Addingham, and four of them, John, Irwin, Lewis and Stanley, all served. By 1919 Irwin was living at Nutclough, Hebden Bridge, with his brother Lewis.

Served as Private 200286 in the West Riding Regiment.

TOPHAM: John

Born on 28 March 1895, he was the son of parents Thomas and Sarah Jane. In 1911 the family lived at 23 Southfield Terrace.

TOPHAM: Lewis

Born in 1899, Lewis was mobilised on 8 January 1917 when aged 18 years and 6 days. At that time he was living with father Thomas at Commons Farm, Wadsworth, near Hebden Bridge, and was a twister by trade. Served in the Army Service Corps as T 39403 and 39403 and later transferred to the Agricultural Company of the Labour Corps on 20 August 1918 as Private 546119. He appears to have been "in service" before his 18th birthday as his record shows him to be on "home service" from 24 June 1916 in Reserve until he was mobilised on 7 January 1917.

After the Armistice men were given priority for de-mobilisation if they had employment waiting at home. There is a letter dated 17 January on Lewis' file from his former employer Hayles of Acre Mill, Hebden Bridge, saying that he was in their employ prior to 4 August 1914 and offering him employment as a twister in cotton warp immediately on his return to civilian life. Lewis was then Private 546119, 2nd Section School of Cookery, Army Barracks, York.

Four brothers served.

TOPHAM: Stanley

Born 1900 and ineligible for military service until April 1918 at the earliest. There is no medal card or service record for him.

In 1911 Stanley lived at 23 Southfield Terrace with father Thomas.

Four brothers served.

TOPHAM: William Throup

William died of wounds on 23 April 1917 whilst serving as a Driver in the Royal Engineers 9th Division; Service Number was 44463. Buried at the Duisans British Cemetery at Etrun, Pas-de-Calais, France. His medal card shows that William served in France from 12 May 1915 and that he was awarded the 1915 Star.

Born on 24 September 1885, William was the son of butcher Alfred and Grace. All of their three children were born in Addingham. William was a groom in 1911, single and living with his parents at 1 Bridge Street, Ilkley. Alfred was now a fishmonger.

Brother Godfrey also served.

TOWN: Harry

Harry died on the 19 March 1917 aged 23 years at Methley Hospital, of pneumonia contracted whilst on war service. Given a military funeral, he is buried at St Peter's Church, Addingham. Henry was Private T4/274290 in the Royal Army Service Corps, serving in the Mounted Transport. The Ilkley Gazette on 11 August 1916 reported that he was in hospital in Le Havre.

Born in 1894, Harry was the son of Edwin and Elizabeth and in 1901 he lived with them and six siblings at 2 Low Mill Street. Edwin was a book-keeper in a silk mill. Brother to Joseph who also served.

TOWN: Harry

Born in 1895, in 1911 Harry was a farm worker and lived at home with his parents John and Maria at 22 Main Street, when John was a boot maker. Boot making was a family tradition and John had been apprenticed to his own father, also John, in Main Street.

Reported in November 1915 to have gone to Leeds to join the Cameron Highlanders. The newspaper also reported in October 1916 that Harry Town, youngest son of John of Main Street, had been wounded in the thigh by shrapnel.

TOWN: John Robert

John was killed in France on 21 March 1918 aged 31 years, when serving as Private 45911 in the 12/13th Northumberland Fusiliers. He is commemorated on the Poziers Memorial on the Somme.

Born in 1887, he was the son of Alfred, a plasterer, and Sarah and by 1911, John aged 24 years, was a weaver and married to Elizabeth. There is a note on the grave record saying "father of Miss E Town of 4 Sterling Street, Silsden".

Not on the Addingham War Memorial.

TOWN: Joseph

Joseph attested on 7 December 1915 aged 24 years, and was still in Reserve when he married Ada Lowcock at St Peter's Church on 29 February 1916 *(a leap year)*. Born in 1891 in Addingham, Joseph was a grocer's assistant and his father was Edwin, a book-keeper.

At the time he enlisted Joe lived at 4 Low Mills. He was 5ft. 7in. tall and A1 fit. In Reserve until 15 May 1917 where he served until 9 September 1919 and de-mobbed on 15 October 1919 to 32 Main Street. Joe served in the Royal Regiment of Artillery as Private 80538 and in 1918 he became a qualified Signaller. There is a note on his file which says "wounded" but no date or details are given.

Brother Harry was killed.

TOWNSON: Alfred

Born on 27 May and the son of James, a farm labourer, and Margaret. In 1911 Alfred lived with his mother and sister at Southfield Terrace. Alfred married Elizabeth England in February 1915 and in 1918 they lived at 7 Southfield Terrace.

Brother to William who served and James who was killed.

TOWNSON: James

James was reported killed in action on 3 July 1916 when serving as Private 5982 in the 1/5th Battalion Duke of Wellington's West Riding Regiment and aged 22 years. Buried at Aveluy Wood Cemetery at Mesnil-Martinsart, Grave Reference I.C.7. A report on 11 August sent to his family said he had been severely wounded on 3 July, but was still alive when he arrived at the Dressing Station.

Born on 19 May 1894 to James, a farm labourer, and Margaret Ann. In 1901 the family lived at 7 Chapel Lane and later at 7 Southfield Terrace. Brothers Alfred and William also served.

TOWNSON: Robert Wetherill

Robert was killed in action on 2 March 1916, aged 27, when serving in the 9th Battalion of the Duke of Wellington's West Riding Regiment as Private 12818. Recorded on the Menin Gate. "Craven's Part in the Great War" has Ben Townson with exactly the same death and regimental details.

Robert, born 1888, was the son of butcher John and Betsy Townson of Main Street, Addingham. In 1901 they lived at 108 Main Street. In 1909 Robert married Elizabeth Bancroft and in 1911 lived at 133 Main Street.

TOWNSON: William

Born in 1884 William was one of the three sons of James and Margaret Ann to serve. Enlisted on 27 March 1916 at Halifax when he lived at 1 Southfield Terrace. William was a gardener and served as Private 28674 in the 20th *(Reserve)* West Yorkshire Regiment. In France from 2 September 1916 until 9 June 1917. It is likely that he was wounded in June 1917 with gunshot wounds to his buttocks and lower back. Treated in England from 10 June until 7 November 1917. There was another posting *(illegible)*, then transferred to Reserve on 23 February 1919 and six weeks later was discharged having served 3 years and 308 days.

TREVOR: Arthur

In September 1917 a Sergeant A Trevor wrote to Mr Flint in Addingham to thank him for the parcel, so we must assume that Sergeant Trevor had Addingham connections. However, can find no evidence of this. In November 1915, the same man wrote to say that he had just become a Sergeant and in 1917 said that he was serving in Salonika.

There are two medal cards in this name and the most likely is for a Sergeant in Army Service Corps – first as Private R4/62556 and then as Sergeant To Reserve 13.6.19. Served Egypt from 27 November 1915. Several ASC units went to Salonika.

TUNNICLIFFE: Harold

Born in 1895, Harold enlisted on 5 September 1914 when aged 19 years and 8 months and a single motor engineer. Initially he served in the Duke of Wellington's West Riding Regiment but this was only for 4 days and then he transferred to the Royal Engineers. Service Numbers 12887 and WR 280475. In October 1916 Harold was posted to the Railway Operations Division of the Royal Engineers and was still with them when promoted to Acting Corporal on 1 June 1917. Had problems with synovitis several times in 1916. Served abroad, probably in France, but the dates are uncertain, and spent time in hospital from 11 February 1918 to 4 March 1918. Promoted to Corporal. In August 1918 Harold was treated at Chelmsford Hospital *(no details)*. Passed Superior and Very Superior skills examinations.

Brother William also served and son of grocer John and Annie.

TUNNICLIFFE: William Henry

Born on 19 September 1887 in Silsden, son of John and Annie who had a grocer's shop in Church Street, Addingham. William became a domestic motor driver and in 1911, when aged 23 years, he worked for Eustace Holden Illingworth, manufacturer, at Pinewood, Oakworth. William was one of their seven servants.

Brother Harold also served.

WADE: Albert

Albert volunteered on 2 September 1914 at Ilkley when aged 21 years and 11 months and an engine cleaner of 18 Rose Terrace. Initially declared fit, Albert was later found to have "vascular disease of the heart" and discharged from service. He had served as Private 12776 in the West Riding Regiment.

Born in 1893 to cabinet maker William and Hannah. Brothers Robinson, Tom and Harry also served.

WADE: Harry

One of the four sons of William Henry and Hannah to serve and born in 1890. In December 1912 Harry married Ethel Barnes in Ilkley and at the time he lived at 18 Victoria Terrace.

There is a newspaper report of September 1916 saying that Private H Wade was in hospital and may be there for some time as a shell exploded only ten yards away from him and he had leg injuries.

WADE: Joseph Gill

Joseph, born 15 February 1880, was the son of Charles and Sarah who, in 1901, lived at 79 Main Street. Both father and son were cabinet makers. In August 1912 when resident at Ivy Cottage, Addingham, 32 year old Joseph married Ethel Dick. His sister Lucy, a schoolteacher, corresponded with Addingham men serving at the front. Joseph was cousin to the four Wade brothers who served.

WADE: Robinson Hargreaves

Born 19 March 1884 to William and Hannah and one of their four sons to serve. The 1911 census had Robinson Hargreaves Wade living at Bramham Park, Boston Spa, aged 26 and a "helper" in what may be a single man's quarters on the estate. There are three helpers, a domestic coachman and a kennel man living there.

There is one medal card for Robinson H Wade and that is for Private 99520 in the Royal Garrison Artillery.

WADE: Tom

According to newspaper reports Tom served in Mesopotamia with the Royal Engineers. In April 1915 he was reported to have joined the Howitzer Brigade of the "Leeds Engineers". In March 1916 he sent a letter saying that they had chased the Turks "all the way to Baghdad".

Tom, born 1888, was the son of William Henry and Hannah and one of four brothers to serve.

WAGGITT: Frederick

Served in the West Riding Regiment as Private 204156.

Born in 1899 in Catterick and the son of John and Jane Ann who farmed at Moorside. In the 1911 census father John is listed as William but it is clear from other records that this is an error.

Brother John and William both died in the war.

WAGGITT: John

A John G Waggitt, born at Catterick in 1893, sailed from Liverpool to Canada in March 1914. His age is given as 23 but should be 20. He was a labourer. Brother to Frederick who served and William who also died.

John served in France with the Canadian Expeditionary Force and died whilst on furlough to visit his family.

Buried in Addingham churchyard, his gravestone says "87051 Gunner. J G Waggitt. Canadian Field Artillery. 30 July 1917 aged 23". There is a death for John T Waggitt born 1894, recorded in Wharfedale in quarter ending September 1917 and a burial in St Peter's Church records for a John Thomas Waggitt on 3 August 1917, aged 23, of Moorside, son of John Waggitt, farmer.

The circumstances surrounding John's death are unusual and the Coroner's report can be read in "Timeline for 1917".

WAGGITT: William

Killed in action on 4 October 1916 aged 26 years, his death is recorded

on Thiepval Memorial Pier and Face 6A and 6B. Served as Lance Corporal 12901 with the 10th Duke of Wellington's West Riding Regiment and before that, in 1915, with the 9th Battalion. Wounded on 26 November 1915 and had a finger amputated. After his death a comrade wrote to say that William was badly wounded when a bomb dropped on their trench. He died shortly after, having said "treat *(tend to)* the others first", then "cheer on lad, best of luck, I'm going".

Born in 1889 at Catterick and the son of John and Jane, farming at Moorside. Brother John and Frederick.

WALKER: Abraham Jackson

Born in 1898 at Foster Cliffe, Silsden and the son of John and Elizabeth who, for a time, had the Craven Heifer. After the war Abraham married Ethel Garforth at Harrogate when he was a 25 year old farmer of Green Farm, Addingham. Recorded in 1918 at 1 The Green.

Brother William also served.

WALKER: William

Born 30 July 1895, the son of Jackson and Elizabeth Walker. Sons Abraham and William both served. In 1911, William aged 15, lived with his parents at The Craven Heifer and father John was an innkeeper and farmer. They had two bar servants, two farm servants and a boarder. In 1918 he was registered at 1 The Green.

WALL: Arthur

Born in 1888 when his parents lived at Harts House which was the family home of his father Robert *(close to Sanfitt on Skipton Road)*. The family still lived there in 1911 when Arthur was a single, 23 year old farm worker. In 1918 he was recorded at 10 Main Street.

WALL: Clifford Parnell

According to the National Archives, Clifford served in the Royal Naval Air Service from 1917, Service Number F45137. His birth is given as

April 1887, son of Thomas and Eliza.

Middle name Farnell in some records. In 1908 Clifford married Mary Fletcher at St Peter's Church. His father Thomas was a labourer and her father Isaac Fletcher was a huntsman. In 1911 Clifford, an overlooker, lived with Mary at 3 High Mill Lane. In 1918 recorded at 5 Parkinson Fold. Brother Leonard also served.

WALL: Edward

In 1901 Edward, born 1879, was the 22 year old son of widow Mary Wall, a maltster and an employer managing the business after her husband Richard died.

Edward may have served in the East Yorkshire Regiment and the Duke of Wellington's Regiment. There is a card indicating that he was awarded a "clasp", number 8063, and had been in service from 8 August 1914.

Edward was uncle to Richard Wall who served. Recorded in 1918 at Stockinger Lane.

WALL: Herbert Flesher

In 1911 joiner Herbert, born in 1890, was the son of widow and farmer Margaret Ann of Town End Farm. Brother Joseph of 159 Main Street was Herbert's next of kin.

Served in the 4th Battalion of the Yorkshire and Lancashire Regiment, Service Number 204632. Attested on 14 January 1916 aged 26 years. Posted to Reserve, then mobilised on 22 March 1917. He also served in the 2/4th and the 1/5th Battalions. Served in France from 20 July 1917 to 17 October 1917 and received gunshot wounds to his buttocks and thighs on 10 October 1917. Transferred to UK a week later, he returned, after convalescence, to his unit and served until 28 May 1918 when discharged as unfit. Total service 2 years 135 days. A pension was granted for the portion of his service spent overseas.

WALL: Leonard

The Ilkley Gazette reported in June 1915 that Gunner Leonard Wall had been gassed very badly some weeks before and his eyesight had been impaired; he later returned to the front.

A Leonard Wall served in the Royal Garrison Artillery as a Gunner and was in France from 19 April 1915. Enlisted on 14 December 1914 and discharged on 23 March 1919. Awarded the 1915 Star and a Silver War Badge. His Service Numbers were 1820, 311799 and 755396.

As well as serving in the Great War, Leonard served in the 1939-1945 war as a merchant seaman and was awarded a service medal. His date of birth is given as 25 February 1882, Service Number R69035.

Born in 1882 and the son of Thomas and Eliza. In 1901 Leonard lived with his parents at 1 Church Street and was a quarry labourer. Brother to Clifford who also served.

WALL: Richard

Born 18 June 1896 and the son of Foster, a coal merchant and Sophia née England, who in 1901 lived at 12 Ilkley Road. By 1911 Foster was a maltster. Richard was the nephew of Edward Wall who also served and in 1918 was recorded at 142 Main Street.

In October 1916 Richard was reported to be wounded by shrapnel in his knee and thigh and was being treated at Beckett's Park Hospital in Leeds.

WALTON: Harry Percival *(Reverend)*

Born in Silsden in 1887, the son of John Smith Walton and Sarah. In 1909 Harry lived with his sister Catherine Hudson and her husband John, a grocer. Harry was employed by G H Walton & Co of Addingham and in 1911 his half-sister, Henrietta Thompson, was a nurse in Norwich. Crockfords Clerical Directory lists him as educated at Durham and awarded a BA in 1910 and Curate at St Marks, Jarrow, from 1913 and to the forces from 1916 to 1919.

In January 1916 he was accepted for a Chaplaincy with the forces. In France from June 1916 he was wounded in the shoulder in 1918 when with the Shropshire Regiment.

Not on the Scroll of Honour.

WARD: John Linford

Born March 1899 at Wakefield, the son of Lily Ward and stepson of William Henry Smith, a house painter. In 1911 the family lived at 152 Main Street.

Enlisted on 17 April 1917, just after his 18th birthday, when he was a farm servant working at Laithe Farm, Earby. Transferred to Reserve and called up on 19 June 1918. Served as Private 54897 in No. 3 Company in the 3rd Battalion of the Duke of Wellington's West Riding Regiment. Discharged on 29 January 1919 as no longer physically fit due to "debility" following pleurisy "aggravated by service". Awarded the Silver Badge. The record indicates that he did not serve overseas.

John emigrated to Canada in 1921, leaving Liverpool for Quebec when a 22 year old labourer.

WARD: Samuel

Born 1874, Samuel served as a Gunner in RGA. Enlisted 30 June 1918 at Halifax aged 44 years and 5ft. 1in. tall. Allocated medical category of B1 as over 40 years of age.

Bricklayer's labourer Samuel married Eleanor Emmott at Addingham on 10 May 1898 and in 1901 lived at 14 School Lane.

Not on Scroll of Honour.

WARD: Thomas

A Thomas Ward is recorded on the Scroll of Honour and as a serviceman voter in 1918 and 1919 at 27 Southfield Terrace.

WATERS: Mark

Born 20 September 1890, the son of gardener William and Ann who lived at 1 Cockshott Place in 1901. Mark became a spinner and in May 1915 married Annie Haigh when he was a 24 year old mill hand.

WATSON: Joseph

Born in 1890. Father Joseph was a silk spinning mill manager born in

Glasgow and in 1911 he lived with wife Martha Ann at Crow Trees, Addingham. A large house with thirteen rooms. Son Joe was a mechanical engineer. Brother-in-law Frank Smith also served.

WATTS: Archibald

Born in 1887, the son of Frederick and Annie and brother to Frederick who also served. The family lived for a time in Wesley Place when 14 year old Archie was a grocer's errand boy.

Motor driver Archie enlisted in March 1915 aged 28 years and served as Private 054507 in the Army Service Corps Mechanical Transport Section. Home until 8 May 1915, went to France with the ASC 9th D F Ambulance and had several postings there including in September 1918 to the HQ of the 4th Army. Whilst in France spent time in hospital in September 1916 and in January of the same year had sent a letter to Lucy Wade saying that "Mr Flint tells me you are working hard for the boys from the old village". He was hospitalised again for three weeks in February 1917. Demobbed in June 1919. Awarded the 1915 Star.

Brother Frederick also served.

WATTS: Frederick

Born 1893, Frederick was a Territorial with the 4th West Riding Battalion of the Royal Field Artillery and signed on the 12 June 1912 at Ilkley for a four year term when a weaver at G Walton & Co of Addingham, aged 18 years and 9 months. Went to France on 16 April 1915. Service Number 576 and later 776245. Treated for scabies at Etaples for two months in 1915, which was as a result of service in the field. Shortly after joined the 245th West Riding Brigade of the RFA in the field. Awarded a £15 bounty in June 1917 for signing on for further service and served in France until 18 December 1918. He had home service from 19 December 1918 to 31 March 1920 giving total service of seven years. Awarded the 1915 Star.

In 1918 recorded at 15 Southfield Terrace which was the address of his parents Frederick and Annie. Brother Archie also served.

WHITAKER: Albert

Born in 1896 and the son of William and Mary who lived at 93 Main

Street in 1901. By 1911 Mary was widowed and 15 year old Albert, now a silk weaver, lived with her and his youngest sister Phyllis at 5 Druggist Lane.

WHITAKER: David

Son of Robert and Ellen of Chapel Lane. Bricklayer's labourer David married Annie Merritt in 1900 when he was 19 years old. In 1901 they lived at 11 Bolton Road.

Served in France, he wrote home to say he was in hospital in Boulogne after being at Thiepval. Suffering from eczema and other skin conditions as he had been unable to bathe for over three weeks.

WHITAKER: Harry

Born in 1887, the son of joiner Laurence and Amy of 4 Stockinger Lane and brother to Laurence who also served.

WHITAKER: James

James died of wounds whilst serving in Mesopotamia as Private 18423 in the King's Own Royal Lancaster Regiment 6th Battalion. His name is recorded on Panel 7 A1 Basra, Iraq.

Born in 1886, he lived at 72 Main Street in 1901 and 1911 with parents John and Harriett where John was in business as an ironmonger. James became a plumber.

WHITAKER: John

John died in May 1918, aged 26 years, and was buried at Nine Elms British Cemetery, Grave reference XIV.D.5. He was a Trumpeter with "D" Battery, 245 Brigade 49th West Riding Division. A newspaper reported John's death and that he first went to the front in 1915. The actual date of his death is recorded as 12, 13 or 14 May in the various records.

Born in 1894 in Patricroft. In 1901 John lived with parents Jonathan, an engine cleaner from Leeds, and Emily at Back Beck. In 1911 the family lived at 64 Main Street. John was their only child not to have been born in Addingham.

WHITAKER: Laurence

The Ilkley Gazette reported in November 1915 that Laurence went to Leeds with five other Addingham men to join the Cameron Highlanders. He served with them as Private 2969 and S 41008 and in April 1917 was wounded in both legs and arms when blown up by a shell. It appears that Laurence did not apply for his medals until 1940 and at that time lived at 7 Wharfedale View.

Born in 1891, the son of Laurence and Amy and brother to Harry who also served.

WHITAKER: Richard

Born in 1890, he lived with parents John and Harriett at Cross Ends in 1901 when John was an ironmonger and employer. In 1911 John, now widowed and still an ironmonger, lived at 72 Main Street. Brother to James who was killed.

WHITAKER: William

Killed in action on 5 February 1917 in Mesopotamia when serving as Private 20547 in the 6th Battalion of the East Lancashire Regiment. Recorded on the Basra Memorial, Panel 19. Enlisted in Rochdale when he lived at Lostock, near Bolton.

Born in 1881, the son of David and Hannah and in 1901 he was a mason's labourer living with his parents at 7 Bolton Road.

WHITAKER: William

Enlisted in September 1902 at Keighley when aged 19 years and 9 months, single and a labourer. At that time he was a Territorial and signed as a Regular for 12 years. It is not clear if in 1914 he had transferred to Reserve as his full 12 years would not expire until 24 September 1914. In Athlone on 4 August 1914, went to France with the British Expeditionary Force. As Private 27239 served with the Royal Regiment of Artillery, enlisting on the same day as Ernest Norris and in the same regiment. They have consecutive service numbers. Whilst in France William served with the 88th and 184th Batteries and in June 1916 was with the 183rd Brigade of the RFA. In November 1917 transferred to the Italian Front and re-joined his unit in France in March 1918. Hospitalised twice in 1919, he may have been discharged in March 1920 to 156 Oakworth Road, Keighley. Served over 17 years plus his years as a Territorial.

William, born in 1882, and son of Robert Whitaker who, in 1901, lived at Chapel Lane, Addingham.

WHITAKER: William T

Believed to be William Tomlinson Whitaker born in 1887. His father, a boot maker, had the same name, and his mother was Maria. In 1901 this family lived at 2 Victoria Terrace and 14 year old William was still at school. William senior lived at Cragg View in 1911 and was a retired boot maker. William junior is not in this census in Addingham.

WHITEOAK: Allan Buckley

Born 1896, the son of Craven Buckley Whiteoak and Martha who in 1901 farmed at Gildersber. All their children had Buckley as a middle name. In 1910 Craven farmed at Gildersber but by 1911 Craven farmed at High House Farm with new wife Marianne. Four of their sons served in the war. In 1911 Allan and four of his siblings lived together in Silsden at Chapel Street and are described as "sons and daughters" but no parents are listed. The summary sheets shows the "occupier" to be C B Whiteoak.

WHITEOAK: Charles Buckley

Charlie was killed in action on 13 April 1918 when serving as Private 45316 in the 1/4th Hallamshire Territorial Battalion. Buried at Tyne Cot Cemetery at Zonnebeke, Flanders.

Charlie lived in Addingham when he enlisted in Halifax and in 1911 was a farmer's son at High House Farm, Addingham, where father Craven farmed. One of four, possibly five, brothers to serve.

WHITEOAK: Frank Buckley

Born in 1899, the son of Craven and Martha, Frank had a "Territorial Forces Attestation" on 31 May 1915 when only 16 years old. This was Service Number 4372 when he was in the 3/6th Duke of Wellington's West Riding Regiment. *(Formed at home stations in March 1915 to provide training for "third line" units with a view to preparing men for future active service").* Later transferred to the 6th Reserve West Riding Regiment and posted to France, when 18 years old. Service Number 24952. In March 1917 admitted to 20th General Hospital with trench fever and returned to UK. Returned to France in July 1917. Wounded again in April 1918. After hospital treatment re-joined his unit in June 1918. Wounded again in October 1918 and spent two weeks in hospital at Etaples. Shortly after Armistice was promoted to Lance Corporal in the field and then in June 1919 returned to the UK. His record stated that on 7 June 1919 his age last birthday was 21 and he joined the army on 31 May 1915.

In 1918 registered at High House Farm.

Not on Scroll of Honour.

WHITEOAK: Fred Buckley

Born in 1885, the son of Craven and Martha. In 1911 Fred was married to Annie and they lived at Aire View, Silsden.There is no evidence of service; however, his name is on the Scroll of Honour, whilst that of his brother Frank, who did service, is not. The wrong brother may have been listed.

Four brothers, Allan, Charles, Frank and Harry, served.

WHITEOAK: Harry Buckley

Born 22 May 1891 and his birth recorded as Henry.

A Henry Buckley Whiteoak served as Private 10058 in the Duke of Wellington's West Riding Regiment and whose service continued beyond 1919 in India and Afghanistan with the North Western Frontier Forces.

In 1918 recorded at High House Farm.

WHITHAM: Ernest

Born 1885, the son of tailor William and Martha who, in 1891, lived at Main Street. Draper Ernest married Ethel and in 1911 lived at Wharfedale View. Recorded at 1 Wharfedale View in 1918.

WILD: William

Died in service on 25 November 1918 when aged 30 years, and buried at Walton Wrays Cemetery, Skipton. Served as Corporal 29864 in the Machine Gun Corps *(Infantry)*. His entry in "Craven's Part in the Great War" says William was the son of Mrs Wild of Lambeth Street, Skipton, and that he died of pneumonia in hospital at Grantham.

In the 1901 census, William, born in 1889, was the 12 year old son of Edwin, an overlooker, and Mary, living at 3 Chapel Street, Addingham.

WILKINSON: Carling

Born 1873, Carling was one of the oldest men from Addingham to serve in the war. Under the Military Service Act of 1916 Carling was called up for service on 27 July 1918 when aged 45. There is a note on his service record to the effect that he was "not to be placed in a medical category higher than B at any time during service". This would effectively debar him from active front line combat. Carling served in the Royal Engineers as Private 370576 and arrived in France on 28 November 1918. Two months later he was "dispatched to the UK as a Group 33 – Occupation in Group 3 – coachman".

Married to Emma, he lived in Victoria Terrace, Addingham, with their two sons, one of whom, Thomas, also saw army service. Married Elizabeth in 1906.

WILKINSON: Harry

Born 17 July 1882 to Joseph, a clogger, and Jane née England. In 1891, as Henry, he lived in Main Street where Joseph was a clogger and also a mail cart driver. Harry married Florence Smith in 1915 and six of her brothers served in the forces. Recorded at 6 Ilkley Road in 1918.

Brother Herbert also served.

WILKINSON: Herbert

The son of Joseph and Jane, in 1901 15 year old Herbert was a drug errand boy and the family lived at 147 Main Street. Born in 1885, in 1911 Herbert worked as a warehouseman and at 25 years old was unmarried and living with his parents. His mother Jane was a confectioner.

Recorded as a military voter at 23 Southfield Terrace.

Brother Harry also served.

WILKINSON: James

Born in 1886, James was the son of Albert and Annie and brother to William who also served. Albert was a carter and the family lived at 108 Main Street.

WILKINSON: Thomas

Born 1898, Tom was the son of Carling and Emma who lived at 7 Victoria Terrace. By 1911 Tom and brother Joe lived with Carling and his second wife Elizabeth at Lomashaye Road, Burnley, where Carling was a domestic coachman.

Father Carling also served.

WILKINSON: William

A newsletter for staff at Listers Mill published around 1960 reported:

> "William Wilkinson died in his 67th year after months of ill health. He had been lodge man and time keeper from at least 1932 then worked in the weaving department. Handicapped by WWI wounds, he was a cheerful and popular man. He leaves a widow and family"

Born in 1894, in 1911 William was a 17 year old cotton weaver of 108 Main Street, living with parents Albert and Annie. Brother to James who served.

WOOD: James

Born on 2 June 1900, James would not have been 18 until June 1918. He was one of the four sons of Matthew and Eliza to serve.

WOOD: John

The son of Matthew and Eliza who farmed at Ling Park, Nesfield for many years. John was born in 1898 at Middleton. John and three brothers, James, Richard and Tom, all served during the war.

WOOD: Richard

In 1901 Richard was the 6 year old grandson of John and Theresa Wood and lived with them at 18 Church Street. Born 1893, in 1911 he lived with parents Matthew and Eliza. Richard worked on the farm and later became a chauffeur.

WOOD: Tom

Tom died from the effects of gas poisoning on Armistice Day, 11 November 1918, aged 22 years, at Whalley Hospital. He had served in France for over three years. Buried in the north-west part of St Peter's Church graveyard. Gunner 795226 in the Royal Field Artillery Territorial Forces and served with "D" Battery in the 108th Brigade. This Territorial unit was also known as the 4th Howitzers before the war.

Born in 1896 at Middleton, in 1901 Tom, aged 5 years, was the son of Matthew and Eliza and one of four brothers to serve.

WOODRUP: Robert Henry

Born 1889 at Bolton Abbey, the son of William and Ellen who, in 1891, lived at Wharfedale View. William may have been coachman at Farfield Hall.

By 1911 Robert was a 22 year old Regular serving in India with the 67th Battery of the Royal Field Artillery. Robert served throughout the war and until February 1924. Held the rank of Gunner 44357 and T/Corporal and later had the Service Number 1018823. Served in India and Afghanistan as part of the North West Frontier Force for which he received a medal, Roll 17390.

In 1924 his address was The Hydro, Ben Rhydding, which is where his father was a coachman. Brother to William who served.

WOODRUP: William Richard

Born in 1896 William was with the West Riding Regiment, Service Number 12791, and served in France from 15 July 1915. This was the date when the 9th *(Service)* Battalion landed in Boulogne.

Brother Robert also served.

WOOLSTON: Alfred

Born in 1896 in Skipton and son of Eli and Sarah. In 1901 the family lived in Main Street, Addingham and Eli was a quarryman.

Enlisted on 8 November 1915 at Bradford when 19 years old and a blacksmith living at Hambleton House, Bolton Abbey. As a blacksmith he was granted Class II pay from the date he enlisted. Served in the 59th Siege Battery of the Royal Garrison Artillery as Gunner 67587. After home service until 9 November 1916, went to France and was there until 19 May 1917.

Brother Eli also served.

WOOLSTON: Eli

Born 24 December 1894 and son of Eli and Sarah. Quarryman Eli senior married Sarah M Smith in 1893 in Addingham. In the 1905 to 1910 Electoral Roll Eli owned a house in Main Street, Addingham. By 1911 the family lived at Mullaglass, Armagh, Ireland, but by 1915 lived at Hambleton House, Bolton Abbey.

Served in the Army Ordnance Corps as Private 027513.

WRIGHT: Harold

Aged 20 years was wounded and died of those wounds on 15 July 1916 whilst in hospital in the UK. Served in the 18th Battalion Price of Wales Own West Yorkshire Regiment as Lance Corporal 18/189. This number indicates that he was the 189th man to enlist when recruitment began for this battalion.

Born in 1896 he lived in Addingham in 1901 with uncle and aunt Joseph and Annie Clemmie at 11 Low Mill Street and later in 1911 he went with them to live in Manningham. Joseph was a silk mill operative. Harold became a butcher.

WRIGHT: George

Born in 1890, in 1901 George was living with uncle and aunt Joseph and Esther Bodwell at Armley. In 1911 he lived with cousins, sisters Alice and Ada Bodwell, in Armley. George was a carter.

Although born in Addingham there is no local address for him.

WYNN: Anton

Born 1892 and one of the three sons of James and Ann Elizabeth to serve. All were born in the village.

Anton enlisted on 29 January 1916 when aged 24 years and 7 months and lived at 5 Southfield Terrace. Served in the 2/6th Duke of Wellingto's West Riding Regiment as Private 4991. Served in France from 5 January 1917. A newspaper reported that Anton was in hospital with chest wounds in December 1917 having been wounded on 27 November 1917 when he had been in France for 11 months. His injuries were such that he was discharged as unfit and awarded the Silver Badge and a King's Certificate.

WYNN: Barnard

Born 8 April 1893 and the son of James and Ann Elizabeth.

Served in the navy and is in the Register of Seamen as Service Number M18144 as E.R.A.3 enlisting in 1915. Awarded medals but there are no service details. In early March 1917 he wrote to Mr Flint thanking him for the parcel. Serving on HMS Crane, Barnard said that they had a "lot of fog this month", presumably in February.

Recorded in 1918 at 5 Southfield Terrace.

WYNN: James

Born 1898, James was serving in the Grenadier Guards when he wrote to Mr Flint thanking him for the parcel and later the same year, in August, said that they had "chased the Huns over the coral as we put up fire overhead barrage". This may indicate that he was serving somewhere close to the sea, and warm.

There are two medals for a James Wynn in the Grenadier Guards, one as Guardsman 27266 who was discharged unfit and awarded a Silver Badge and one for Private 31572 with no additional information.

Recorded in 1918 at 5 Southfield Terrace.

Brothers Anton and Barnard also served.

WYNN: William

Enlisted when living in Bradford and was killed in action on 19 September 1918, aged 36 years. He is commemorated on the Vis-en-Artois Memorial, Panel 3. Served in the 2nd Royal Fusiliers City of London Regiment as Private 92987 when he was killed and earlier in the 2/4th London and the 7th Kings Royal Rifles as R/1176.

Born in 1882 he lived in Main Street, Addingham, in 1891 as Willie Winn, aged 8 years and a boarder with a Spencer family. By 1901 he was 18 years old and lived with father John and his second wife Mary Ann Wynn in Manningham.

Not on Addingham War Memorial.

YOUNG: William

Born 1882 in Hazelwood, in 1911 William lived at 1 Smithy Fold with widowed mother Sarah. Aged 29 years, William was a coachman and single. In 1901 Sarah lived at 1 Kitty Fold and was a charwoman.

William is on a 1914 photograph of Addingham and Bolton Abbey new recruits, taken outside Addingham Post Office. They had enlisted in the 9th Battalion and were assembled to leave for Halifax.

Classified lists of those who served

1. Regulars and Reservists

The first men from Addingham to see active service were the Regulars who were already serving somewhere with the colours. Some of these men have been identified:-

-Hanson Binns
-George Clayton
-John Clarke
-George Fisher
-Bernard McRink
-John McRink
-Percy Roe
-Alexander Sutherland
-Oliver Sutcliffe
-Albert Tighe
-Godfrey Topham
-Arthur Ryder
-Robert Woodrup
-William Whitaker

Soldiers still under contract but in Reserve were recalled to their regiments on 5 August 1914 and five have been identified as leaving that day. All were in France within a few weeks:-

-Walter Emmott
-James Harrison
-Edward Hudson
-Ernest Norris
-James Lister

2. Territorials

The Territorials were mobilised on 5 August 1914 but none of the men from either of the two local units, the 1/6th Duke of Wellington's, West Riding Regiment, or the 4th Howitzer Brigade of the Royal Field Artillery based at the Drill Hall in Ilkley, saw overseas service until early 1915.

These men are believed to have gone that day:-

1/6th Duke of Wellingtons

- Charles Atkinson
- Frederick Bell
- Emanuel Benson
- Harry Chambers
- Herbert Craven
- William Dove
- Arthur Foster
- Thomas Flynn
- Norman Holmes
- Charles Hood
- Percy Hustwick
- Charles Pass
- William Pass
- James Townson

4th Howitzer Brigade

- John Brown
- Philip Brown
- Fred Hall
- Frank Keighley
- Jack Kettlewell
- Tom Lancaster
- Thomas Lodge
- John Oldfield
- William Pocklington
- George Robinson
- Roy Smith
- Thomas Sutcliffe
- Charles Swales
- Fred Watts
- John Whitaker
- Tom Wood

3. Places Men Served

Whilst the greatest numbers served in France, some served in other theatres of war, for example:-

-	Fred Adams	Sierra Leone
-	Harold Brown	Basra, Egypt and India
-	John Cunliffe	Gallipoli
-	Harold Emmott	Gallipoli
-	John Goulding	Gallipoli
-	Ernest Hustwick	Gallipoli
-	Alf Ideson	Gallipoli
-	James Hellen	Italy and Salonika
-	Wilfred Holmes	Egypt and Gallipoli
-	Ellis Kettlewell	Egypt
-	Thomas Lodge	Italy
-	Michael McCarthy	Ireland
-	Oliver Sutcliffe	Mesopotamia and India
-	Thomas Throup	Egypt
-	Arthur Trevor	Mesopotamia
-	James Whitaker	Mesopotamia
-	William Whitaker	Mesopotamia
-	George Robinson	Palestine

4. Naval Personnel

Men known to have served in a branch of the Royal Navy were:-

- Charles Clarke
- John Clark
- Harry Dickenson
- Harold Hillbeck
- Thomas Styles
- Edward Sutcliffe
- Bernard Wynn

5. Lord Derby Recruits

Men who enlisted in late 1915 or early 1916 under the Lord Derby Scheme:-

- Fred Adams
- Robert Akers
- James Burke
- Fred Carline
- Alfred Cook
- Abraham Dewhirst
- Richard Goulding
- Joseph Bickle
- John Holt
- Ben Hodgson
- William Kendall
- John Lister
- John Lowcock
- Michael McCarthy
- Cornelius McCarthy
- Alfred Midwood
- Hedley Richardson
- William Richardson
- Marmaduke Storey
- Joseph Town
- Alfred Woolston

6. The Ultimate Sacrifice

There were 83 men who died, listed below in date order. Not all are on the village war memorials. At least a further 3 men who served died shortly after the war.

1914

-	Arthur Ryder	24 August
-	John Clarke	26 August
-	John P Cunliffe	14 September
-	William Ogden	26 September
-	Charles Clarke	1 November
-	George Clayton	6 November

Total 6

1915

-	Norman Beck	16 March
-	Walter Emmott	20 March
-	Mark Dobson	3 April
-	Harry Chambers	5 May
-	Fred Ryder	5 May
-	Clifford Fawcett	9 May
-	Charles Ellis	24 May
-	John C Cunliffe	4 June
-	Edwin Tighe	15 June
-	Francis Spencer	13 August
-	Ernest Hustwick	21 August
-	John Goulding	21 August

Total 12

1916

-	Robert Townson	2 March
-	Harry Leach	4 March
-	James Whitaker	3 April
-	Fred Fisher	5 May
-	Wilfred Holmes	1 July
-	Percy Hustwick	1 July
-	James Townson	3 July
-	Hedley Richardson	4 July
-	Harold Wright	15 July

-	Wilfred Blackburn	29 July
-	Joseph Merry	31 July
-	Carl Moulding	3 August
-	George Bailey	6 August
-	James Dove	8 August
-	Charles Atkinson	18 August
-	Frederick Bell	3 September
-	Charles Hood	3 September
-	Ralph Smith	27 September
-	William Waggitt	4 October
-	Mathias Dove	4 October
-	Joseph Burke	12 October

Total 21

1917

-	William Whitaker	5 February
-	John Brown	3 March
-	Harry Town	17 March
-	James Lister	2 April
-	William Topham	23 April
-	Wilfred Holmes	27 April
-	Philip Brown	11 May
-	Denis Holgate	17 May
-	Henry Hobson	7 June
-	Reuben Smith	11 June
-	John Waggitt	18 September
-	William Horsman	26 September
-	Sydney Hadley	18 October
-	Norman Bell	22 November
-	Norman Holmes	27 November
-	Thomas Hodgson	30 November
-	Arthur Foster	31 December

Total 17

1918

-	Harry Bellerby	21 March
-	John Town	21 March
-	Ambrose Emmott	25 March
-	Percy Jones	26 March
-	Patrick McShea	30 March

- Edward Kidd — 10 April
- Charles Whiteoak — 13 April
- Tom Foster — 14 April
- William Skirrow — 19 April
- John Whitaker — 13 May
- Alfred Tiffany — 20 July
- Alfred Cresswell — 23 July
- Edward Sutcliffe — 3 August
- John Lister — 26 August
- John Lister — 1 September
- William Smith — 2 September
- Lawrence McRink — 18 September
- William Wynn — 19 September
- William Gale — 1 October
- William Dixon — 28 October
- John Lowcock — 30 October
- William Kendall — 30 October
- William Ellis — 10 November
- Tom Wood — 11 November
- William Wild — 25 November
- Alex Sutherland — 10 December

Total 26

BIBLIOGRAPHY

Books and other publications
'A History of Addingham School from 1875' – Mr Lemmon
(see addingham.info/story-addingham-schools/)
'Addingham - from Brigantes to Bypass' – Kate Mason
'Ilkley Past and Present' – Alex Cockshott & Denise Shillitoe
'Recollections' – Martha Heaton
'The English – a Social History' – Christopher Hibbert
'The Workhouse Encyclopaedia' – Peter Higginbotham
'A History of Keighley' - Ian Dewhirst
'Kendal and District Otterhounds' – Private Publication
Mother & Home magazine
'Great War Fashion' – Lucy Adlington
Great War Exhibition at Scarborough Art Gallery July 2014
Whitby Lifeboat Museum
'Boy Soldiers of the Great War' – Richard van Emden
'Craven's Part in the Great War' – published circa 1920
The 'Somme' – Robin Prior and Trevor Wilson
'1914 to 1918 - A History of the First World War' – David Stevenson
'The Bradford Pals' – David Raw
'Priestley's War' – Neil Hanson
Unpublished diary of Brumfitt Atkinson
(see addingham.info/cpl-brumfitt-atkinson-diary/)
Memoirs of J B Priestley

Local & National Records
Addingham Parish Council Minutes
Census Records 1851 to 1911
National Archives and penal records
Military and Naval Service records
Red Cross International Archives
West Yorkshire Tax Evaluation 1910

Newspaper Archives
The Times
The Bradford Telegraph & Argos
The Daily Telegraph
The Craven Herald & Pioneer
The Ilkley Gazette
The Keighley News
The Yorkshire Post

Websites

Addingham village website - addingham.info
aircrashsites.co.uk
Ancestry.co.uk – service records/medical cards/POW records
Craven's Part in the Great War - www.cpgw.org.uk/

We Who Served...

FOOTNOTE

The photograph on the back cover was taken outside Addingham Post Office of "1914 Recruits" and is hanging in the Old School room above the library and on it are 28 men.

The names of the men are given as:-

Back Row: Geo. Robinson, Tom Roberts, Alec Nelson, Eli Woolson, J Mitchell, R Townson, Charley Binns, J.Hargreaves, Wm Hall.

Middle Row: Fred Chaplin, J Lister, Wm Young, Albert Wade, Walter Nelson, H Spencer, N.Nelson, Wm Roe.

Front Row: Harold Tunnicliffe, Frank Hartley, J Kettlewell, Harry Leach, Frank Burk, Fred Fisher, C S Moulding, Geo. Bailey, W Spenceley, Chas. Fisher.

Reclining: Harry Horsman.

Most of the men have been identified as being of Addingham; however, the caption indicated that some are recruits from Bolton Abbey. The men who may be of Addingham and have not been traced are:-

W Spenceley
Charles Fisher
Tom Roberts

Details of the others who have been traced and are from Bolton Abbey are recorded below as none of the men are in the preceding alphabetical list:-

BINNS: Charles

As Charley, born in Burnsall in 1895 and in 1911 lived at Barden and an estate worker, son of George and Mary.

MITCHELL: John

Enlisted Addingham and became a Lance Sergeant in the 9th Service Duke of Wellington's Regiment. Born Bolton Abbey and son of John

Mitchell, a forester of Strid Cottage. Killed by sniper in September 1918 aged 36 years and buried at Gouzecourt New British Cemetery. Service Number 11091. Brother William, born 1886, was also killed.

THE NELSON BROTHERS:
All born at Beamsley and in 1901 lived there at Summerscales Farm. In 1911 **Walter**, born 1890 and **Norman**, born 1892, lived at home but **Alex**, born 1894, was a footman at Crookhey Hall, Garstang, and he married in Skipton in 1911.

An Addingham man who may have served in the war, but not proven is:-

STEEL: William
In 1911, aged 18 years, he was at HMS Excellent Gunnery School at Whale Island, Portsmouth and in the Royal Navy. The son of Alfred and Emma of 13 Low Mill Lane, baptised at St Peter's Church and born in May 1892. By marriage the family was connected to the Hillbeck and Pass families.

Printed in Great Britain
by Amazon.co.uk, Ltd.,
Marston Gate.